Synagogues in a Time of Change

Synagogues in a Time of Change

Fragmentation and Diversity in Jewish Religious Movements

Zachary I. Heller, *Editor*

Published by the Alban Institute in cooperation with the
National Center for Jewish Policy Studies and STAR
(Synagogues: Transformation and Renewal)

THE
ALBAN
INSTITUTE

Herndon, Virginia
www.alban.org

The Alban Institute
2121 Cooperative Way, Suite 100
Herndon, VA 20171

Cover design by Signal Hill.

Cover art: *Aaron's Breastplate* by Sandra Bowden. In Exodus, Aaron's priestly garments are described as being made "for beauty and for glory" and his breastplate as having been inset with twelve stones inscribed with the names of the twelve tribes of Israel. In this collage assemblage, not only are the names of the twelve tribes inscribed, but the Hebrew text of Jacob blessing his twelve sons is also encoded into the textured paper. Just as this work of art recalls these tribes of Israel, so does *Synagogues in a Time of Change* explore and acknowledge the divisions and differences in the forms and structures of synagogue life that exist in America today.

Library of Congress Cataloging-in-Publication Data

Synagogues in a time of change : fragmentation and diversity in Jewish religious movements / Zachary I. Heller, editor.
     p. cm.
  Includes bibliographical references.
  ISBN 978-1-56699-389-0
  1. Judaism--United States--History. 2. Jewish sects--United States--History. 3. Synagogues--United States--History. 4. Intergroup relations--United States--History. 5. Jews--United States--Identity. I. Heller, Zachary I.
  BM205.S955 2009
  296'.0973--dc22
                              2009014388

  09   10   11   12   13   VP   5   4   3   2   1

Contents

120494

PART 5
INDEPENDENTS AND THE TRANSITIONAL GENERATION

Acknowledgments

This volume has been developed under the joint aegis of The National Center for Jewish Policy Studies, and STAR (Synagogues: Transformation and Renewal).

As editor of *Synagogues in a Time of Change: Fragmentation and Diversity in Jewish Religious Movements*, I would like to acknowledge the cooperation of the many outstanding contributors to this volume whose thinking and writing have greatly enriched this discussion. I am particularly grateful to Dr. David M. Gordis, now president emeritus of Hebrew College and founding director of the National Center for Jewish Policy Studies, Rabbi Hayim Herring, Executive Director of STAR (Synagogues: Transformation and Renewal), and Rabbi Sanford Seltzer, Director of the Interreligious Center on Public Life and formerly Associate Dean of Hebrew College's Rabbinical School, who have placed their confidence in me and entrusted me with the development of this project. They have always been available for consultation, sharing their wise insights, and have functioned as an informal editorial advisory committee. The National Center for Jewish Policy Studies acknowledges its indebtedness to Hebrew College, Newton Centre, Massachusetts, of which it is an independent affiliate, for its continued hospitality and administrative support during the past fifteen years.

A special note of gratitude to Dr. Maury and Joyce Hoberman whose personal commitment to this project was expressed in their tangible support that helped make its development and editing possible. Their support is another expression of their desire to contribute to the creation of a vibrant Jewish community, rich in spirit and ideas.

Our appreciation is expressed to James Wind, Richard Bass, and Kristy Arnesen Pullen of the Alban Institute, who have understood the significance of this volume and have undertaken to bring it to print and distribute it to a wide readership. The editorial skills of Andrea Lee have been especially valuable in enhancing the precision of language and style of this text that is the product of so many hands.

Introduction

Zachary I. Heller

This volume is, first of all, an attempt to describe the development of contemporary religious movements or denominations in American Jewry and their interrelationships and tensions. It will be evident to the reader from several essays that Jewish life and the development of the synagogue in America have continually adapted to the new and ever-changing environment. They have been influenced by the unique characteristics of American society, whose democratic and populist nature set the tone not only for its political and social structures, but for religious expression and institutions as well. In conjunction with this exploration, dynamics within American Christianity are also examined because, as a reflection of the American experience, they serve as background for what has occurred in the Jewish community. This book also explores the contemporary scene in which the position of Jewish movements appears to be challenged by several factors—from unaffiliated Jews to emerging spiritual communities to non- or transdenominational congregations. This volume has been organized in five thematic sections that take the reader from the historic perspectives through the contemporary scene to consideration of long-range challenges. The five parts are as follows:

- The history and context of Jewish religious life in America
- Fragmentation or diversity?
- Prescriptions
- Personal reflections and community stories
- Independents and the transitional generation

1

The Issues and Context

Jewish life, law, traditions, and modes of observance since the Rabbinic Era have been marked by fluidity, by creative interpretations of classic texts, and by responses to the changing conditions of each age, although some fundamentalists may not readily accept this historic perspective of religious development. The evolutionary process may be more apparent during certain periods of Jewish history than others. For example, the period beginning with the Enlightenment in Europe has seen several significant attempts to formulate responses to the doors that it opened as well as strong defensive reactions to those trends. Attempts to formulate new interpretations and expressions of Jewish law, philosophy, and practice, and the resultant responses to them, formed a contrapuntal dynamic in the nineteenth century, first in Europe and then transplanted to North America. Out of this dynamic developed organized movements in which like-minded individuals and congregations could find mutual support and opportunities to advance shared agendas.

While the new American organizations had some structure, their individual component congregations maintained general autonomy, having only an agreement to subscribe to a basic set of core principles and common identity. This was in contradistinction to some precedents in Europe in the previous century, perhaps most significantly in Great Britain where the Orthodox United Synagogue, like the Anglican Church, maintained strict control over the functioning of its member congregations, controlling the appointment of clergy and even having legal ownership of synagogue buildings and cemeteries. The American setting was so different from the British and other models that when Solomon Schechter, who had reorganized the Jewish Theological Seminary of America in New York after a scholarly career at Cambridge, brought together leaders of twenty-two synagogues in February 1913 to form a network of Conservative congregations with the model of the British United Synagogue in mind, no mention of any centralized authority was made. This pattern of organization was similar to the Union of American Hebrew Congregations (now the Union for Reform Judaism [URJ]) founded by Rabbi Isaac Mayer

Wise in 1873 and of the Union of Orthodox Jewish Congregations of America (originally the Orthodox Jewish Congregational Union of America, now known informally as the Orthodox Union [OU]) founded in 1898.

Those common bonds among Jewish congregations in North America and the formal organizations that represented them had no precedent in the Jewish lexicon; they were quite different from the German *gemeinde*, an overarching community. As Jewish immigrants became more Americanized and as English became their new language, they sought a descriptive term for this new organizing concept. For lack of a more accurate one, they often adopted a term from the world of the American Protestant churches—*denomination,* despite its differing implications. Those who had greater linguistic sophistication, and understood the implications of *denomination* in its American Christian usage, often used the term *movement* instead, which they felt reflected the new reality more precisely and, unlike *denomination*, did not have implications that suggested a centralized authority and clerical hierarchy. But in common practice, these two terms, *movement* and *denomination*, were often used interchangeably. Yet, when there arose the desire for a term that would identify a program or an identity as inclusive of the major movements or as transcending the bounds of their organizations or institutions, the one used most often is *transdenominational.* When there is the desire for a term suggesting the concept goes beyond the current state of the established religious movements, it is *postdenominational.* Those who identify themselves as independent of any of the movements or denominations are *nondenominational.*

Throughout this volume we have generally adopted the common usage *American Judaism, American,* or *America* to refer to both the United States and Canada where applicable or without specific designation to the Jewish community in the United States. Mexican Jewry that identifies as a Latin American community is generally not under consideration except as part of any reflection of the issues of world Jewry. While Canadian Jewry has much in common with the Jewish communities in the United States and has been aligned with the organizational structures of the synagogue movements headquartered in the United States, there is much that differentiates it. Historically, Canadian Jewry has been much more conservative and traditionally oriented than members of the same movements south of the border. Many Canadian Reform and Conservative congregations have often not adopted some of the more liberal practices espoused by their counterparts in the United States, and recently several significant Conservative synagogues in the Toronto area have decided to abandon their membership in the United Synagogue of Conservative Judaism for multiple reasons, including ideology and some organizational issues.

Some Challenges to Contemporary Jewish Movements

The spectrum of Jewish religious communities today share a number of challenges. One challenge is from is the vast numbers of Jews who are generally unaffiliated. Some claim to be secular and are therefore distanced from what the synagogue represents, while others do affiliate for limited periods when they make use of the synagogue to meet the needs of their lifecycle celebrations and transitions. Both the 1990 and 2000 National Jewish Population Survey (NJPS) indicated a significant group of American Jews who are unaffiliated or who self-define as secular. Yet the reality is that many of those who apply the term *secular* to themselves are not professed atheists or agnostics but people whose secular identity is a reflection of their lack of adherence to regular Jewish religious practice, whether in private or communal settings, yet who do admit to some elements of traditional faith that are deeply personal. The various religious movements may indeed experience a greater challenge attracting those who describe themselves as unaffiliated, as having no denominational connection, or even as secular than they do attracting those across denominational lines. Those who are "unaffiliated" or "secular" are often dropouts from synagogue life. According to some estimates, only up to 30 percent of American Jews are synagogue members at any particular time while up to 80 percent have a synagogue connection during their lifetimes. One of the major challenges of Jewish life in this era is how the vast resources of synagogues and the movements with which they associate can be directed to capture the hearts and minds of those who seem alienated and disinterested.

The second challenge is a qualitative one from those who are often among the outstanding products of the synagogue movements and their educational institutions and programs. These people seek to transcend the movements and find expressions of Judaism and modes of behavior not bound to either the organizational frameworks or the modes of behavior that characterize the denominational realities. They seek to create independent, collaborative religious settings that meet their needs, whether by going beyond what they find in existing formal congregations or by stretching the bounds of accepted ritual practice that typified the congregations in which they were raised and trained. These groups are often referred to as "emerging spiritual communities."

The reality is that despite supposed clear lines of demarcation among the movements, their boundaries have a great deal of permeability. Members move across denominational lines at will, sometimes several times during a lifetime. Synagogue affiliation is determined by multiple factors, including philosophy, geography, social relationships, personal comfort with modes of religious practice, charisma of clergy, and economics. Many times over the past decades suggestions have been made that some denominations should consider merging, despite their well-articulated differences in philosophy about and attitudes toward core issues in Jewish practice and belief. Such notions about merger have been rejected quickly, not just because of organizational considerations, but also as a reflection of the belief that the denominational postures do have merit and express distinct views that should be maintained.

Congregations, ranging from small to large, not affiliated with the organizational structure of any movement and that consider themselves independent certainly exist. Many have existed this way for a number of years; some have previously been part of a particular movement but left it for various reasons; others never affiliated from the outset or declared that they were movement neutral at the time of a merger with another synagogue when a community faced demographic decline. Some, though, have purposely espoused a non- or transdenominational position with the intent that it would permit them to define themselves broadly with an eclectic posture that might be attractive to a wider range of potential members. These congregations are noted as distinct from the independent *minyanim* prayer groups or emerging spiritual communities referred to above and are described in this volume as a new contemporary phenomenon.

Despite these ideological and practical stances, denominational dividing lines are often blurred as the ideas raised and implemented as innovations in one movement sometimes find their way across boundaries, slightly redefined but unmistakably recognizable. But the pendulum eventually swings in both directions. Traditional observances previously deemed antiquated and therefore cast aside as part of liberal responses to modernity reappear at later date, perhaps with some modification, as the magnetic poles of the Jewish world reenergize each other.

Some significant examples of this include, first, the movement toward gender equality and inclusiveness in the synagogue—both in the pulpit and the pew—which began first in the Reconstructionist movement and then in the Reform movement. In the early 1970s the Reform seminary Hebrew Union College–Jewish Institute of Religion began to ordain women. The Conservative movement moved towards egalitarianism in the synagogue somewhat later; only after more than another decade of debate did the faculty of the Jewish Theological Seminary of America decide to ordain women as rabbis and then certify them as cantors. This was greeted with derision by Orthodox authorities and their followers. Yet, as one examines the countless steps that have been taken since then expanding the various rabbinic-type roles for which women are being trained within "modern" Orthodox institutions, both in Israel and in America—women serve as legal pleaders before rabbinic courts regarding divorce; as counselors in matters of Jewish family life, with expertise in issues of sexuality and reproduction; and as spiritual guides and educators in synagogues—it is evident that this train has left the station and is moving down the track, not to be turned back. The recent phenomenon of somewhat equal, although separate, advanced Jewish education, including mastery of classic legal texts and interpretive commentaries for young women in modern Orthodoxy, represents initial steps toward greater inclusiveness, if not actual egalitarianism, in some

Orthodox congregations and independent prayer groups referred to in the chapters that follow.

Issues of gender have been followed by soul-searching struggles of both religious conscience and personal emotion as movements consider, both openly and more discretely, issues of homosexuality. The issues are not just ideological, rooted in classic texts that are subject to debate, but are also human realities that demand sensitive concern and responses. Here too there is much interchange, overt and covert, across denominational and ideological lines, despite the often-rigid public positions taken by the more traditionalist camp.

Other issues such as instrumental music in synagogue services and other innovations in liturgical and even legal practice are examples of influences of the liberal upon the more traditional Conservative movement.

But this stream has in reality begun to flow in the opposite direction as well. Consider the following examples:

- One of the first major moves of Classic Reform, even in Germany, was the reduction or elimination of Hebrew as the language of Jewish liturgy. That has been greatly reversed in the last two editions of Reform prayer books.
- Zionism was rejected initially but is now a significant core value of Reform ideology.
- *Kashrut*, the dietary laws, was derided as an irrelevant ancient practice incompatible with modernity, yet is slowly returning to Reform synagogues and homes.
- Traditional symbols of Jewish worship such as *tallit* and head coverings were set aside in favor of appearing like our non-Jewish neighbors. While not yet required in all Reform synagogues, they have become the norm in many.
- The Reform movement has joined its Orthodox and Conservative coreligionists in establishing day schools and summer camps that provide an intensive Jewish curriculum and experience.

One must take note here of the Jewish Renewal movement that has coalesced around the leadership and personal model of Rabbi

Zalman Schachter-Shalomi and has focused on spirituality, kabbalah, and neohassidic thought and practice. These approaches have certainly had an effect upon all denominations. The Renewal movement has a diffuse organizational structure that makes no claim to being a new denomination but does try to be an inclusive umbrella that brings together somewhat diverse elements that share common interests.

Influences across denominational lines go only so far. Elements in the Orthodox Jewish world that espouse an isolationist posture are moving continually towards greater religious fundamentalism and portraying themselves as the inheritors of the authentic mantle of traditional Judaism as supposedly practiced in pre-Holocaust Eastern or Middle Europe.[1] Despite their rejection of innovation and adaptation in matters of religious practice, Orthodox Jews are actively involved in the worlds of contemporary business and technology. Their claim of religious authenticity has often attracted the newly observant *ba'alei tshuvah* (literally "returnees in repentance") for whom the notion of absolute truths is mesmerizing and fixating. Many of them, who have had little contact with traditional Jewish observance, often gravitate to the more dogmatic and less flexible elements within Orthodoxy, unable to distinguish between core and custom, principle and tradition.

The more moderate positions found in modern or centrist Orthodoxy have been challenged by those of the right wing portrayed above. An example is the recent questioning by the Chief Rabbinate in Israel of the authority of most members of the Rabbinical Council of America (the majority of whose members were ordained by the Rabbi Isaac Elchanan Rabbinical School of Yeshiva University) to conduct divorces and conversions. The Chief Rabbinate viewed these products of American Orthodoxy as tainted by modernity and liberalism. This challenge has served to put great pressure upon those espousing moderate positions within Orthodoxy to conform to the inflexible ideology that rejects any possibly tempered response to the realities and challenges of Jewish life in America. In this crucible, modern centrist Orthodoxy faces its greatest test.

Each of the movements faces its own internal challenges as well as the contemporary response from the many unaffiliated, in the spirit of "a plague on all your houses," who want to say, "We are just Jewish." Many contributors to this volume note that the movements or denominations grew out of responses to issues whose roots are traced directly to Jewish life in Middle Europe in the nineteenth century. In the twenty-first century, not only have the answers changed but also the original questions are no longer relevant. The purpose of this volume is to explore "where we have come from, where we are going, and to whom we are ultimately accountable" for the future of Judaism in America.

Origins of This Volume

The nascence of this volume is to be found in a one-day consultation at Hebrew College in Newton Centre, Massachusetts, in June 2006, the purpose of which was to explore the position of contemporary denominations in Jewish life and the issues of trans-denominationalism. Sponsored by Hebrew College and STAR (Synagogues: Transformation and Renewal) and chaired by Rabbi Sanford Seltzer, at that time an associate dean of the Rabbinical School of Hebrew College, the conference combined the presentation of several formal papers with informal roundtable discussions. Several of those papers, with further editing by their authors, have been incorporated in this volume. The balance of the chapters have been solicited in order to fulfill the purpose of this book.

In December 2006 the Association for Jewish Studies (AJS), which is an association of scholars of Jewish studies on the university level, convened its annual meeting, and it was announced beforehand that one of the myriad sessions would be a roundtable discussion on "Denominationalism in a Post-Denominational World." A distinguished panel of discussants was announced, including among others, Dr. David Ellenson, president of Hebrew Union College–Jewish Institute of Religion (the seminary of the Reform movement) and a noted scholar of Jewish history, and Dr. Arnold Eisen, at that time still at Stanford University, a highly regarded scholar of Jewish religion and religious behavior who had recently been selected to be the new chancellor of the Jewish Theological Seminary of America (Conservative). The organizing committee had asked them to participate as independent scholars and not as representatives of their institutions or movements. They have edited their oral remarks from the transcript for inclusion in this volume.

This volume is wide-ranging in its exploration of the state and future of the religious movements, often called denominations in Jewish religious life, especially in America but with worldwide implications as well. Its contributors reflect a diversity of scholarship, personal experiences, and insights regarding contemporary Jewish life. Those involved in the book's conception have not sought a preconceived trajectory that would demonstrate predetermined conclusions, but rather want to share the concerns and insights of the contributors and include the reader in a work whose unfolding process was brought to a close only by the need to target and then meet a publication date.

The editor and his colleagues in this endeavor hope that this book will stimulate much thought and discussion about the future of organized Jewish religious life in America, and the roles of the various movements in it and their relationships with each other. Do they provide ever-expanding options and opportunities for Jewish expression that enhance the Jewish future, or do they attempt to protect and promote organizational interests and positions that reflect concerns of the past, rather than responding to unfolding challenges? Institutions and movements must answer whether they are defenders of the status quo or visionaries, unifiers or divisive. How can they keep their program and message vital for succeeding generations, especially those of the transitional postuniversity-age generation? How do they speak to those who do not identify with their formulations of Jewish identity and expression? How do they understand the concerns of those for whom formal theology and sacerdotal language and symbols are not relevant and therefore consider themselves secular?

We set these challenges before those who are members and leaders of synagogue communities and movements as well as those who are currently uninvolved and uncommitted. We trust that this volume will be a catalyst for personal reflection and public discussion, and that will provide our satisfaction and reward.

PART 1

The History and Context of Jewish Religious Life in America

CHAPTER 1

History as Prophecy
Narrating the American Synagogue

David B. Starr

The synagogue remains a central institution in Jewish life as a place of study, worship, and assembly. Those three activities remind students of Jewish life that since ancient times Jewishness contains some definite if imprecise admixture of ethnicity and religion, a worldview of rituals and values that generate behavior, belief, and modes of belonging. In the *longue durée* of diasporic post-Temple (70 CE) Jewry this spelled a rough but perceptible consensus about the boundaries and content of Jewish life, horizontally in relation to non-Jews; vertically in relation to a sense of Jewish history, destiny, and purposes.

Yet the centrality of the synagogue notwithstanding, its precise place in Jewish life varied throughout the ages. Many in the Jewish community may nostalgically pine for the lost world of traditional Jewish society, which involved a larger communal construct of governance structures, leaders, and institutions—a Jewish body politic in which the synagogue numbered as but one of many communal institutions. It shared the burden for Jewish life, since Jews practiced their rituals demarcating time and space as much if not more in the home and in the street as in any demarcated sancta. Even the notion of sancta hardly applied to the synagogue, since it contained no functioning priesthood, no cult of purity reminiscent of the ancient temple. Its leaders—the sages—dominated by their earned intellectual talents rather than any inherited prescribed ritual role. These sages worked with and competed against lay leaders, together with whom they led Jewish religious and social life.

Like any institution, the synagogue demands historical scrutiny since it never stands outside of its context: it reflects as much as it leads larger trends in Jewish and indeed general society. One has to look only at a nineteenth-century German Reform temple to see Lutheran influences; the family pews of twentieth-century North American non-Orthodox temples and synagogues to see the hand of trends in gender, family, and religion.

Much of the best history writing on the United States began with the time-honored notion of U.S. exceptionalism. But rather than blithely assuming and asserting that as fact, many scholars now linger over this notion, asking and critiquing that if the United States has been different, how so? This approach suits Jewish historical study to a tee, since that method always demands that history be considered in twin contexts: that of its locale and of placing any given place and time within the sweep of the Jewish historical story. After all, it is fair to ask whether a synagogue in my hometown of Brookline, Massachusetts, or any U.S. synagogue resembles more its non-Jewish house of worship that stands down the street than it does a synagogue that existed there in 1920, or a synagogue in Salonika in 1935 or 1535?

The Synagogue in Twin Contexts

Haym Soloveitchik has written about evolution in modern Orthodoxy in the second half of the twentieth century. His work suggested that synagogues become part of larger trends occurring in Jewish life. In Orthodoxy this included the decline of organic communities that relied upon tradition and custom, which gave way to enclaves of tighter, more doctrinaire and rigid approaches to learning and to life. Orthodox synagogues have benefited from this swing to the right by increasing lay rigor; yet the rabbis of those synagogues may feel pressure from laity desiring even more fixity than the rabbi may deem correct or advisable.

Soloveitchik's work incorporates understanding of both the Jewish and U.S. dimensions of his story. A student of Jacob Katz, he knows that Orthodoxy exists as a modern traditionalist ideological construct, not to be equated with a traditional society. He knows that it responded to various shifts that affected modern Jewry, like the nineteenth-century Emancipation movement and the Jewish Enlightenment in Europe, migration, and acculturation.

He charts the ways in which internal cultural production like rabbinic legal texts reflected these shifts by compensating for the decline of traditional society. New assertions of codificatory power
emerged at the expense of the local, the customary, the mimetic
dimension of traditional praxis.

He recognizes that this trend reflects the twentieth-century
North American world as well: the world of the university, the
progressive emphasis on the rational and the expert, the linear
teaching that the technology of books and the Internet delivers, all
of which tend to flatten out the textures of the traditional society.
Add to that the socioeconomic upward mobility of modern Orthodoxy, and the modern Orthodox synagogue comes into view:
as posh as liberal synagogues, yet filled with young families desiring greater observance and commitment to Orthodox educational
institutions like *yeshivot*, at the same time seeking the Ivy League
acceptance letter for their children.[1]

American synagogue study reflects a classic tension within the
study of American religious history. This may be termed a clash
between the declinists versus transformationalists (perhaps the latter incorporates a revival-decline dynamic). Perry Miller, the great
historian of the Puritans, may be seen as an exponent of the decline
school. He read the Puritans as tragic figures, unable or unwilling
to cope with the challenge that social change posed to their Calvin-
ist religious worldview. Their "errand into the wilderness," as the
seventeenth-century minister Samuel Danforth described it, gave
way to the commercial revolution that transformed that wilderness
into America, from a periphery of empire to an emerging country
in its own right, from Puritans to Yankees. In this scheme religion
lost, defeated by capitalism's power and its own inability to respond
adequately. Puritan declension, symbolized by their acceptance of
the "halfway covenant" rather than the full covenant liberalizing
who could be considered as "saved," came too late to salvage their
religious project of building religiously ordered community.[2]

Different Jewish camps deployed the declension thesis to understand and critique the Jewish response to modernity. Zionism
judged modern denominationalism and the modern synagogue as
the wrong solution to the challenge posed by Jewish cultural and
political integration into European life. Rather than striving for

equality as privatized religious communities, Zionism insisted that Jewish equality must be national and cultural, the creation of a Jewish space, civic ethos, and a new Jew.

Orthodox historiography looked askance at Jewish Enlightenment and Emancipation as harbingers of secular modernism and liberalism, which bequeathed to the Jewish community manifold ills: the sovereign self, which undermined traditional notions of community and communitarianism, and the shattering of the consensus about canonical culture. According to this interpretive line, Jews lost their center: their commitment to commonalities of behavior, belief, belonging, and their sense of purpose.

All modern Judaisms contrived responses to this crisis, and they etched their worldviews in the synagogues they created. Reform Judaism, the boldest in affirming modern liberalism, sought to recast Judaism through a newfound autonomy granted to the choosing individual. The synagogue became the showplace for Jew and non-Jew alike to witness the new Judaism, more decorous and priestly, featuring a new sort of rabbi edifying the congregation through sermons that blended Jewish sources with bourgeois definitions of culture.

In response to Reform, Orthodoxy viewed itself as self-consciously *halakhic* in ever-expansive ways, trying to make Jewish life panhalakhic in policy and in life. As Moshe Halbertal wrote in a supercommentary on the historian of Orthodoxy Jacob Katz's work: "Katz noted the paradoxical phenomenon that, as the community's commitment to the *halakhah* shrank, the power of the halakhic authority over those who remained in the framework expanded. The challenge to tradition created a more profound dependence by the community's members on the rabbi, who, in this period, became Judaism's central mediator. Moreover, since the power of the halakhic authority became restricted to those who had survived the crisis, the rabbi no longer had to compromise with other powers functioning alongside him."[3]

Though the rise of Orthodoxy formed the subject of Katz's analysis, one might profitably substitute the word *synagogue* for *rabbi* and for that matter all modern synagogues, not just of the Orthodox variety. The key here is the paradox Halbertal placed at the center: that the synagogue, and the rabbi, accrued more and more power over less and less vis-à-vis the implosion of traditional society. In the vacuum caused by the loss of the community structure, its institutions, its sacred rhythms of time and public spaces, only the synagogue remained, a semipublic institution. Within its walls it labored to reunite ethnos and religion, as it has struggled to create a community delivering meaning in a world often filled with a privatized search for religious authenticity.

Cautions, Assumptions, and Exceptions

The above analysis rests on the world of Central and Western European Jewry. It leaves much to be desired, both on its own terms and as a means of explaining North American Jewish life. For starters, it makes a lot of assumptions about the structure and content of premodern Jewish life that need to be tested. As with state-established churches—and the medieval model of Jewish community was a kind of state-established church—a distinction needs to be made between their institutional standing and people's felt connection to them. Could it be the case that contemporary Jews still think too typologically about the premodern and the modern, assuming the former to be the age of religion and the latter to be the age of reason, one epoch giving way to a new age, with little to connect them?

There can be little doubt about the impact of the Enlightenment and Emancipation upon Jewish life. Jews, like everyone else, experienced the dizzying effects of the industrial revolution, modern nationalism, migration, urbanization, technology, modern capitalism, and the like. Yet one must not assume that if the world lacked those dynamics prior to the advent of modernity, piety must have filled the void—for that would be committing the historian's sin of anachronism—projecting the present back into the past. Even with the corporate semiautonomous world of the Jewish *kehillah* of the Middle Ages, tensions roiled communities. The synagogue existed as one institution, and it may be the case that it competed with other forms of cultural expression acted out along lines of class and gender, or in the uneasy relationship between rabbinic elites and their ways and the folk and their ways.

The North American context also yields complex and confusing evidence, cautioning the scholar about drawing a unified field theory explaining it all. From the perspective of Jewish history, it seems easy to dismiss North American Jewish history—and its synagogues by extension—as pale imitations of the real thing. Judaism redux: cathedrals catering to a largely unlettered, apathetic community led by clergy unlikely to be recorded in the annals of Jewish letters.

Yet the notion of American exceptionalism carries with it the normative judgment that transformation rather than decline went on here, including in the religious sphere. This more Whiggish view takes fullest expression in the recent synthesis *American Judaism* by Jonathan Sarna. Sarna—a student of Sydney Ahlstrom, a leading scholar of American religious history at Yale—eschews Perry Miller's declension thesis, seeing the United States instead as a world of revivals and declines. Freedom, democracy, congregationalism, ethnic and religious pluralism, separation of church and state—all of these produced a competitive yet tolerant marketplace that gave rise to various Judaisms and various sorts of synagogues. Viewed against that background, the notion of postdenominational synagogues seems almost inevitable, one more example of the marketplace at work.[4]

The American perspective brings us back to Alexis de Tocqueville, who saw the United States clearly as a place unto itself. This included the spirit of tremendous volunteer boosterism distinguishing the civic and religious spheres. With cheap, plentiful land came the ability to expand ever outward from metropolis to periphery, challenging old communities and cultures to remain relevant, enabling new versions to grow up. The ground beckoned to its settlers: build lives here, church this land, forge the city—and temple—on the hill. Out of this encounter, American Christianities, and Judaisms, emerged entrepreneurially, housed in ever-evolving and multiplying houses of worship.

Religion as Counterpoint

Synagogue building reflected American and Jewish imperatives and the common commitment to the idea of religion, even if the reality sometimes seemed to pale in comparison to vestigial traditionalism linking immigrants to their European homes. Politics affected the felt need for some sort of religion as a counterpoint to the cultural confusion brought on by capitalism, the gospel of science, and the threat of godless bolshevism. Religion reminded people that their country worked not solely on account of its material circumstances, but also because of its Manifest Destiny—the grace God shed upon it. Over time that included not only Protestants, but also Catholics and even Jews. Hence President Eisenhower's pronouncement after his election in 1952, "Our government makes no sense unless it is founded on a deeply felt religious faith—and I don't care what it is."[5]

Sarna's book tells this story with a scholar's eye for the main lines and the writer's eye for the small detail. And it all rests upon the American foundation: a state and society characterized by democracy, freedom of religion and conscience, church-state separation, and voluntarism, all of which spurred church building. This matched up with Jewish imperatives: a people with a penchant and need for ethnoreligious community building.

Structurally and culturally, North American synagogues tended to take their cue from the environment around them. Early Sephardic immigrants in the colonial world imported their traditions, including hierarchy and ecclesiastical authority, only to see that centralized synagogue community model founder. It fell victim to North American reality: The relatively small number of Jews that came to America socially integrated rather easily and quickly, which challenged and effectively overturned an older notion of centralization and authority. America made itself felt culturally too: here women went to synagogue because American women went to church, something these women and their mothers had not done in a previous life in Amsterdam.

Democratic Norms

The American Revolution rewrote the synagogue. New charters spoke the gospel of the new world: houses of worship—like the state in which they lived—would henceforth be governed via democratic norms. The absence of an early North American rabbinate accentuated this impulse. Here too Jews mimicked their neighbors: as Protestant patterns encouraged family seating, so too more liberal congregations embraced the family pew.

By the age of President Andrew Jackson in the 1820s and '30s, it became clear that America was producing a new kind of Judaism, structurally at least. The age of fervent territorial and economic market revolution inspired mobility, new communities, and a marketplace of ideas and institutions. A new generation of Jews, most famously early lay reformers in Charleston, South Carolina, created new synagogues embodying their American values. Dramatic expansion of the Jewish community, bringing it from 10,000 in 1825 to 230,000 by 1880, created new ethnic diversity in American Jewish life. One could now speak of multiple Jewries, grouped around countries of origin, languages, and varying religious customs. One could hear Spanish, Ladino, German, Polish, Yiddish, and other languages in any given Jewish home or house of worship.

The United States' ordeal by fire brought disunion but in the end a more perfect union. In a postwar wave of optimism, the growing American Jewry built its grand "temples," monuments to its declining inhibitions about being out in American society. The great Reform temples of Cincinnati and elsewhere suggested that Zion existed not in Jerusalem but on the banks of the Ohio River and any place else in the last best hope of man on earth. Just as newer churches became "institutional churches" dedicated to a social gospel and organizations of communal voluntarism, so too the temple as center now constituted itself as both a social mission-driven organization as well as a house of worship.

That trend increasingly defined and described the American synagogue of the late nineteenth and early twentieth centuries. Jews frowned upon religious mores that separated them from their neighbors; they embraced social work that connected them to the larger society. This endangered the centrality of worship and study, which in turn paved the way for the American vision of the right sort of rabbi. He came to his work charged with doing the near impossible: making the life of the mind and the spirit relevant to the life of action.

By the 1950s North American Jewry saw itself at a crossroads. Now overwhelmingly Eastern European by origin but mainly middle class in position and outlook, these North American Jews knew they now occupied the center of the Jewish world. With the European center destroyed by Nazi genocide and the Jews of the land of Israel facing an uncertain future, only North American Jewry seemed secure in its place. Their institutions would have to play multiple roles.

Now living in suburbs, no longer dwelling in densely settled and thickly textured urban neighborhoods, Jews built new synagogues mirroring their anxiety and their pride. Aesthetically more imposing than the city *shteiblach* they had fled, these edifices and their rabbis and professionals needed to reach increasingly acculturated Jews. These temples faced a new burden, not only creating Jewish life where none existed, but replacing ethnic neighborhoods and an array of Jewish cultures, some secular and Yiddish, some religious.

Diverging Centers

The synagogue center of Mordecai Kaplan's imagination now took on increasing relevance and popularity: a place of prayer, study, schooling, socializing, and social work. The synagogue center continues to be a powerful idea; it embodies the tensions and connections of the Jews: an entity comprising both a nation and a religion, existing as both a social group and a church. No wonder, then, that its central institution embraces the assembly hall, the classroom, and the house of God.

Just as the synagogue always mirrored broader social trends, so too it served as a theater for the dramas within Jewish life. With new ideologies of Judaism came competing platforms for the substance of Jewish life—what should Jews practice and why. These questions became the province of the synagogue. The twentieth century witnessed the contest between two claimants to the mantle of modern traditionalism: Conservative and Orthodox Judaism. The *mechitzah* separated not only men and women, but Conservative synagogues from Orthodox ones. It more than anything else symbolized and concretized this Jewish disputation. So too the question of the location of the synagogue: would it stand at the geographic center of a physical community or not? The Conservative innovation permitting driving to synagogue on the Sabbath in effect decentered the synagogue, making it a kind of nonspatial entity, potentially existing in the middle of nowhere, as in the case of the new building of Congregation Mishkan Tefila that had moved in 1957 from a densely populated area in Roxbury, Massachusetts, to a new location on Hammond Pond Parkway in suburban Chestnut Hill, a parkway at the intersection of a shopping thoroughfare, but not a neighborhood.

All of these activities leave the unmistakable impression that North American Jews worked busily at their Judaism. But before adopting the optimism of the transformationalists, a few questions remain. Synagogue history, as with the study of any institution, begs the question of meaning: what difference do synagogues make in people's lives, seen in the context of other sources of meaning— the public school, civic associations, and the like? Much of the best recent religious history tries to get at this by studying lived religion, the patterns of ritual observance that come from or directly touch parishioners.[6] In North American Jewish life, one may argue that each movement places its own emphasis on the synagogue and achieves different results. I would argue that, historically, Reform centered itself on the synagogue, investing it with high prestige, whereas Orthodoxy relied more on the emerging day-school movement as a tool for building community.

The evaluation of the valence of the synagogue stems as well from broader social trends. In a society that accords high respect for technology, rationalism, and professionalism, if not intellectualism, the synagogue and its professionals continue to struggle against the perception that if they possessed true talent they would be working on Wall Street rather than serving as clerics for often unappreciative congregants.

From the Jewish perspective, as with much else we struggle against our own messianic expectations: we operate as if the synagogue effectively replaces the mythic world of traditional Jewish society. We lack the means to grapple with that loss and its implications, the shattering of a common covenantal unity and a belief in a shared purpose. It remains unclear how Jews individually or collectively will grapple with freedom and historicism, two pervasive phenomena that shape how we live and how we think.

Transformationalism may describe the reality of religion in America, but normatively speaking it fails to reveal anything about the quality or implications of those changes. Transformationalism often avoids the normative questions: What of the content, boundaries, and quality of leadership within a community? How does it mediate contemporary culture and the challenge of individualism? To what extent has America produced a creative, yet in some ways deeply incompetent, Jewish community as measured by traditional standards of competence in Jewish study and life? Such flux may function better for large religious faiths like Christians or Muslims rather than smaller communities that have difficulty replenishing themselves, particularly after the Holocaust, what with intermarriage and a stagnant birthrate.

These two means of thinking about synagogues may or may not bear relevance for the new age of postdenominationalism and unaffiliated congregations. We cannot yet know what they mark: either the creative energy that transformationalism insists lies at the heart of the history of American Jewish experience or the continuing mediocrity of much of Jewish cultural life. New rabbis, new schools, new congregations—might they spell the desire for a new commitment to Jewishness or a rejection of the old for no good reason? The past only provides a perspective upon the future; foretelling belongs in another province altogether.

CHAPTER 2

Denominations in American Judaism
The Dynamics of Their Relationships

Lawrence Grossman

During the first century-and-a-half of its existence, American Judaism had no "denominations." The earliest Jewish communities, established beginning in the late seventeenth century and during the eighteenth century in New York, Newport, Philadelphia, Charleston, and Savannah, were based on the *kehillah* model prevalent in Europe, whereby all Jews living in a defined location were members, the synagogue functioned not only as a place of prayer but also as a social and cultural center, and communal authorities asserted the power of religious coercion over the members. Since the founders of these communities were mostly Sephardim, the liturgical traditions of Spain and Portugal were followed, even when subsequent immigration would make Ashkenazim the numerical majority.

This communal structure could not survive the legal separation of church and state in the new United States and the spirit of freedom and individualism that accompanied it. The notion that a religious community could monitor and discipline its members' behavior became obsolete, and religious practice came to be seen as a purely voluntary matter. In the early nineteenth century new synagogues formed, first, by breaking away from the old ones and then through the immigration of new groups of Jews, who established their own places to pray, both in the older cities and in new locations.

Even at this stage, divisions were not yet of a denominational kind. Rather, the new arrivals, who were overwhelmingly Ashkenazi, tended to separate along the lines of origin: those coming from the same European town or province, and thus sharing common prayer customs, opened their own synagogues. Such differences—although important to the people involved—were relatively minor and did not denote ideological or theological variety. Judaism was universally conceived in its traditional form, even as large and growing numbers of North American Jews were abandoning its practices.

The First "Denominations": Reform and Orthodox

The first denomination to emerge was Reform, officially adopted in the 1820s by Congregation Beth Elohim in Charleston, South Carolina. But the new wave of German Jewish immigrants arriving in the country over the next two decades was what made Reform into the predominant form of Judaism in America.

Reform *temples*—the term used instead of *synagogues*—stressed decorum in the services; used organ music as an accompaniment to prayer; replaced or supplemented the original Hebrew of the prayer book with English (and sometimes German) material; and employed rabbis who dressed in modern clerical garb, had secular educations, and could deliver edifying sermons in English. Reform temples also had a tendency to alter or eliminate elements of the liturgy that did not comport with modern ideas, such as references to the miraculous resurrection of the dead, the messianic restoration of Jews to their Palestinian homeland, and the renewal of sacrifices. Reform radically downgraded the importance of such Jewish practices as keeping the kosher laws and observing the Sabbath, deeming rituals less important than ethics.

The success of Reform in America was due to two factors. One was its adaptability to the values and the real-life needs of many Jews, who wanted to shake off old-world ideas and restrictions. The other was the charismatic leadership of Rabbi Isaac Mayer Wise (1819–1900), who shepherded the movement from his home base in Cincinnati for decades. Reform growth put defenders of tradition on the defensive. Led primarily by Isaac Leeser (1806–1868) of Philadelphia, traditionalists fought a seemingly losing battle to maintain the old practices while adapting to the American environment.

It was in the 1840s, then, that one first could speak of denominations in American Judaism: there was Reform and there was Orthodoxy—the word that was being increasingly used to denote the traditional way of doing things. Naturally, the question emerged of how to reconcile the existence of such divergent visions of Judaism with the ideal of Jewish unity, a dilemma that has dogged American Jews ever since.

Close to twenty rabbis, including Leeser and Wise, convened a meeting in 1855 in Cleveland in order to create an overall organizational structure for American Jewry. But the sharp religious differences already evident in the community doomed this effort. After the Civil War, in 1873, the Reform movement, under Wise's direction, proceeded to create its own congregational body. Assuming that it would come to represent all of American Jewry, it adopted the name Union of American Hebrew Congregations (UAHC). The Union initiated a rabbinical seminary in 1875, Hebrew Union College (HUC), whose name also connoted nondenominational unity, as did the name of the Reform rabbinical association, Central Conference of American Rabbis (CCAR), organized in 1889.

Ironically, at the height of its self-perception as normative American Judaism, Reform sowed the seeds of new denominationalism. The serving of unkosher seafood at the banquet celebrating HUC's first graduating class in 1883 was followed two years later by Reform's promulgation of the so-called Pittsburgh Platform, which flatly denied Jewish peoplehood, rejected the authority of all ritual, and identified the messianic doctrine with human progress. By then a good number of traditionalists had concluded that they had no place in the network of institutions associated with Reform.

These dissidents founded the Jewish Theological Seminary (JTS) in 1886. Its avowed purpose was the training of *traditional* rabbis—in contrast to the HUC graduates—but its leadership and constituency was not all of one piece, including individuals of unimpeccable Orthodoxy as well as moderate Reformers who believed that the Pittsburgh Platform had gone too far. At first JTS was sometimes referred to as an "Orthodox" seminary, and it was supported by the Orthodox Jewish Congregational Union of America (now known as the Union of Orthodox Jewish Congregations of America, or OU), created in 1898.

A Third Way: Conservative Judaism

By 1902, however, JTS had few students and little money, and a small group of wealthy Jews recast the institution with the goal of producing rabbis trained to modernize and Americanize the East European Jews who had begun to arrive in the country in large numbers in the 1880s. To serve as JTS president they brought from England the world-renowned rabbinic scholar Solomon Schechter (1847–1915). Neither old-line Orthodox nor Reform, Schechter espoused modern critical approaches to Jewish texts and utilized the term *Catholic Israel*, that is, the experience of the Jewish people, as the touchstone for determining normative Judaism, even while maintaining allegiance, at least in principle, to *halakhah*. Schechter enjoyed collegial relationships with Reform scholars, referring to their movement as "His Majesty's loyal opposition." He assumed, as did many others at the time, that Reform and emergent Conservative Judaism would mark out the two viable religious options open to twentieth-century North American Jews.

Under Schechter's influence, JTS gradually found itself at the vanguard of a new movement, Conservative Judaism, which found a mass constituency among the children of the recent Jewish migrants from Eastern Europe. Eager to retain a traditional atmosphere in the worship service while eliminating from it what they saw as old-world vestiges, these Conservative Jews established synagogues that followed the standard liturgy, but where men and women sat together, English readings supplemented the Hebrew prayers, and Americanized rabbis delivered sermons in English and often on the relevance of Jewish teachings to current issues. Some of these synagogues went so far as to copy Reform in using organ music during services. The Conservative congregations, many served by rabbinical graduates of JTS, organized as the United Synagogue of America in 1913. The OU by then had withdrawn its support from JTS, perceiving accurately that it was no longer an Orthodox institution.

Despite the rapid growth of Conservative Judaism—which would replace Reform as the largest Jewish group by the 1950s— the assumption that the East European immigrants would, en masse, Americanize their religious practices proved mistaken.

Whether these immigrants were personally observant of the religious laws or not, the image of Judaism that many of them had was the unacculturated Orthodoxy of their homes; the Westernized traditionalism of the Conservatives had no greater authenticity in their eyes than did the completely alien Judaism of the Reformers. As small Orthodox synagogues proliferated, primarily in the urban centers where these newcomers settled, their rabbis created in 1902 an organization to represent them, the Union of Orthodox Rabbis (Agudath Harabbonim).

Nevertheless, Americanization affected even the Orthodox. A synagogue movement, the National Council of Young Israel, begun in 1912, insisted on decorum in its services and promoted the full participation of young men in leading prayers, neither of which had characterized Judaism in the "old country." The Rabbi Isaac Elchanan Theological Seminary, which had started as a traditional yeshiva on the Lower East Side of Manhattan, transformed itself in the 1920s and 1930s into Yeshiva University, with a secular college and graduate schools. The university trained English-speaking rabbis at home in modern culture to compete with the Conservative movement. In 1935 such rabbis, popularly known as "Modern Orthodox," founded the Rabbinical Council of America to represent them.

Reconstructionism and New Divisions

A tripartite Orthodox-Conservative-Reform framework had emerged, but it was complicated by the development, beginning in the 1930s, of yet another approach to Judaism, Reconstructionism. It was the creation of Rabbi Mordecai Kaplan (1881–1983)—originally an Orthodox rabbi—who did not intend to promote it as a separate denomination, but rather as a religious conception that would eventually permeate North American Judaism as a whole. Reconstructionism centered on Jewish peoplehood (what is today called ethnicity), understood Jewish practices as folkways of Jewish civilization, and rejected all supernatural elements, such as miracles. It had considerable influence within the Conservative and Reform movements. Not until the 1950s did Kaplan's disciples launch Reconstructionism as an independent movement, with its own rabbinical school and congregations. It has always remained quite small but highly influential.

Since the end of World War II, a number of trends have pushed the Jewish religious movements further apart. The most significant change has been the growing cleavage between the Conservative movement and Orthodoxy. In 1950 the Conservatives, for the first time, announced an open break with the Orthodox on a matter of Jewish law, permitting driving to synagogue on the Sabbath. A series of other liberal rulings would follow over the years, many of which expanded the role of women in the synagogue far beyond that allotted to them by Orthodoxy—counting them in the *minyan*, allowing them to receive *aliyot* and other synagogue honors, and providing a mechanism for civilly divorced women to remarry in cases where their husbands refused to give them religious divorces. Capping this series of advances, JTS in 1983 approved the ordination of women as rabbis, and subsequently as cantors.

Through these changes, as Conservative Judaism gradually defined itself as a movement separate and apart from Orthodoxy, American Orthodox Judaism came increasingly under the influence of more rigorous rabbis, many of them yeshiva heads and Hasidic leaders who arrived in the United States to escape communism in Russia or later, the ravages of World War II and the Holocaust. Religious standards—in the area of *kashrut* supervision, for example—became more stringent and, for the first time in America, exposure to secular culture, including a college education, came to be seen as dangerous to Orthodoxy. One matter of particular concern to these rabbis was what they saw as the overly collegial relations that prevailed between modern Orthodox groups and their non-Orthodox counterparts. These, the more sectarian Orthodox believed, bestowed unmerited religious legitimacy upon heterodox groups.

The matter came to a head in the mid-1950s over Orthodox membership in local rabbinical boards, which encompassed rabbis of all denominations within a particular community, and in the Synagogue Council of America, a national body that included the synagogue organizations of all three of the then-existing branches of American Judaism. In 1956 ten leading yeshiva heads officially banned Orthodox membership in such transdenominational groups. While adherence to this edict was far from universal among the Orthodox, its promulgation did put those in favor of interdenominational cooperation on the defensive. In addition, it effectively scuttled negotiations that were taking place at the time between leading talmudic scholars at Yeshiva University and JTS for the creation of a rabbinical court that would handle matters of family law for both movements.

Orthodox exclusivity was also transatlantic: relations between religion and state in Israel became another stumbling block to denominational comity in the United States. American Orthodoxy, much to the chagrin of other American Jews, has consistently backed the monopoly that Orthodox rabbis maintain on Israeli Judaism. The periodic conflicts in Israel over who is a Jew and the recognition of non-Orthodox conversions to Judaism, pitting American Orthodoxy against the non-Orthodox movements, have provided perhaps the sharpest episodes of interdenominational tension.

Since the 1950s American Orthodoxy has grown both in numbers and in self-confidence. For the first time since the dawn of Jewish emancipation in the eighteenth century, Orthodox families—which are larger than those of other Jews—seem able to transmit strong religious commitment to their children, drastically minimizing the ravages of secularization that plagued previous Orthodox generations. Orthodoxy has also turned more sectarian. Attempts to rebuild a modern Orthodoxy that would interact fruitfully with non-Orthodox Jews have not succeeded. Edah, an organization founded with considerable fanfare in 1996 with such a goal in mind, lasted ten years and then folded.

A Balkanized Map

Another major shift in the denominational picture was the complex transformation undergone by the Reform movement. Reform, which had already shed its earlier hostility toward Zionism, became increasingly traditional in terms of religious practice. Maintaining kashrut in some form, using primarily Hebrew in the prayer service, and wearing a *tallit* and covering one's head in the synagogue—all previously rejected by Reform—began to gain acceptability in the 1960s, a trend that has accelerated since. This phenomenon—all other things being equal—would have enhanced interdenominational relations by narrowing the gap between Reform and Conservative Jews.

At the same time, however, Reform veered far from traditional notions on matters of personal status. As intermarriage rates rose in the 1960s, an unknown but undoubtedly increasing number of Reform rabbis performed mixed marriages, sometimes together with non-Jewish clergy. Under the leadership of its president, Rabbi Alexander Schindler, the UAHC launched outreach initiatives to the intermarried in the 1970s and in 1983 adopted patrilineal descent, meaning that someone might be recognized as a Jew if either parent was Jewish and if the individual performed acts (which were left unspecified) that indicated Jewish identification.

This decision, one aspect of Reform's broad policy of openness to intermarried families, has undoubtedly helped Reform grow. By the 1990s Reform had once again became the largest denomination, outstripping the Conservatives. But in making this breakthrough, the movement had also struck a heavy blow against denominational harmony. Since traditional Jewish law, recognized by Orthodox and Conservative Jews, viewed only the child of a Jewish mother as Jewish and would require a child of a Jewish father and a non-Jewish mother to undergo formal conversion in order to enter the Jewish faith, this decision taken by Reform created a category of "Jews" who would not be considered such by the more traditional movements.

In the 1980s, then, the denominational map seemed balkanized, showing an increasingly sectarian Orthodoxy having little truck with the other groups and a Reform movement at odds both with the Orthodox and with Conservative Judaism over the issue of patrilineality.

Conservative Judaism Redefined

Recent developments in the Conservative movement, however, have altered this picture. Already in 1984, when JTS voted to ordain female rabbis, some rabbis and laypeople belonging to the movement's more traditionalist wing broke away and founded the

Union for Traditional Conservative Judaism. By 1990 it had set up its own small rabbinical school and dropped "Conservative" from its name, becoming the Union for Traditional Judaism, located ideologically somewhere between modern Orthodoxy and Conservatism. The abandonment of the Conservative movement by its former right wing had the effect of empowering Conservative forces that advocated more changes in line with the temper of the times, which would have the effect of moving the denomination even further away from Orthodoxy and closer to Reform.

The issue that provided the battleground for a redefinition of the Conservative movement was gay rights. For Orthodox Judaism, homosexuality was, in biblical terms, an "abomination." Reform, which had never been bound by Jewish law and its proscription of homosexuality, had declared sexual orientation Jewishly irrelevant in 1990, endorsed civil marriage for gays in 1995, and came out in support of rabbis who conducted commitment ceremonies for same-gender couples with appropriate Jewish ritual in 2000. How would the Conservative movement, committed both to continuity and change, respond?

In 1990 the Rabbinical Assembly, the rabbinic association of Conservative Judaism, voted to oppose civil discrimination against gays and lesbians and welcomed Jews of any sexual orientation into Conservative synagogues. The next year the movement's Committee on Jewish Law and Standards produced two diametrically opposed opinions on the question of whether homosexuals might be appointed as rabbis or to other positions on religious influence, one for and the other against. The issue simmered for a decade, until 2002, when the president of the United Synagogue called for liberalizing the movement's stand on gay rights and JTS students sought to pressure the administration to admit open homosexuals into the rabbinical seminary. JTS chancellor Ismar Schorsch adamantly opposed them, arguing that the very identity of Conservative Judaism as a movement committed to Jewish law was at stake.

In December 2006, the Committee on Jewish Law and Standards ruled that individual Conservative seminaries might decide on whether to admit homosexual rabbinical students and that individual rabbis could opt to perform same-sex commitment ceremonies.

The following March, with Chancellor Schorsch having retired, JTS officially opened its rabbinical program to gays and lesbians.

In the discussions at JTS and within the broader Conservative movement, some influential voices called for an end to what they viewed as the fiction that Conservative Judaism was *halakhic*, that is, obedient to Jewish law. There have even been calls to denote Conservatism as *"aggadic"*—motivated by the nonlegal textual tradition of Judaism, as opposed to the legal tradition. The strength of such sentiments will be tested when the movement confronts its next divisive issue, the status of children of mixed marriages. There are Conservative voices that are already calling for some form of Jewish recognition for children of Jewish fathers, along the line of Reform's patrilineal decision. Indeed, a time may come when the two movements become indistinguishable.

Fading Frameworks

Another distinct possibility is the gradual disappearance—aside from Orthodox separatism—of denominational lines. Many younger Jews, motivated by individual spirituality or personal self-fulfillment, find no meaning in the old institutional frameworks of Judaism. This would account for the growing number of congregations unaffiliated with any movement and for the emergence of a "nonmovement" under the name of Jewish Renewal. Clearly, the denominational pattern of today—which was itself, as we have seen, the result of historical trends—is likely to change beyond recognition over the next generation.

CHAPTER 3

Denominationalism and Its Discontents

The Changing Face of Synagogue Affiliation

Sanford Seltzer

Nearly 150 years ago, Isaac Mayer Wise, the grand architect of American Reform Judaism, called upon the synagogues of his day to embrace a new prayer book of which he was the principal editor. Aptly named *Minhag America* (American Custom), he saw it as replacing the estimated eight other prayer books then in use in congregations in the United States, thereby bringing order into what he deemed to be liturgical chaos. *Minhag America* would, he believed, not only address the spiritual needs of the total Jewish community but also, as he wrote in 1870, "become the cornerstone of a complete union of American Israel."[1] So convinced was he of the inevitability of this union that he followed the traditional custom of prefacing his prayer book with an abstract of the *halakhic* rules governing prayer. To underscore the non- or transdenominational quality of the prayer book, he wrote the preface in unvocalized Hebrew, which had neither an English nor a German translation, under the heading *dinim hashayakhim lehilkhot tefillah*, meaning "rules applying to the laws of prayer."[2]

He was to be sorely disappointed. His dream of a nondenominational American Judaism consisting of a single union of congregations led by rabbis trained and ordained at a common rabbinical school was soon shattered. That occurred when a significant group for whom the tenets of Reform were simply too radical for their tastes seceded from this fragile association. Their own deliberations resulted in the emergence of Conservative Judaism, or the Historical School as it became known, and the creation of the Jewish Theological Seminary. Wise's prayer book would not even enjoy the readership he had envisioned within the Reform movement. For it was replaced by one bearing the imprint of his colleague and rival David Einhorn, when the first edition of the Union Prayer Book authorized by the Central Conference of American Rabbis, which Wise had also founded, appeared in 1894.

In retrospect, Isaac Mayer Wise's vision seems naïve and out of touch with reality. From its very inception, the theological differences, not to speak of the political and geographic divisions, within Wise's initial union of synagogues and rabbis were overwhelming. Moreover, by the end of the nineteenth century, the influx of vast numbers of Eastern European Jews resulted in the demographic transformation of the American Jewish community. These immigrants were committed to far more traditional modes of custom and observance than what Wise and the Reform leadership of the day were prepared to accommodate, making his dream utterly untenable.

Wise's efforts notwithstanding, the earlier pattern of independent congregations has remained a part of the landscape of American Judaism. Congregations opting to remain unaffiliated have done so for varying reasons. These include a disinclination to be identified by the positions espoused by the different movements as well as an unwillingness or inability to meet the financial obligations attendant to movement affiliation. Nevertheless, they have never represented more than a distinct minority of the synagogue community.

While it has earlier nineteenth-century European precedents, the American Jewish scene, to a degree unparalleled anywhere else in the world, has been characterized by the existence of definitive branches of Judaism, each ultimately with its own congregational structure, seminary, and rabbinical body. In the United States, these movements have flourished unimpeded by the imposition of governmental regulations and controls, as was the case of their European antecedents. All have modeled themselves largely upon the nineteenth-century structures Wise introduced.

The first major twentieth-century institutional challenge to the seeming hegemony of denominational Judaisms in the United

States was the effort of Rabbi Stephen S. Wise to found a rabbinical school in New York, one that would be nondenominational and serve the total Jewish community. In 1920, in explaining why a need existed for what he called the Jewish Institute of Religion (JIR), Wise criticized both the Jewish Theological Seminary in New York and the Hebrew Union College in Cincinnati for what he saw as their inadequacy and shortsightedness.

"Both alike," Wise wrote, "seemed to us committed to an uncatholic sectarianism, which in both cases seemed more a survival of yesterday rather than a prophecy of tomorrow. Wherefore, the founding of the Jewish Institute of Religion in a community that was itself a Jewish cosmos."[3] One cannot help but notice the barely disguised barb directed at Solomon Schechter and the famous phrase he coined, "Catholic Israel," in Stephen Wise's use of the words "uncatholic sectarianism."

He went on to say that he reluctantly assumed the presidency of the new school only after the three individuals to whom he had offered the position, Emil G. Hirsch, Israel Abrahams, and Mordecai Kaplan, had each refused. What prompted him to consider three such philosophically diverse personalities for the post, and what the future of the school might have been had one of them accepted, remains a tantalizing mystery. As it was, JIR survived as an independent institution for roughly thirty years until it became a part of the Reform movement when it merged with Cincinnati's Hebrew Union College in 1951 as its sister school in New York City.

Demographic Shifts

Now at the onset of the twenty-first century, despite the transformation of the American Jewish community from a population of immigrants to one able to trace its native-born roots back three and even four generations, denominational Judaisms still appear to be flourishing. What has changed is the growing body of literature and research pointing to new and significant nondenominational aspects of synagogue life that may well challenge this long-standing denominational primacy. It is almost as if the aspirations of both nineteenth- and twentieth-century Wises have been revitalized in a contemporized format. To be sure, the available data remain both limited and contradictory in their portrayal of this phenomenon.

For example, statistics drawn from the National Jewish Population Surveys of 1990 and 2000 reveal that the number of adult Jews who do not identify with a formal synagogue movement has increased from 20 percent to 27 percent over that decade. But as the noted sociologist Steven M. Cohen has observed, in contrast to Jews who are denominationally attached, these same individuals were disproportionately raised by intermarried parents, are themselves married to non-Jews, and score far lower on all measures of conventional Jewish engagement than those identified with one of the existing synagogue movements.[4] These findings are hardly encouraging and do not of themselves bode well for nondenominationalism, let alone for the future of the synagogue.

On the other hand, recent studies of the affiliation patterns of young adults in their twenties and thirties who are active Jewishly indicate attitudes that are totally disdainful of denominational labels, even when the respondents are members of congregations identified with a particular movement. As one young woman put it, "What am I? Am I Orthodox? Conservative? Whatever. I'm Jewish. I want people to feel comfortable expressing their Jewishness however they feel comfortable. My friends express their Judaism across a spectrum."[5]

The authors of the study describe this population as consisting of "young adults who have come of age in an increasingly pluralistic and global society, with little patience for anyone who tries to lionize one path above others and who see denominational distinctiveness as a source of divisiveness."[6] The fact that many of them are members of affiliated congregations despite their stated aversion to denominational ties is fascinating.

Why this is so is not clear. It may simply be due to the absence of any nondenominational synagogues in the communities where these young people live. More likely this younger generation's membership is a result of the farsighted determination of the congregations in question to welcome them and allow them to develop their own independent programming, under synagogue auspices but without interference, in the hope that the congregation will grow accordingly.

Ignoring Nondenominationalism

Given the history of the American synagogue, it is not surprising that until recently few sociological studies of the American Jewish community addressed denominationalism and its discontents in any detail, if at all. In contrast to concerns regarding Jewish education, intermarriage, philanthropy, the Jewish family, the decline of a sense of *klal yisrael* and support for Israel, denominationalism has not been viewed as a priority item but rather as something meriting at best a passing mention.

A case in point is Calvin Goldscheider's still significant volume, *The American Jewish Community: Social Science Research and Policy Implications*, published in 1986. It features a series of brief commentaries authored by distinguished members of the Jewish community representing a variety of disciplines, including the rabbinate, academia, and the social sciences. Goldscheider solicited their reactions to what he refers to in his book as "the goals and arenas of policy for a voluntaristic community in a pluralistic society."[7]

While the specific issue of denominationalism is conspicuous by its absence and is not mentioned in the book's table of contents, two contributors' statements, which are responses to the concerns posed in the volume, are noteworthy. The late Rabbi Wolfe Kelman, at that time executive director of the Rabbinical Assembly, comments that most of the existing structures, ideologies, and institutions on the American Jewish scene predate World War II, and in some instances World War I, and thereby may no longer be relevant to a postwar generation of American Jews. "The same," he writes, "is also true of the three or four major denominations depending on how you count them, which arose in response to specific American conditions at the beginning of this century and have become trapped by the taint of denominationalism which separates rather than unites."[8]

In a similar vein, Bernard Reisman, then the director of the Hornstein Program in Jewish Communal Service at Brandeis University, challenges Goldscheider's assertion that since the younger generation of American Jews was increasingly secular in its outlook, the future basis for Jewish continuity hinged upon ethnicity and fostering communal ties with Israel. Disagreeing, he argues,

"Young people are forming their own Jewish networks . . . to seek out Jewish religious definitions which are both authentically Jewish and consonant with their modern intellectual values." He adds that his contacts with younger generations of American Jews suggest that they have great interest in "Jewish religious/spiritual links although not necessarily in the same way Jewish religiosity and spirituality have been expressed by prior generations."[9]

A decade ago, the initial report from a study of the Jewish attitudes and behaviors of the "moderately affiliated," a term coined by Steven M. Cohen and Arnold M. Eisen, was also conspicuous by its failure to address nondenominationalism. Titled *The Jew Within: Self Community and Commitment Among the Variety of Moderately Affiliated*, the initial report included responses by a number of highly regarded individuals, two of whom had been quoted in Goldscheider's work a decade earlier.[10] Again, denominationalism generated little discussion, save for the comments of Cohen and Eisen in their concluding summary: "Not only are the boundaries between the major Jewish camps of less significance, so too are the boundaries separating Jew from non Jew. Denominationalism is out."[11]

Jewish sociologists were hardly alone in their disregard of the subject. Over the years, the major branches of Judaism also paid little attention to the possibility that nondenominationalism would ever threaten the congregational status quo. There seemed to be no reason to act otherwise. The few congregations beyond the organizational pale were essentially disregarded by the major movements, especially Conservative and Reform. It was justifiably assumed by them that whatever other benefits were to be derived from formal affiliation, at the very least, when a congregation needed a rabbi it would have no recourse other than to turn to one of the major branches of Judaism for placement, a service requiring affiliation as a prerequisite.

Similarly, rabbis who had been ordained at a specific seminary linked to a particular movement understood that serving a congregation that had no intention of affiliation could mean putting their future careers in jeopardy. They were well aware that if and when they chose to seek another pulpit and would have to call upon that rabbinical body's placement apparatus for assistance, it would either not be offered or given grudgingly in retaliation. In addition, that body's restriction of their placement opportunities to the least desirable of available openings was a very real possibility. That knowledge, compounded by the recognition that the number of unaffiliated congregations financially able to support a full-time rabbi was limited, was a powerful deterrent.

Unaffiliated Rabbinical Schools

What then has changed in a relatively brief period to account for the current emphasis upon nondenominationalism? The emergence of new rabbinical schools having no links to the established branches of American Judaism, taking pride in their total autonomy, defining themselves as transdenominational, and attracting both well-qualified students and distinguished faculty is a critical factor. Their existence, should they all not only survive but also prosper, may well change the synagogue scene by challenging the near-monopoly on rabbinic ordination and placement heretofore enjoyed by those seminaries linked to the historic branches of Judaism in North America.

The presence of these new seminaries may have also increased the probability that rabbinic institutions will, in the future, find themselves in direct competition with one another for students and staff and most tellingly for congregations in which to place their graduates. This is a reality that congregations will be quick to perceive and undoubtedly use to their own advantage, as some already are. One need but peruse the pages of such newspapers as the *Forward* to find congregational ads placed by synagogues. Often affiliated with a specific movement and potentially subject to penalization, at least in theory, for having bypassed the movement's placement procedures, these congregations announce openings for rabbis, cantors, and other synagogue professionals.

The need to compete has also resulted in the fashioning of expensive, sophisticated, eye-catching, glossy descriptions in full color, extolling the virtues of the specific seminary. These ads appear not merely in the Anglo-Jewish press but in magazines and periodicals published in the United States and in Israel. These appeals bear a striking resemblance to a similar pattern of sleek advertisements now being produced by secular universities and medical centers, which in an age of scarcity and financial strain find themselves competing for students and even for patients. The mystique once engendered by academia and by medicine has given way to the laws of supply and demand.

It remains to be seen whether the utilization of Madison Avenue sales techniques by rabbinical schools pressed for funds and appealing to a limited market of congregational consumers will result in the demystification of the institutions as well and will be regarded as just as another professional school promoting its wares. To what extent the image of the rabbi as spiritual leader, teacher, and religious exemplar will suffer in the process is another unknown.

Moreover, as the number of students ordained as rabbis increases and competition for positions crossing denominational lines becomes more frequent, rabbinical schools will have to choose between resentment and hostility toward one another or exploring avenues for working cooperatively in their own best interests and those of the synagogues. Of the three non-Orthodox major rabbinical bodies in the United States—the Rabbinical Assembly (Conservative Judaism), the Reconstructionist Rabbinical Association, and the Central Conference of American Rabbis (Reform Judaism)—the latter is the only one, as of this writing, to have even begun to seriously consider ways of devising a cooperative approach to the problem.

Ideological Flexibility—Big Tents

Among the factors accounting for the turn toward nondenominationalism is the ideological flexibility operative within the contemporary American synagogue. With the possible exception of Orthodoxy, the other branches of American Judaism—Reform, Conservative, and Reconstructionist—have essentially ignored their official theological postures as articulated in their historic documents and respective platforms. Instead, they have chosen a modus operandi best characterized in images borrowed from politics, as large tents open and welcome to a diversity of religious beliefs and practices. The message to their respective constituencies is that no one will be rejected and that everyone can coexist comfortably within the same institutional walls.

Arnold Eisen has captured this theme when he writes:

> I think we can also say on the basis of contemporary behavior that more and more Jews have become practitioners of what anthropologist Samuel Heilman has dubbed "traditioning" the movement into and out of tradition as demanded by one's lifestyle and one's commitments of the moment. . . . One fully participates neither in Tradition—a given all-embracing pattern of beliefs and observances held to be the way of being Jewish determined by God or by age old authority—nor in what we might now call Tradition, a self-selective pattern of observance.[12]

This triumph of personal autonomy and the Heilman definition of "traditioning" as hallmarks of contemporary Jewish practice regardless of denominational allegiance are also the subject of Michael Meyer's commentary. Meyer has written about the custom of the generational passing of the Torah during a bar mitzvah, now very much in vogue in Reform synagogues. He notes that the Torah scroll becomes the most visible symbol of Jewish identity even though "none of the three generations involved has more than passing familiarity with the content of the scroll nor has or will ever practice most of its specific precepts."[13]

In an environment where faith and practice are governed mainly by the personal preferences of individuals whose knowledge of Judaism is limited and whose degree of observance is equally scant, terms such as *transdenominational* and *nondenominational* are not especially inspiring as indices of the future, if this is to be the primary constituency to which they will apply. Once again, Steven M. Cohen suggests a very different scenario for the nondenominational future in his assessment of why the Conservative movement, once the largest branch of Judaism in America, has been numerically surpassed by Reform.

He contends that Conservative Judaism's numerical decline is in no small measure a consequence of its failure to retain the loyalty of a substantial coterie of its younger members. Disillusioned by the movement's failure to sustain a generation dedicated to "the virtues of a modern halakhic Jewish life," many have gone else-where.[14] Having allowed itself to succumb to the temptation of the "big tent" philosophy, the Conservative movement became a pale imitation of Reform. In so doing, it alienated those who took seriously the message conveyed in the Historical School's camps and by its teachings.

This younger generation, he adds, whose ideological commitments no longer allowed them to remain within Conservative Judaism, are the ones who assumed the leadership of a select number of successful, dynamic, Jewishly vibrant congregations eschewing denominational labels. If Cohen's analysis is correct and the success of these synagogues is to be construed as a dissident response to the internal policies of Conservative Judaism, it implies that had the Conservative movement been true to itself, these synagogues would never have come into being.

If so, the logical inference is that a return to its principles by the Conservative movement would result in the retention of a younger generation of men and women who have embraced a halakhic way of life and the ensuing decline of the postdenominational synagogue. But should this occur and Conservative Judaism in the twenty-first century reevaluate its philosophy, it remains to be seen whether the growth of these congregations will be slowed as Conservative Judaism's younger adherents no longer feel the need to leave.

Others have argued that given the momentum of nondenominationalism, congregations espousing it will continue to grow and to attract new disciples drawn from all of the established branches of Judaism. Men and women who, regardless of their personal practice, have become disenchanted by the burden of labels and who deem them anachronistic and counterproductive will opt for places of worship and study where they can be identified as just Jewish.

Unlimited Access to Educational Resources

A third factor discouraging denominational affiliation is the availability of educational materials, books, and audiovisual aids on Judaism for all ages produced on the open market. At one time, such items not only might have been difficult to acquire without formal affiliation, but the availability of such resources beyond the publishing houses linked to the movements was also limited. Neither situation is a factor any longer. Now, by and large, the only requirement is one's personal or institutional interest and a check or a credit card to cover the cost of a given order taken from a catalogue or purchased on the Internet. Together, all of these developments have helped set the stage for the drama unfolding before us.

The Benefits of Denominationalism

No discussion of the current denominational scene would be complete without some recognition of how the various movements of Judaism have contributed to the dignity and stature of both the American synagogue and the rabbinate. Establishing procedures over the years for rabbinical placement, pensions, tenure, the resolution of disputes between congregations or between a rabbi and a congregation, relationships between rabbis and cantors, and a host of other matters have become part of the ethos of congregational life.

Achieving these goals was not a simple matter. A long and arduous undertaking, the effort resembled similar struggles in the business world between corporations and unions and between employers and their employees. It took time before both lay and religious leaders acknowledged that whatever the economic and business aspects of rabbinic-congregational relationships, their interaction also had an inherent spiritual dimension. Without it, the proper conduct of synagogue life was imperiled. The following excerpt taken from the placement guidelines of the Reconstructionist Rabbinical Association, a selection that could just as easily have been cited from similar guidelines of the Reform and Conservative movements, is illustrative of that accomplishment:

> The relationship between God and the Jewish people imagined by the writers of the Bible is named a *brit* (covenant) which is also used to signify a solemn pact between individuals. The term implies mutuality and suggests that each party in a relationship

has obligations towards the other. In addition to being a contractual record of promises, a *brit* is a combination of expectations, trust, loyalty and affection. The relationship between rabbi and congregation should be understood as a *brit*, in which each party covenants with the other in mutual devotion for a common sacred purpose.[15]

At present, the absence of any formal organizational structure involving unaffiliated congregations, independent rabbinical seminaries, and rabbis ordained from the latter or ordained privately has precluded the preparation of similar documents setting forth standards of relationships couched in religious terms. Consequently, rabbis negotiating with unaffiliated congregations are essentially on their own. Lay leaders of these congregations, either out of ignorance or a disinclination to do otherwise, are prone to draft contracts and negotiate settlements predicated upon how employees are treated in the business and professional worlds with which they are familiar. These agreements favor terms such as *employer-employee* and are often void of any religious terminology or a sense of the synagogue as something other than a business venture. The rabbi is viewed as a salaried executive, the synagogue's chief operating officer rather than its spiritual leader.

Nondenominational communities may introduce such standards, either due to their consultation with affiliated congregations in their area or at the behest or insistence of the rabbi interviewing for the pulpit. Others may do so out of a congregational desire to what is right and Jewishly appropriate. But the lack of a connection with a movement makes it more problematic that such standards will be implemented. Lamentably, the absence of standards demeans rabbis, all synagogue professionals, and congregations alike.

As nondenominational congregations increase, they may find it necessary to create synagogue bodies of their own, realizing that total autonomy has its shortcomings as well as its pluses. There already are voluntary associations of rabbis and congregations who identify with the Renewal movement: OHALAH, *Agudat HaRabbanim L'Hithadshut HaYahadut* (Association of Rabbis for Jewish Renewal), and ALEPH (Alliance for Jewish Renewal). In the future these associations may provide the impetus for similar endeavors for non- or transdenominational rabbis and congregations.

The newly established transdenominational seminaries will also be called upon to examine the responsibilities they bear in furthering an ethical agenda based upon the Jewish values they have been teaching to those whom they will ordain, who in turn will be preaching these same values to their congregants. In doing so, these seminaries will also be forced to evaluate whether this can be achieved without some form of linkage with OHALAH, ALEPH, or other congregational and rabbinic groups that may emerge in the years to come.

Because one cannot foresee what the coming years will bring, one can only speculate about the role nondenominationalism will play in the world of the synagogue. Those predicting its triumph and either the diminution of the power of denominations or their ultimate demise are as premature in their prognostications as are those dismissing it as a passing fad. How the organized movements will respond to this phenomenon, as they surely will, is also an imponderable. One thing is certain: Not only is the American Jewish experience at another exciting and pivotal moment, but once again the synagogue holds center stage.

CHAPTER 4

American Dissonance
Christian Communities in the United States and Their Cultural Context

Rodney L. Petersen

I remember reading sociologist Peter Berger's 1969 book *A Rumor of Angels* at a time when many academics in a range of disciplines were preaching the soon demise of religion. The academic heirs of social theorists from Karl Marx to Sigmund Freud to Max Weber believed that as societies became more modern, religion would lose its capacity to inform, console, or direct. History has not come round—at least not yet. Instead, according to a recent Pew Forum on Religion and Public Life survey, religion in the United States has become more fluid and diverse, a consumer product with an array of choices set out in denomination, nondenomination, and postdenomination churches and other transdenomination bodies.[1] What is true for Christians, and particularly for Protestants, is also a reality for other religious groups.

The palpable reality of such fluidity and choice came home to me in 2008 in a church sanctuary packed with people age thirty-five and under who had been assembled by the Boston Faith and Justice Network (BFJN). Director Rachel Anderson welcomed progressive evangelical Jim Wallis on the occasion of his book tour for *The Great Awakening*. She drew attention to the need for the wider religious community, a transdenominational reality, to come together to deal with issues of economic disparity, environmental degradation, and an American propensity for violence. This gathering was a vox populi with religious denomination leaders seated in the benches.

Hosted by a local Vineyard church in west Cambridge that meets in an ornate Catholic church whose population has changed, the group appeared to embody all that the Pew Forum reported. Present at the gathering were representatives from established and evangelical religious communities in the Boston area: Park Street Church, the Massachusetts Council of Churches, Roman Catholic and Eastern Orthodox churches and a variety of ethnic groups affiliated with urban Emmanuel Gospel Center (EGC), nursing mother to more than thirty new and ethnic congregations in Boston. Another group present that day, the International Community Church, an American Baptist Church, is now better known for the "baker's dozen" congregations that meet in its Allston, Massachusetts, building.

What is remarkable is how normal this gathering of religiously diverse groups felt to me. In my work with religious movements and students, I often meet people whose life paths demonstrate a similar diversity, like one young man who is now on his way to seminary. Having been born a Roman Catholic and having journeyed by way of neopaganism to Pentecostalism, he now considers himself a confirmed Roman Catholic and a confirmed United Methodist. Another I know was born Jewish, had traveled by way of Buddhism to messianic Judaism and is now considering which Presbyterian body, or none, with which to affiliate. This movement and ferment among people looking for religious identity comes after frequent and well-publicized defections of others from evangelicalism to Eastern and Antiochene Orthodoxy or to Roman Catholicism or to Judaism. As with other contemporary religious expressions, Christianity has become a movement of great fluidity and diversity in the twenty-first century.

Contemporary Communities of Faith

Religious "border crossing," as evident in popular journals or as seen at the particular BFJN event referred to above, is not unusual but in fact represents much of postdenominational Protestantism and the wider religious currents of which it is a part. The purpose of this chapter is to set such phenomena in the context of North American denominational history.

Aaron and Amy Graham, pastor and youth leaders of the Dorchester (Boston) Quincy Street Missional Church, are cofounders of BFJN with Rachel Anderson. They represent the interracial and intergenerational character of a growing postdenominationalism—churches that are young, vibrant, and committed to connecting faith and justice as fresh models of religious authenticity, but not particularly associated with denominational or nondenominational predecessors. Aspects of this movement reach back to the civil rights movement of the 1960s, as with Ralph and Judy Kee, founders of the Greater Boston Church Planting Collaborative. Other roots reach to college campus fellowships over the past century as well as to the dynamics of intercultural relations, economic, and technological change in social life in the United States, and to globalization. While postdenominationalism finds a certain locus within Protestant groupings of churches, it is a social reality that can be discerned across all branches of Christianity, in Judaism, and among other faiths. It can take the form of small intentional communities or megachurches. Postdenominationalism may participate in forms of transdenominationalism.

Postdenominational Christianity

The Vineyard represents part of a fourth stage in American denominational life. The first stage was the planting of European churches on American soil in the seventeenth century. Certainly, a second stage was represented in the emergence of the denominational ideal early in the new nation's history. A third stage coalesced around the nondenominational movement that was part of the fundamentalist-modernist debates, leading to their pinnacle in the 1920s. Postdenominationalism is a fourth stage of church self-perception and remains a porous category. Often spontaneous and lay driven, this expression resorts to clergy leadership at some point in a given community's evolution. However, leadership is as often trained in the local congregation's setting and structures, as it is in theological seminaries or similar religious institutions. Many for whom denominationalism means little have forsaken the formal worship of their parents for an ease and immediacy in worship. The porous institutional boundaries of the Cambridge Vineyard, in which the Wallis event took place, is characteristic of the Vineyard association of more than 750 churches in 47 countries worldwide.

Begun spontaneously in 1974 in the Los Angeles area, Vineyard Christianity was first given shape by Kenn Gulliksen. Congregants met in fellowship and worship to experience God as a living, life-changing friend, not just a theory. The group grew quickly. By 1982 they found in John Wimber, a former professional musician who celebrated God's miraculous work, one who could help give leadership to the rapidly growing fellowship. After spending several years training ministers at Fuller Theological Seminary in Pasadena, California, Wimber and his wife, Carol, began meeting with a small group of Christians who, like those under Gulliksen's leadership, were looking for a more dynamic, supernatural experience of following Jesus Christ. With Wimber as leader of West Coast Vineyard churches, Gulliksen moved to Boston to start an East Coast Vineyard community.

What is true in Boston is true in the Bronx: New York Faith and Justice (NYFJ) started when a small group of Christians met at a Sojourners conference in 2006. They began to meet regularly and developed a plan for Christians pursuing justice in the city of New York. With a mission inspired by Isaiah 61 ("The spirit of the Lord GOD is upon me . . ."), the group envisioned an urban community centered on the life of faith as a life committed to social justice, "a New York where resources are shared and just policies are practiced because God's people are no longer dependent on the dollar—they are oaks of righteousness—dependent on God alone."[2] BFJN and NYFJ are sister organizations, pursuing social justice as an expression of faith. "Gone are the days in which what happened in some small village in El Salvador was unrelated to any other world event," reminded Latin American theologian and educator Ruth Padilla DeBorst, urging a recognition of U.S. interdependence with others.[3] Many in the contemporary postdenominational world see their discipleship as global and local, characterized by such mission interests as Micah Challenge, a global Christian campaign intended to deepen engagement with the United Nations Millennium Development Goals, and *Lazarus at the Gate*, a twelve-session small group study developed by Evangelical Covenant pastor Gary VanderPol that invites prayerful lifestyle change to enable generosity to the poor.

Informal and contemporary in setting and worship, Vineyard churches have become known for helping people find a fresh experience of God—and Vineyard songs are sung worldwide across many denominations. Wade Clark Roof writes in his study of baby boomer spirituality, *A Generation of Seekers*, something that might be said of the Vineyard: Their "concern is to experience life directly, to have an encounter with God or the divine, or simply with nature and other people, without the intervention of inherited beliefs, ideas, and concepts."[4] When Wimber died in 1997, he left behind a congregation of almost seven thousand and an association of churches reaching more than a hundred thousand people.

Such postdenominationalism lacks the edge of nondenominational Christianity, the latter often forged in opposition to mainline Protestant denominations and their perceived liberalism. The leaders of postdenominational communities of faith tend to be drawn from the wider culture. An example of this is Vineyard pastor Dave Schmelzer who, before participating in the founding of the Boston Vineyard, worked as a successful playwright. A graduate of Stanford University, Palo Alto, California, and Fuller Theological Seminary, he became a follower of Jesus later in life and became interested, together with his wife Grace, in fostering a church that would be helpful to spiritually interested skeptics, as he once was. "Following God is shockingly interesting, powerful and reorienting," he writes.[5] Similar characteristics can be seen in leaders of the New York City Vineyard fellowship, called "The River." Senior pastors Charles and Caroline Park, with degrees from Massachusetts Institute of Technology and Columbia University respectively, report that their life with the Vineyard is much more fulfilling than the pursuit of the American dream; so also for mathematician and executive pastor Kevin Oro-Hahn.

The Schmelzers, the Parks, and Oro-Hahn are not unusual examples of the leaders found in such contemporary faith communities: successful at elite colleges and universities or in their careers, they have found meaning in the world of Christian fellowship frequently made up of congregants who have tried everything—money, alcohol and drugs, or promiscuity and infidelity. At the same time, they are not the full story of how such communities come into existence. Through the Alpha Course,[6] offered both within and apart from the church, and through self-help groups derivative of Alcoholics Anonymous and prison fellowships, spontaneous groups continue to emerge, but often move toward some form of denomination or association affiliation.

Postdenominational Christianity has the feel of the orders of renewal that have frequently been a part of the church's history. The medieval church, sometimes referred to as a modality of faith, was often challenged by sodalities or new-formed fellowships that brought an immediacy of meaning into people's lives.[7] *Modalities* are the characteristic forms of the church by which the institution serves the spiritual needs of a settled folk in a regularized fashion. *Sodalities* are the orders, forms of monasticism, and volunteeristic Christian associations in search of renewal and deeper spiritual authenticity that have appeared through history. Greek Orthodox theologian Petros Vassiliadis writes that whereas the first thousand years of church history were characterized by unity, the second thousand years were shaped by division—that of the Eastern Orthodox and Latin Western churches, the Protestant Reformation of the West, and further divisions seeking reform and renewal. The third millennium of the church will be one, Vassiliadis envisions, of growing reunion and unity.[8] It is as if centuries of European Christian tradition and habit are now being swept away in the face of new forms of worship and belonging. Leith Anderson of Wooddale Church in Eden Prairie, Minnesota, writes that the culture is suspicious of old-church "European" atmospherics, ritual, and language—of old institutions in general. Yet aspects of the older tradition are not discounted in such "new monasticism" as associated with the Lindisfarne Community, an international community based in Ithaca, New York, but incorporated in an eclectic way "with a heart for spiritual renewal and service."[9]

The Mustard Seed and the Megachurch

Concerns for social consciousness and a quest for authenticity and spiritual immediacy have often been a part of renewal movements; however, they seem heightened in postdenominational Christianity. In a similar way, one can talk about intentional efforts to build community. Robert Putnam's thesis in *Bowling Alone: The Col-*

lapse and Revival of American Community on the breakdown of community in America, which he feels undermines the active civil engagement a strong democracy requires, is countered by the effort to build community in Cambridge and Boston, in New York City, in Chicago and Minneapolis, on the West Coast, and elsewhere.

One way this plays out is in groups such as the Mustard Seed Associates, based in Seattle, or the Simple Way in Philadelphia. The latter is a neomonastic group committed to radical communal life, as outlined by Shane Claiborne in *The Irresistible Revolution: Living as an Ordinary Radical*. Located in a destitute Philadelphia neighborhood, adherents call themselves "ordinary radicals" because they attempt to live like early followers of Jesus, ignoring social status and unencumbered by material comforts.

Another way the quest for community plays itself out is more affirming of traditional American culture, as with the Mariners Church. The Mariners Church of Irvine, California, is a postdenominational church that strongly emphasizes the importance of community building. With more than 3,500 people in attendance at four services every weekend and through its array of services to different demographic groups, Mariners Church is almost a 24–7 community. Soft-rock orchestral music, casual California dress, and a cappuccino cart off to the side of the worship space welcome people to worship, and an array of ministries continue the fellowship through the week. However, community building is not unique to the world of postdenominational Christianity, though it may characterize those churches. First Presbyterian Church, Orlando, Florida, is an example of a denominational church with postdenominational verve. Through its array of ministries, tailored not only to its own flock but also to the needs of Orlando, the church successfully carries off a megachurch community model but within a denomination. Another is Pollard United Methodist Church in Tyler, Texas. It sees itself as a church of options for people of different worship and lifestyle preferences. The Fellowship of Las Colinas, Grapevine, Texas, tailors its services and orientation to its targeted population, following the lead of management theorist Peter Drucker. Drucker's work has taught churches to be clearer about their mission, their intended audience, and what the "customer" considers to be of value.

Many successful megachurches, whether they are denominational, nondenominational, or postdenominational, practice community building by following a model for small group participation developed by Willow Creek Community Church, South Barrington, Illinois. Willow Creek's development was pioneered by Pastor Lee Strobel, who wrote one of the best-selling books of megachurch literature, *Inside the Mind of Unchurched Harry and Mary*. He stresses the need for large organizations to develop small group ministries, groups and fellowships within a large church that can foster personal relationships and deep meaning. Most of the members of Willow Creek's more than fifteen thousand worshipers are in such cell groups, and the model has been successfully developed for and exported to other large churches. In the face of community instability, one member put it like this: "Our government has let us down. Our workplace is not secure. Our communities are falling apart. Churches and synagogues are serving the community."[10] Helping to give direction to a growing sense of anomie in American culture, megachurches such as Saddleback Church under Pastor Rick Warren have authored materials like *The Purpose-Driven Life: What on Earth Am I Here For?* If half of all churchgoing Americans are attending 12 percent of the nation's four hundred thousand churches—presumably megachurches— then the community-building characteristic of such churches like Wooddale or Willow Creek is worth watching.

Transdenominationalism

Among Protestant and other Christian churches, the term *transdenomination* began to emerge at the end of the nineteenth century with the first networks of churches forming councils of churches and then the nascent ecumenical movement. In recent years the term has taken on greater specificity as churches have explored various forms of church unions. For example, in 1997 the Church-wide Assembly of the Evangelical Lutheran Church in America (ELCA) approved a "Joint Declaration on the Doctrine of Justification," which resulted from years of Lutheran–Roman Catholic dialogue. This decision might be termed *transdenominational*, as are decisions by the ELCA to enter into "full communion" with other churches or denominations. Various groups among the Christian Right and Left have worked to produce a transdenominational theology, such as Christian Reconstructionism (Right) or the Center for Progressive Christianity (Left), with the ecumenical movement representing a centrist Christian thrust. Issues of identity with respect to the larger American culture, institutional representation, and funding come into play in the formation of transdenominationalism.

Themes of social justice, authenticity, spiritual immediacy, and community that course through contemporary religious movements are not unique to postdenominational Christianity, or even to Christian mainline denominational efforts, but they become places for transdenominational identity to locate itself. So do such Roman Catholic movements as the Focolare Movement and the Community of Sant'Egidio, a social justice and renewal effort. In the United Methodist Church, the emergence of the JUSTPEACE Center for Mediation and Conflict Transformation is a possible transdenominational contender, as is the Cooperative Baptist Fellowship, which sees itself not as a denomination but rather as a fellowship of churches and Christians seeking social justice and renewal. Many other denominational and postdenominational efforts, as well as those further adrift from mainline traditions, are marked by similar social characteristics. Examples include the following:

- Engaged Buddhism and the work of activists like Thich Nhat Hanh
- The Soka Gakkai movement
- Proponents of Islamic renewal, a diffuse but growing movement whose goal is reform of Muslim societies and polities (as with Abdulaziz Sachedina, author of *The Islamic Roots of Democratic Pluralism,* or with Karamah, Muslim Women Lawyers for Human Rights)

These all are a part of the fluidity and variety of the North American religious scene. With 271 church bodies listed in the annual *Yearbook of American and Canadian Churches,* religion in North America has become a consumer product with a wide array of choices. However, even this diversity of choice needs contextualization, as more than thirty-seven thousand denominations worldwide understand themselves to be Christian today.[11] Many of these are outgrowths of groups that began in the United States, but many did not. In this light it is helpful to see contemporary postdenominationalism in its historical context. Clearly, the world of contemporary faith communities is vast and variegated.

The Formation of Denominations

While the term *denomination* has not always been attractive to all Christians or other groups, it has served into the present a useful social purpose as generally implying the social acceptance of a particular religious group in the political culture of the United States in a context of religious pluralism. As such it has been picked up by Judaism, although not with complete acceptance by the Jewish religious community.[12] It will be interesting to see whether the same process extends to Islam and then to other non-Christian religions.[13] The term *denomination* coalesced during the Christian religious reform of the sixteenth-century and European Enlightenment and was brought forward by social forces unleashed during that time. The subsequent breakdown of a universal Christendom and further religious dissension in late seventeenth-century England led to a settlement of religious groups united in general theological agreement but differing in church government, or polity. In 1702 the Presbyterians, Baptists, and Congregationalists formed "the body of the Dissenting Ministers of the Three Denominations in and about the City of London." This "Old Dissent" employed the term *denomination* to counter the pejorative use of *sect*, a term applied to religious deviancy.

Taking root in the North American colonies, the term *denomination* became increasingly useful as the unifying social experiences of religious awakenings, or revivals, and the American War of Independence brought together in a widening circle of social acceptance disparate religious communities reaching back to different European patterns of church life.[14] What was true for Christian churches was true for other religious societies, including Jewish communities, early in U.S. history, as recognized by

Hannah Adams's 1817 *Dictionary of All Religions and Religious Denominations: Jewish, Heathen, Mahometan, Christian, Ancient and Modern*.[15] Yet, the term acknowledges the church bodies' success in achieving legitimacy as institutional forces for social change in the United States. That success may be one that will soon recede in significance. Christian religious diversity, the waning of the European religious heritage in the United States, and the growth of both non-Christian religious identity and no defined religious identity are eroding the usefulness of the term. Today many Christian groups, such as the Vineyard fellowships, communities, and megachurches, see themselves as entering a postdenominational phase of history.

Elements Forming the Denomination Idea

The idea of denominational Christianity in the United States was first a necessity that grew out of the interplay initially between inherited Protestant Christian churches and colonial attempts at restoring an original Christianity. This was true in early New England as well as elsewhere on the eastern seaboard. A second impetus was the progressive establishment of religious liberty in the colonies and, then more dramatically following the American Revolution and the establishment of a national government with its Constitution and Bill of Rights, which protect the free association of persons as members of legally sanctioned religious societies. These factors created an additional impetus toward what would emerge in the United States as a new pattern of religious organization, the religious denomination.[16]

Third, religious associations proliferated in the years of the Second Great Awakening (ca. 1787–1825); then, with further awakenings, revival and Pentecostal awareness into the contemporary period continued to increase. These spawned renewal in modalities of faith, but also new sodalities of Christian expression that often resulted in new denominations and movements for social renewal (prison reform, child labor restrictions, home and foreign mission endeavors).[17] They offered a moral agenda for the nation that shaped social and political life. They provided a way of organizing and unifying national life as waves of new immigrants engulfed the nation and could have overwhelmed it.[18] Religious associations, initially focused on communal religious identity, evolved to focus on the free association of persons for moral ends, who often coalesced through religious revival. Lamentably, such free association in religious society often also meant growing segregation in religion along color lines. Such participation through free association provided a further trajectory into the contemporary period—well represented in the *Sojourners* community.[19]

Toward the close of the nineteenth century, a fourth trajectory emerged that merits attention into the twentieth century: the growth of networks of organizations or federations. This is seen preeminently in the emergence of Protestant councils of churches and associated religious bodies to promote a common social or ecumenical agenda. Roman Catholicism had generally not been as fissiparous as Protestantism through the nineteenth century, and Orthodoxy generally was not numerically significant. Despite differences in forms of national Catholicism, a common Latin liturgy and pastoral allegiance, and sometimes hostile Protestant culture, tended to support a unified Catholic Church.

The formation of denominations was accompanied by the development of seminaries and schools of theology that were, in the main, designed to raise and defend the particular theologies and polities germane to the different denominations, as with Andover Seminary, Newton Centre, Massachusetts (1807, Congregational), Princeton Theological Seminary, Princeton, New Jersey (1812, Presbyterian), The Seminary at Newbury, Vermont, and Concord, New Hampshire (1839, Methodist; to become Boston University's School of Theology), and Newton Baptist Seminary, Newton Centre (1807).

Nondenominationalism

Significantly, those churches that stood apart from an emerging consensus among the denominations for a pressing social agenda in an urbanizing America, to be called a "social gospel,"[20] or in disagreement with the extension of an Enlightenment understanding to religion and seminary preparation, as seen in modernism, began to form a nondenominational movement. In the context of the fundamentalist-modernist debates, this process continued through the twentieth and into the twenty-first century, often taking root around heresy trials in seminaries (in relation to the emergence of imminent signs of history's end, as with premillennialism, or in relation to urban revivals). Defended in pulpit and on the "sawdust trail" of popular piety, the turn-of-the-century Bible School movement, as with the Boston Missionary Training School, the Moody Bible Institute (Chicago), and the Bible Institute of Los Angeles loomed large in continuing American religious history. This "fundamental" and often independent Christianity posed a growing challenge for mainline denominationalism.

Nevertheless, religious organization in the United States, whether in denominationalism or in its oppositional nondenominational form, was largely oriented around a denominational model into the mid-twentieth century. The initial tension between inherited patterns of European Christianity with new sodalities of faith, development of the denominational model, the social significance of choice in patterns of religious association, and the beginnings of religious networks across ecclesial boundaries gave definition to faith communities in the United States. These four trajectories are not alone in shaping denominationalism; they continue to have an impact on religious organization in the twenty-first century and upon the breakdown of denominationalism as it has been known.

Tension in the Denominational Model

Through the social evolution of North American religious life, denominations had become the means for free religious association coupled with mutual respect toward other expressions of religious commitment among Protestants, the dominant faith community in the United States. For many, the appearance of Will Herberg's 1955 book *Protestant–Catholic–Jew* not only affirmed the sociological significance of denominationalism but now the extension of the social concept of denominationalism to Catholicism and Judaism. What had been a largely Protestant phenomenon was now openly acknowledged as an *Americanizing* phenomenon of religious experience, one that carried with it not only questions of social acceptability but often those of social stratification as well.[21]

This phenomenon also had global implications in the emerging efforts at global religious freedom subsequent to the United Nations Universal Declaration of Human Rights (1948) and Article 18 affirming the freedom of religion.

Two significant movements to challenge Protestant denominational life at the time of its very pinnacle of influence as a concept were movements that themselves had helped form denominationalism—the ecumenical movement and a new evangelicalism. Both grew out of the same revival and mission movements that had so shaped denominationalism, the ecumenical movement more oriented to modalities of faith, the normative pattern of denominational Christianity, and the new evangelicalism to sodalities of faith, many that mistrusted theological modernism as it had taken root in a number of denominations.

Ecumenism

Ecumenism takes its name from the Greek term *oikomene*, meaning "the inhabited world" and from the first empirewide councils of the church that were called by Constantine (325 CE) and his successors to settle matters of doctrinal debate. The term became used in the twentieth century to denote the quest for church unity among Christians amid European and global conflict.[22] The reaction of European churches to World War II led to the erosion of church boundaries as they had been known since the sixteenth century. In the general population's opposition to the Nazis and to European fascism, where it existed, whether one were a Protestant or a Roman Catholic mattered less than if one were a member of the underground—and the growing horror and impact of what had been done to European Jewry had an added impact upon all Christian churches worldwide. Despite people's greater or lesser expressions of opposition, some Christians realized how complicit European society, if not Christian faith and church life per se, had been in the death camps. These factors associated with the war fostered an effort to transcend boundaries and promoted the growth of the ecumenical movement that had begun in prewar years.

The Holocaust's impact upon all Christian organizations was profound. For Roman Catholics, it is one of the influences leading to the Second Vatican Council (1962–1965). Documents such as the *Dogmatic Constitution on the Church* (1964), the *Decree on Ecumenism* (1964), and the *Declaration on the Relation of the Church to Non-Christian Religions* (1965), which together proposed a form of Christian inclusivism, promulgated and opened the way forward not only toward Christian ecumenism and a positive reorientation toward Judaism but also to all religions.

As much as ecumenism was an expression of Christian denominational triumph in the unific sense as set forth by nineteenth-century theorists such as Philip Schaff,[23] it also raised several challenges for then-contemporary Protestant denominationalism, for Eastern Orthodoxy, and for postconciliar (post-Vatican II) Catholicism: What was the future of the church? Was it to be found in a union, conciliar, coalition, or confessional model? Was the end in view simply some form of mutual recognition? Wartime cooperation, efforts at postwar spiritual renewal, and reactions to the Holocaust created a new nondenominational climate, different from oppositional Protestantism, that fostered various forms of church unions and the erosion of boundaries among religious groups. Such ecumenical momentum within Christianity, at times interfaith in nature, promoted a new *transdenominationalism*, a term yet to find settled meaning but often connoting the freedom of interreligious, in some cases at least intracommunal, flow of ideas. Schools of theology, seminaries, and university divinity schools—many dating back to the period of denominational formation—found themselves increasingly shaped by such thinking.

Evangelicalism

If World War II stimulated an ecumenical current within Christianity that diminished the importance of denominational distinctions, it also served as a catalyst for a new evangelicalism. As the United States faced the Cold War, evangelicalism preserved and shaped a particular view of Christian and Protestant American history. Several events forged evangelicalism as a movement: the leadership of Park Street Church in Boston, the revivals of Billy Graham, publication of the new fortnightly *Christianity Today*, and the development of a set of seminaries and schools of theology that would advance its cause. As a movement, evangelicalism was uncertain of denominations and their ecumenical intent. It held to the fundamentals of the faith, such as the infallibility of the Bible, but rejected much of earlier twentieth-century forms of fundamentalism, such as an individualism that was blind to concerns of social justice. The appearance of Carl F. H. Henry's 1947 book, *The Uneasy Conscience of Modern Fundamentalism*, served as the new evangelical movement's manifesto to bring the fundamentals of Christian faith appropriately to bear upon contemporary culture.

The leadership of Harold John Ockenga of Park Street Church and the emerging National Association of Evangelicals signaled tendencies in this movement which were Congregational in terms of polity and independent with respect to denominational structures.[24] While often nondenominational in its oppositional self-understanding, such Christianity, from a sociological perspective, often appeared as a new form of denominational life. The ways evangelicalism sought authenticity were through its connection with a history of American revivalism extending back to D. L. Moody, Charles Finney, and Jonathan Edwards to the Puritan origins of American religious culture. *Christianity Today* became the answer to *The Christian Century*, even as Fuller Theological Seminary; Trinity Evangelical Divinity School, Deerfield, Illinois; and the emerging Gordon-Conwell Theological Seminary, South Hamilton, Massachusetts, set the stage for a new academic leadership.

The Civil Rights Movement

Both the ecumenical and evangelical movements, and the tensions they represented for Christian denominations, were affected by several social factors: the growing civil rights movement in the United States, increasing unease over the war in Vietnam, and new recognition of U.S. and global economic inequalities. This movement of civil rights and heightened social awareness distilled from the ecumenical and evangelical movements new political tensions that carried the faith communities into the twenty-first century. In the United States, these tensions often took on the characteristics of regional differences.

Mainline Protestantism and the civil rights movement became almost synonymous. The civil rights movement (1960–1980) was a galvanizing issue for mainline Protestantism. Church support for the movement began in many of the mainline Protestant churches, and also among some Orthodox (notably Archbishop Iakovos), Roman Catholic, and Jewish groups (notably Abraham Joshua Heschel). Important in itself, the civil rights movement was the natural extension of a human rights agenda that could be traced back through the Enlightenment to the Reformation itself. Most clearly linked to spiritual renewal in the more ecumenical-oriented churches, Christian social witness came to be seen as integral to it. This began with matters of race and carried over to the women's, Latino, Native American, countercultural, sexual, and environmental movements. As an appeal to common social witness transcended denominational boundaries, such an agenda undermined a denomination's influence. This result was not unlike the forces at work in engendering the first ecumenical movement between European Roman Catholics and Protestants in general during World War II. This added social component promoted both postdenominationalism and emerging transdenominationalism, the latter perhaps first discerned in black and Jewish efforts at desegregation in the South.

Evangelicals were not unaffected by these movements, although they tended to embrace them more cautiously. The reasons for this point in several directions, including the following:

- A heightened conception of personal rather than structural sin
- A conception of the inerrant nature of biblical authority as focused more on personal rather than social morality
- Loyalty to a perception of American history and American national identity framed by the concerns of the Cold War
- A premillennial sense of history that was focused on the imminence of the end of history

While each of these issues might be seen as factors that limit social engagement, the first two, at least, germinated and emerged as an evangelical left (for example, Jim Wallis and *Sojourners Magazine*, Tony Campolo, Ron Sider). An evangelical Right became caught up by concerns of traditional family life, the politics of abortion and sexual practices (James Dobson), the Moral Majority under the influence of such persons as Jerry Falwell and presidential aspirant Pat Robertson of Regent University, and the social-conservative ethics and political life as framed by the Institute on Religion and Democracy.

By the 1980s what has been called the "two party" system of American Protestantism had emerged, whereby each denomination, and ecumenical and evangelical movements as well, divided into two groups—roughly liberal and conservative Christians.[25] This division not only occurred around critical sociopolitical issues but often also drew in questions of the priority of the state or the church in matters of religious allegiance.[26] Alliances between conservative Catholics and evangelicals became prominent and illustrated new forms of transdenominationalism. So also, after the World Council of Churches (WCC) General Assembly in Vancouver, British Columbia, in 1983, evangelicals softened their categorical rejection of the ecumenical movement and began to recall their own role in its formation.

Postdenominationalism: 1990s to the Present

The evangelical and ecumenical movements began their challenge to denominationalism at midcentury. As U.S. social life became caught up with the civil rights movement and the further justice and rights movements it spawned, the churches' framing of a social agenda created new divisions and alliances within both ecumenical and evangelical Christianity. These added further stress to the fissures already apparent in North American denominational life. Some Protestants found a new haven in returning to Rome, some to forms of Orthodoxy, others to new forms of monasticism, and some to a new postdenominationalism.

This chapter began by exploring postdenominational Vineyard spirituality, but postdenominationalism is also composed of other strains that have come together, often under the banner of a diffuse evangelicalism. Additional movements that have given shape to postdenominationalism include the church-growth school of thought, the megachurch phenomena, the emerging or emergent church movements, and the Next Church. Much, but not all, of this development has occurred outside of the traditional structures of Protestant denominationalism. Postdenominationalism has further eroded denominationalism, even as some of the new movements that comprise it have become tantamount to new denominations in their own way.

The church growth movement became focused on effective evangelism for the purpose of growing churches. This focus included such business school practices as mission statements, a product orientation, marketing to targeted populations, and an executive bureaucracy. Its goals, as stated by leading proponent C. Peter Wagner, former professor at Fuller Theological Seminary, are "to make more effective the propagation of the gospel and the multiplication of churches on new ground" and thus to "[see] America evangelized in our generation."[27] The roots of the church growth movement can be located in Donald McGavran's earlier missionary work in India with its targeted missiological emphasis on reaching ethnic groups as groups, but by the 1990s this moved beyond its missionary phase. Often defined by its first advocates, McGavran, Wagner, and the Charles E. Fuller Institute of Evangelism and Church Growth, additional persons began to shape its popular appeal.[28]

The megachurch movement is related to and in some ways came out of the church-growth school of thought. Some megachurches, like the Crystal Cathedral of Garden Grove, California (Reformed Church in America), under the ministry of Robert Schuller, have retained their denominational moorings, particularly those related to the Southern Baptist Association, while others such as Willow Creek Community Church or Saddleback Church have developed out of charismatic leadership and spontaneous community Bible studies. Another megachurch with a global reach is the Potter's House, a multiracial, nondenominational church with more than fifty active outreach ministries, led by minister and business visionary Bishop Thomas Dexter (T. D.) Jakes. Founded as the Greater Emmanuel Temple of Faith in 1979 and transplanted to Dallas, the Potter's House is now church home to more than thirty thousand members. Another megachurch leader, also representing success in the media, is Joel Osteen. Osteen and his wife, Victoria, serve as copastors of Lakewood Church, Houston. Begun by his father, a Southern Baptist who became a Charismatic, the church continues an active media ministry, crusades, conferences, mission program, and food distribution. Osteen's second book, *Become a Better You*, was released in 2007 with a first printing of three million copies. Often attempting to reach a society characterized by an increasingly secular public life and privatized personal life, megachurches frequently work to foster personal spirituality against and through the framework of the technological and organizational changes that have altered the North American landscape into the twenty-first century.

The emerging church and emergent church movements have taken root since the end of the twentieth century. They give witness to another form of popular evangelicalism whose five themes of prophetic engagement, postmodern sensitivity, praxis orientation, postevangelical self-understanding, and political consciousness have been identified by North Park University (Chicago) theologian Scot McKnight.[29] Emerging church is a movement that seeks to engage a postmodern generation through deconstructing and reconstructing Christian beliefs, standards, and methods that appeal to a postmodern generation. This is often characterized by a postfoundational approach to epistemology, that is, one that avoids a systematic approach to different truth claims, and a greater recognition accorded to religious pluralism and spirituality. Narrative in sermons; subjectivity in epistemology; a negative approach to creeds, confessions, and statements of faith; and an entertaining style of worship characterize emerging church gatherings, along with the use of new technologies and multimedia recourses. Tony Jones, national coordinator of Emergent Village, a network of emerging churches, writes of the emerging church as something of a reaction to the megachurch phenomenon.

Related in some ways to the megachurch or to the emerging church is *Next Church*, sometimes seen as similar to various evangelical forms of church life. Next Church tends to be independent and entrepreneurial. It draws in many people who have patchy or nonexistent histories of churchgoing. Its champions believe that in its tech-savvy and anti-institutional character, Next Church represents a distinctly North American reformation of church life, one that transcends denominations. It understands itself to be a full service, seven-day-a-week, pastoral or apostolic church. Also called a "new tribe" church or new paradigm, Next Church is seeker sensitive and may meet any place that has an Internet connection and computer monitor.

Concluding Observations

Denominationalism developed together with democratization and the principle of free association in religious life, ideas that took root in the American setting. This church life has developed along with individualism in the modern world, shaped also by increasing technological innovation and change. Evidence indicates that U.S. Protestants are less likely to belong to mainline denominations and more likely to belong to conservative ones than in the past. That they are often a part of postdenominational expressions of community life appears to be a growing social phenomenon worth tracking. That similar denominational stress or organizational tension can be found in Catholicism and Eastern Orthodoxy—as well as in Judaism and perhaps elsewhere—is not surprising, given the shared social setting of religion in North America. While the trusted brands of American Protestant religious life grew through the 1940s and 1950s, their loss of members from around 1965 to the present can be found in many of the movements noted above—megachurch, emergent church, and, in general, postdenomination-alism. But postdenominationalism also represents a discernable outgrowth from the trajectories that formed denominationalism in the United States.

To say that postdenominationalism is anti-institutional is too large a claim. Rather, the importance of institutions is seen in a new light, that of the value they hold in a structure of religious networking for social good and around other specific ends. As with the first expressions of federations and councils of churches at the end of the nineteenth and early twentieth centuries, postdenominationalism is a way of building social capital for democratic societies, even in the context of religious difference. Hence the interest in emerging transdenominationalism, a movement across denominational and even religious borders, is growing. The strength of the American religious setting has been the way in which it has allowed denominationalism to morph into an *Americanizing* aspect of social legitimacy for common civic life. Beyond these observations, something more needs to be said that transcends these influential and positive trajectories in American religious life.

First, American culture has increasingly become one united around work, not celebration. One of the chief ends of religion is celebrating life's transitions. An effect of marginalizing religious life in secular America is marginalizing community celebration. People's quest for religious authenticity in America today is in part a quest for meaningful community celebration—and for genuine community in contrast to the distrust in or the hollowing out they encounter in many other institutions. Religious institutions will continue to play a role in social experience in the United States; understanding them is important to an understanding of American culture.

Second, religious meaning is easily co-opted by the state when the state becomes the only socially unifying force in the life of the nation. The implications of this for the separation of church and state and for a misplaced civil religion are significant, particularly given the emergence of the National Security State following 1947 and the rise of American militarism. By taking themselves seriously, and by taking interfaith dialogue seriously, religious institutions can help promote the well-being of all other institutions in society through their freedom of expression and the vibrancy of the prophetic office. Hence, we are drawn to the importance of postdenomination and transdenomination religious experience and cooperation.

Third, the question of who vets religious truth is one of increasing interest in a postdenominational and transdenominational religious world: one author has said that the Christian faith is becoming more like Wikipedia and less like *Encyclopedia Britannica*—that is, rather then vetting knowledge through a process of learned men and women or by adherence to creeds and confessions, Christianity (or other religious traditions) is "what others are saying." There is something of an inherited truth here, something that takes us back to Peter Berger, whose thoughts began this chapter, and to the thesis in his 1967 book with Thomas Luckmann, *The Social Construction of Reality*, that meaning is embedded in society through patterns of social interaction and does not arise from an infallible truth. The erosion of trust in major institutions, be they banks and corporations, the government, the military, universities and the press—or religion—bears serious reflection as different religious groups in the twenty-first century seek legitimacy, particularly as they take prophetic positions that differ from prevailing political orthodoxy.

PART 2

Fragmentation or Diversity?

CHAPTER 5

Thoughts on American Jewish Denominationalism Today
Culture and Identity

David Ellenson

Several personal observations begin my approach to the topic of American Jewish denominationalism today. I was raised in an Orthodox synagogue, and in the course of time became a Reform rabbi. For many years I belonged to a Conservative as well as a Reform congregation, and all of my children have been educated at some point in Solomon Schechter schools. I am also an associate member of the Reconstructionist Rabbinical Association, and I am in many ways as close to being an "orthodox Kaplanian" as one could be. I still resonate to almost all Rabbi Mordecai M. Kaplan put forth in *Judaism as a Civilization*. I regard Judaism as an "evolving religious civilization," and the notion of peoplehood that Kaplan promoted is central to my own liberal approach to and feelings for Judaism.

I say all of this because, when I was approached to reflect on this topic, I was asked that I do so "just as an academic." However, the fact that I now head the major educational institution of the Reform Movement, the Hebrew Union College–Jewish Institute of Religion, is inescapable, and I am thus surely a partisan in the phenomenon that I am attempting to describe and analyze in these remarks. Having said all this in the interests of full disclosure and as a way of prologue to my comments, I have made these preliminary observations and will, despite all these commitments, attempt to be as objective as I possibly can be in offering these thoughts on the ongoing vitality and utility of denominations in Jewish life.

As we approach this whole question of denominationalism, I concur with Arnold Eisen's remarks included in chapter 6 of this volume. For contemporary denominational differences are undoubtedly more linked for most American Jews on the folk level to matters of style and behavior than to deep theological commitments that distinguish the movements one from another. While sociologist Steven Cohen has often pointed to defining characteristics that do exist today among those who affiliate with different denominations, I suspect these differences are real for an ever-smaller number of persons. For more and more American Jews, the distinctions in theology and ideology so crucial to the elite leaders of the different movements are increasingly irrelevant to "rank-and-file Jews." Many of the debates that occupy the leaders of these movements are probably regarded by many of these Jews as needlessly divisive and extraneous to the larger task: creating a vital and vibrant Judaism in the face of the challenges that modern-day America presents to ongoing Jewish life and commitment. A great many sociological, demographic, and cultural changes have transformed American life in general and Jewish life in particular during the course of the twentieth century. The language of denominationalism may not mean today what it meant when the institutions and practices of these movements were originally formed. Indeed, the permeability among the denominations that has allowed hundreds of thousands of people who claim to have been raised in the Conservative Movement to belong at present to Reform synagogues testifies to the fluidity that marks contemporary American Jews and their religious affiliations.

The German Jewish Religious Experience

However, before continuing with my analysis of the contemporary American scene, let me revert to my role as a historian of the German Jewish religious experience and focus on the birth and growth of denominations there, because I think such considerations provide a backdrop for underscoring the uniqueness that marks denominationalism in the United States today. Quite clearly, Jewish life in Western Europe and later in America was transformed between the time of Spinoza in the seventeenth century and the onset of the nineteenth century. Simply put, the European Jewish community underwent revolutionary political, cultural, religious, and social changes, and Jewish religious denominationalism arose at that point as a way for the Jewish community to cope with these changes.

The Reform Movement, initially under the leadership of layman Israel Jacobson in the second decade of the nineteenth century, and later on under the direction of rabbis like Samuel Holdheim and Abraham Geiger in the 1840s, articulated the first communal denominational response to these transformations in Jewish life. Reform was at first a lay-led movement that aimed principally to recast traditional modes of Jewish worship in accord with nineteenth-century German standards of aesthetics. However, the rise of *Wissenschaft des Judentums* (the science of Judaism) and its attendant ideal that Judaism was not only *in* but *of* history—that is, Judaism developed through time and had to be understood in cultural context—provided an ideological fulcrum that allowed for the growth of a non-Orthodox *Liberales Judentums* (Liberal Judaism) in Germany. Its Reform and positive-historical trends centered around the *Hochschule fuer die Wissenschaft des Judentums* (the academy for the scientific study of Judaism) of Abraham Geiger in Berlin and the Jewish Theological Seminary of Zacharias Frankel in Breslau, respectively. Cultural conditions in Germany were such that these two wings of German Liberal Judaism functioned within a common institutional framework where graduates of both institutions joined the same rabbinical organization. It would take the United States—as I will discuss below—with its cultural-social divisions between Jews of German and Eastern European descent to foster the growth of distinct Reform and Conservative movements latent in the ideological differences that separated Geiger from Frankel.

Orthodox Judaism itself arose in the 1840s, as Professor Jacob Katz pointed out over and over again in his voluminous and insightful writings, as a self-conscious attempt to defend Jewish tradition in an era when neither the beliefs nor the practices of the tradition were taken for granted. The works of a Rabbi Esriel Hildesheimer or Rabbi Samson Raphael Hirsch demonstrate their constant emphasis on a *Torah nitzchit*, an eternal Torah, and the

Hirschian assertion that the Law, both Written and Oral, was closed with Moses at Mount Sinai. This emphasis reflects a polemical struggle with the non-Orthodox varieties of Judaism—both Reform and positive-historical—that were claiming that all of Judaism, including the Law, was in a state of constant flux and subject to the transforming impact of history and ongoing cultural change.

This point is crucial if one is to grasp why it is that denominationalism arose as it did in modern Jewish life in Germany and the United States. The rise and growth of Liberal Judaism in Germany allowed for the birth of such denominationalism precisely because figures like Geiger and Frankel provided a philosophical-theological basis that justified both the patterns of practice as well as the types of changes they desired to introduce into modern Jewish religious life. Orthodox Judaism emerged in response to men such as these because a figure such as Rabbi Samson Raphael Hirsch had to discredit the claims to religious legitimacy that Reform put forth and because he was further compelled to distinguish himself from a man like Frankel, who observed Judaism no less punctiliously than he himself did. Despite their common patterns of Jewish observance, Hirsch condemned Frankel as a *kofer* (a heretic) on the grounds that Frankel's commitment to the notion that Jewish law had evolved throughout time was beyond the pale of acceptable Jewish belief.

America's Difference

Mai nafka minai? Of what significance is all this in shedding light on our topic today—contemporary American Jewish religious denominationalism? It is that while the seeds for modern Jewish religious denominationalism were planted and came to fruition in Germany, the reality was that only two "movements" emerged there—Orthodox Judaism on the one hand and *Liberales Judentums* on the other. No separate Reform and Conservative, Reconstructionist and Renewal "denominations" existed as they do in contemporary America. Men like Hermann Cohen and Leo Baeck, who became the most prominent "spokesmen" for Reform Judaism in Germany, actually attended the Jewish Theological Seminary in Breslau.[1] Men such as Solomon Schechter and Abraham Joshua Heschel, destined to become prominent spokesmen for Conservative Judaism in America, attended the Hochschule in Berlin. Precisely because the Jews of Germany had cultural homogeneity, no separate and distinct non-Orthodox Jewish movements arose on German soil. The nature of denominational responses that initially emerged in Germany to the changed character of Jewish life in the modern world was thus institutionally narrower than the variety of denominational responses that have ultimately come to define American Judaism.

Why was America different? In answering this question, it is critical to recall that when Isaac Mayer Wise came to the United States and established the Union of American Hebrew Congregations in 1873 and the Hebrew Union College in 1875, he avoided the label "Reform" in the titles of his institutions because he did not believe he was a creating a denominationally distinct form of American Judaism. Instead, his intention was to create an American Judaism for a community that was culturally homogeneous—at least prior to 1881. Wise did not aim to form—at least initially—a Reform Movement. Instead, he aspired to speak for all of American Judaism, and he even claimed that the Hebrew Union College would educate both "Orthodox" and "Reform rabbis." However, with the advent of two hundred thousand Eastern European immigrants in the first years of the 1880s to the United States, his dream of a unified American Judaism perished. The Jewish Theological Seminary was established in 1886 after and in response to the infamous Treifa Banquet, and by the early years of the twentieth century two distinct non-Orthodox denominations—Reform and Conservative—existed on American soil. These movements, I contend, reflected the very real differences that distinguished the folk practices and beliefs of German-American Jews from their Eastern European brothers and sisters. The notion of a united American Judaism that animated Wise ultimately came to perish in this country by the turn of the twentieth century. While genuinely distinct ideological and theological positions informed the leaders of Reform and Conservative Judaism, the rise and growth of denominationally distinct forms of non-Orthodox Judaism in America resulted more from the cultural heterogeneity that marked the American

Jewish community at this time than from any other factor. Reform Judaism came to be the denominationally distinct expression of the folk Judaism of German Jews in this country while the Conservative movement came into being to express the folk Judaism of Eastern European Jews in this country, as they successfully integrated into this nation and moved up to "areas of second settlement." Wise's notion of a "union of American Israel" perished principally because of sociological exigencies, that is, the very real differences that distinguished ethnically heterogeneous German from Eastern European Jews. The institutional patterns that emerged from these distinctions remain with us to this day, and the plurality of liberal varieties of American Judaism has even multiplied if we consider the emergence of Reconstructionist and Renewal expressions of Jewish religious tradition in contemporary America.

Yet, by the end of the twentieth century, the sociological and historical factors that led to the growth of two very separate major non-Orthodox movements as well as others have in fact diminished and the American Jewish community—the arrival of Israeli, Persian, Russian, and South African Jews notwithstanding—is more culturally homogeneous today than it has been since the nineteenth century. In the early twenty-first century, it will therefore be interesting to observe whether denominational differences remain as significant as they once were for large numbers of non-Orthodox American Jews, or whether the cultural homogeneity that now marks more and more American Jews will lead them to revert to a nineteenth-century pattern where denominations were less significant.

To be sure, attitudes towards issues like intermarriage and homosexuality will surely separate more tradition-oriented Jews from their liberal brothers and sisters. Indeed, many in this former group may well ultimately identify as modern Orthodox. Yet, the highly individualistic search for meaning and community that marks so many North American Jews, and that has caused Steven Cohen and Arnold Eisen to coin the term *the sovereign self* to describe the dominant orientation of most present-day American Jews,[2] will surely lead to increasingly greater denominational permeability when these Jews do choose to affiliate. Furthermore, I suspect that to many such Jews denominationalism will be irrelevant to them altogether as they explore their Jewish connections. More and more such American Jews, to employ Leo Baeck's felicitous phrase, are likely to move away from "an adjectival Judaism," that is, a Judaism where the adjective—whether it be *Reform, Conservative, Reconstructionist, Renewal,* or even *Orthodox*—is more important than the noun *Judaism.* They will not hesitate to move among movements and individual rabbis and religious teachers as they engage in their own personal religious and communal quests.

This is not to say that denominations are in any immediate danger of extinction. Any elementary course on sociology can tell you that well-established and powerful institutions never disappear quickly. Yet, I am certain, even as a Reform partisan, that many American Jews—for the reasons cited above—will be highly indifferent to denominational labels in their highly eclectic and idiosyncratic search for meaning. Those of us who do champion distinct movements will need to indicate why an affinity between our particularistic denominational commitments and the individualistic orientations that mark a highly culturally homogeneous community should engage American Jews as they look for community and meaning. While the pathways that individual Jews follow will surely be diverse, a homogeneous cultural reality may well now allow for a common Jewish landscape to emerge that will promote a greater degree of Jewish unity beyond denominational lines than at any time since the nineteenth century. I do not think Isaac Mayer Wise would disapprove.

CHAPTER 6

Thoughts on American Jewish Denominationalism Today
A Tradition of Unity and Diversity

Arnold M. Eisen

I have decided that my most useful contributions to these reflections would be a broad, schematic and in part theological sketch about the deep structure of Jewish tradition. Begging forgiveness from the historians, I will neither focus on details, nor will I let nuance distract me. I want to create a schematic view that I hope will indicate something useful about where contemporary Jews stand and why denominations continue to persist in twenty-first-century America.

A Schematic Sketch

First, for the purpose of this discussion, is that for whatever reasons—historical, theological, or covenantal—the fact of the covenant as well as its perception, the story the Jews have told about ourselves, set up on the one hand a set of *horizontal* relations among Jews, political, sociological and communal, and a *vertical* set of relations to God. The latter included diverse meanings of God and revelation, and myriad beliefs and practices related to them.

Let us agree that the covenant texts found in the Torah and in the rest of the Bible establish multiple and competing sources of authority. Let us also stipulate that because of the way the Bible is organized, one cannot possibly arrive at an all-encompassing and detailed creedal formula on which all Jews can agree. Rather, we must as Jews bring together a set of diverse readings of fundamental aspects of the tradition that were built into it from its inception. Think of any page of Talmud or any set of commentaries such as *Mikra'ot Gedolot*. Not an infinite variety, but a significant variety, are there from the very beginning; as far as Bible scholars can shed their insights on it, this is an essential quality of Jewish sacred texts. It demands and imposes diverse interpretations.

Second, let us go forward to the rabbinic period and so to Jewish dispersion (I am aware of course that the Diaspora existed before the destruction of the Second Temple). If we were to approach rabbinic Judaism the way a functionalist theorist such as Emile Durkheim might approach it, we would likely say that in order for Judaism and Jewry to survive its dispersion it *had* to have at its disposal a combination and balance of unity and diversity. That is, some unified system of special behavior and belief had to exist if Jews were going to remain one people and retain the advantages that being one people conferred in terms of sheer survival, whether economic, political, or communal. But some uniformity of theology also had to exist so that Jews could tell themselves convincingly that they were part of one story, members of one extended family, no matter where they were living or what language they spoke daily. Despite their geographic diversity, indeed because of it, they required a tradition that struck them and the Gentiles among whom they lived as more or less unified.

But, the words *more or less* are likewise necessary to that statement, because inside this unity—whether communal, political, or otherwise—an incredible amount of diversity had to be present. In retrospect, looking at it once more from a functional or phenomenological perspective, the Jews could not have "made it" with an unbending creedal structure that demanded absolute uniformity of belief and practice wherever they were on Earth. The diversity of their situation was too immense. Jews in many cases were not entirely aloof from the cultures and societies of which they were a part. This led to diversity that was greater still.

We Jews have a history characterized by broad internal divisions; we talk about Ashkenaz and Sepharad. More than just food and architecture varied. Recall Gerson Cohen's well-known essay about messianism East and West on the ways that the Ashkenazic-Sephardic division plays itself out in terms of messianic beliefs and activism. If time and space permitted here, we could analyze a whole range of such differing Jewish beliefs and practices. We should, I think, regard diversity as well as unity as normal structural features of the Jewish experience in the premodern world. Jewish civilizations could not have arisen and flourished under both Islam and Christianity if Jews had been subject to complete creedal or behavioral agreement. Some room for variation, as well as the possibility of unity, was needed.

Third, now moving ahead to modernity, particularly as it shaped Judaism in the West, we find a third powerful feature making for diversity: *voluntarism*. Jews in German cities and states established new sorts of schools and prayer services in the early nineteenth century because, for the first time really, they *could*. Jewish communal authority had weakened. Gentle rulers allowed or encouraged the changes. The surprising thing, in hindsight, is not that a variety of Jewish options were created, both in communal structure and in religious belief and practice, but that this variety has remained relatively limited. Jews still select the definition of their Judaism or Jewishness from a fairly narrow range of options.

The varieties of Judaism could have been much broader, at least in theory. But—perhaps because Jews remained one people, subject to the same external forces and loyal to one sacred Scripture—their divergences coalesced among a small set of possibilities. How many denominations do Jews have, after all? And how different are they from one another in many specifics? My rhetorical questions are not meant to suggest that the differences among the denominations are either trivial or ephemeral; they are not. But the number of extant patterns is small, and the behavioral overlap among them is substantial.

The Frankfurt society tried in the 1820s to do without circumcision, and quickly got voted down on that matter by other Reform Jews and their rabbis. Although debate about the virtues of circumcision still continues, and many prefer to have it performed by a physician in the hospital, the practice retains near-universal support. I find this remarkable. Experimentation with Shabbat, *kashrut*, and other practices likewise began early in the modern period and goes on today with relatively few variations. The options explored have not changed a whole lot over the past 150 years or so. Debate continues over what Jews should believe and do, what limits they should set to membership in their people, and who should decide these things. This division too seems inevitable. It stems as much from the deep structure I have been examining as from the modern Jewish situation. Diversity is inevitable, given the freedoms of which Jews take full advantage. So is unity, a core of common concern, practice, and even belief, without which it is hard to maintain that we are part of one story, if indeed it is our story, and can plan a role in authoring its future chapters. The drive for unity, as always, must contend with the fact of diversity.

Point four. This unity and diversity is true, most crucially of all, with regard to what is perhaps the most significant division of the Jewish people. This division began a little over a century ago on the question of whether Emancipation (in other words, minority status in diaspora democracies) provided a viable framework for Jewish existence and thriving. Zionism arose from the conviction that it does not. Israelis such as A. B. Yehoshua remain convinced of that; others do not. Either way, it seems virtually inevitable that the longer Israel exists, and the more Jewish tradition figures in the individual and collective lives of its citizens, the greater will be the gap between the forms of Jewish thought and behavior that evolve inside the state and those that develop outside of it. The Israel–diaspora divide adds another layer of complexity to the denominational divides that the authors in this symposium have been considering. Each of the individual denominations is affected by its shape and fortunes in Israel. So too are the relationships among them.

This brings me to my fifth point. A feature of the present situation for Jews that has long been evident to me as a scholar of modern Jewish thought and that stands at the center of my book, *Rethinking Modern Judaism*, is this: often little correlation exists between a person's beliefs about God, revelation, immortality, messiah, and a set of other factors and the behaviors a person adopts. A wide variety of behaviors are permitted and encouraged by Jewish beliefs. There is certainly not a one-to-one direct correlation between them, although neither is there a total absence of correlation. What you believe makes certain behaviors urgent, necessary, or irrelevant. Let us say for example that Martin Buber with his definition of autonomy, his distaste for any religious or behavioral norms, could not serve as the basis for any religious movement in Judaism. If he is going to be a significant presence in any denomination, it can only be Reform. Look at Eugene Borowitz who has used Buber to great and enormous effect but not without ambivalence. Borowitz cannot follow Buber to the end because Borowitz's commitments as a covenantal Jew demand the repudiation of Buber at key points.

Mordecai Kaplan's civilizational model is consummate with a certain definition of Conservative Judaism and perhaps with Reform Judaism, but Kaplan got himself in trouble with other elements inside Conservative Judaism. He was a nonstarter inside Orthodoxy because of his stated desire in *Judaism as a Civilization* to dispense with the category of *mitzvah*. The moment a thinker wants to do that, he or she puts himself or herself much more outside established religious norms than is the case with reflection, however radical, about the nature of God. One cannot imagine Joseph Soloveitchik writing a book called "Folkways Man" as opposed to "Halakhic Man" or a book called "The Communal Man of Civilization" rather than "The Lonely Man of Faith." Soloveitchik's grounding within a firm normative community, and a firm structure of *halakhah*, is precisely what gives him the freedom to be so idiosyncratic theologically. Soloveitchik's existentialism can only take flight because of the grounding that he himself promotes inside *halakhic* authority. Conservative Judaism, if I can put it this way, cannot rely on Kaplan alone. It requires Abraham Joshua Heschel, among others. But the tension between Kaplan and Heschel, to my view, marks out territory on which it cannot only survive but also flourish.

Heschel treated the subject I have been discussing at great length in *Torah Min Hashamayim* (beautifully translated and annotated by Gordon Tucker and Leonard Levin as *Heavenly Torah*). Heschel was trying to say that even though *Torah Min Hashamayim* itself is an *aggadic* concept, it is the basis of halakhah and any movement that dispenses with *Torah Min Hashamayim* has read itself out of the legitimate mainstream of Jewish life. But he also warned against the mistake, which he apparently felt was being made in the Orthodox world, of defining *Torah Min Hashamayim* too narrowly. That flew in the face of the diversity of meaning that he documented in the book. I think what Heschel was doing was nothing less than defining a theology for Conservative Judaism. His commitments—theological, behavioral, communal—define, to my view, the movement still.

Style More Than Theology

It seems inevitable to me that Jews are going to have—and should treasure—such theological variations as those just described. But, in light of what I have said thus far, it seems to me that Jewish denominational divisions are going to rest far more on matters of style and behavior, though these are admittedly linked to theological differences, than they are going to rest on theological divisions as such. It is not my impression that one must have a certain concept of God to engage in a certain kind of Jewish behavior; but it *is* my impression that Jews care greatly about whether men and women do certain things together, what language they do these in, whether separation of meat from milk is important to them or not, what should be taught in Jewish schools, and so forth. Identity is built on these basic things; denominations are built on these basic things. Similarly, while I don't think that Jews are divided merely by matters of style, I do think that style does come into it more than we generally recognize. For style pertains to how we Jews dress, eat, walk, speak; where we spend our time; the story we tell ourselves and others about who we are in the twenty-first century carrying on the covenant in force for three millennia.

Other factors too are operating. Harvard paleontologist Stephen Jay Gould, in one of his more famous articles about evolution, made the point that not every development that occurs in nature is itself functional. Rather, he made useful comparison to the architecture of Gothic cathedrals; certain developments follow from other choices that are made. Once the arches are built a certain way, the columns must take certain forms. Other possibilities are precluded. The same is true to some extent, I think, in the development of religious movements. The denominations tend to develop ideologies to justify, rationalize, and sanctify developments that often take place "on the ground" for institutional reasons or organizational reasons. At times I think we Jews also engage in a sort of species differentiation. We can't do X or Y, because another denomination has done it, and we can't allow ourselves to be mistaken for them. Such considerations also play their part in our people's delicate balance of unity and diversity. They also enter into the way we enact the possibilities built into the covenant and its narrative from the very outset.

Suppose for purposes of argument that the Jewish community were to adopt one of Mordecai Kaplan's most radical and fruitful suggestions, one which it has rarely taken up, and that has virtually nothing to do with God concepts or attitudes toward the commandments. His suggestion is that instead of spending so much money on maintaining separate buildings, denominations make do with far fewer buildings and share them. How would denominations change if they held many kinds of services inside one building or combined multiple schools inside of one building? It seems to me that the question on the table for the Jewish community as we approach the next generation, given that resources now as always are scarce, is this: What do we need to do separately? What could we do much better together? Organizations tend to fear that the minute they do anything together with others they are blurring the boundaries and are going to disappear. That is, of course, not an adequate reason for separate activity.

An Overarching Purpose

It seems to me that if one has confidence in the validity of one's path one can say: certain things can be done much better if done together. Indeed, such shared ventures will clarify the necessity for doing other things separately and differently. What matters, ultimately, is that the Jewish people survives and thrives, that Torah is transmitted as a tree of life, that God's voice is heard and served. Jewish denominations are vehicles to that end rather than ends in themselves. That does not make them any less dispensable. Variety has always been a part of the deep structure of Jewish tradition. But it does mean that denominations must constantly ask themselves whether they are serving their overarching purpose or protecting turf.

All Jewish denominations are historical creations. They came into being in a certain time and they may leave the scene at a certain time. This is undeniable. The question is whether they take their place in the pattern of unity and diversity that has sustained the Jewish people and its tradition for centuries and enables each person to walk that path. My own conviction as a scholar, a lifelong Conservative Jew, and now as chancellor at Jewish Theological Seminary is that our denominations at their best can do these things, and that they must. The differences among us make us stronger, if only we can muster the cooperation and mutual respect that has for so long maintained Jews despite and in their differences.

CHAPTER 7

Jewish Denominations
Transformation or Demise?

David M. Gordis

Though reflecting a range of perspectives on the past, present, and future of Jewish denominations at the threshold of the twenty-first century, thoughtful observers, many of whom have contributed to this volume, agree that the Jewish community generally and the denominations in particular have undergone significant transformations over the most recent decades. Does this signal an inevitable decline and the ultimate disappearance of denominations from Jewish life? Alternatively, do these transformations represent the normal evolution of a living community? Is the persistence of denominational differences healthy and constructive, or is it time to rethink the paradigm that structures the Jewish community's religious life? I propose to reflect on these questions here, as a person who has been nurtured within the Conservative movement in Judaism and who now characterizes himself as no longer fitting comfortably within the denominational framework but who prefers to view himself as transdenominational.

I use the term *transdenominational* advisedly, intentionally opting for it rather than for other terms that are sometimes and inaccurately used synonymously with it, namely *postdenominational* or *nondenominational*. By choosing this term, I want to convey the continuing relevance of denominational differences, albeit in the context of a widening inclination within the community to soften lines of difference between denominations and a growing disinclination to accept denominational labels.

I will focus on three emerging developments: a move towards ideological and stylistic convergence, particularly in the non-Orthodox community; a persistent and deepening divide within Orthodoxy between modern Jewish interpretations and Jewish fundamentalist views; the growth of institutions in the community that cross denominational lines.

Ours has been characterized as a postideological age in which decisions about values, behaviors, identity, and social and professional connections are taken on other than ideological grounds. This characterization is largely accurate and is relevant to the phenomenon of Jewish denominationalism, which was born in an unequivocally ideological context. All contemporary Jewish denominational expressions originated as reactions to the impact of the Enlightenment on traditional Judaism. What had been by-and-large accepted as axiomatic for traditional Jews, though in nuanced and more varied ways than is sometimes recalled, were the existence of a personal God who is the source of revelation, Hebrew Scripture as the content of the divine core of Sinaitic revelation, and the empowerment of generations of traditional interpreters to shape a binding legal tradition as articulated in authoritative codes of Jewish law. Underlying this ideology was the affirmation of the Jewish people's unique and chosen status in the divine scheme and the perception that the Jewish drama was in some way the central human drama and the core narrative in the divine plan.

The Enlightenment challenged these traditional axioms primarily through subjecting them to the prism of historical consciousness and critical methodology applied to canonical texts. Responses to the challenge were embodied in the development of the Jewish religious denominations. Translating the conclusions of historical and critical methods to a rejection of the authority of the postbiblical Jewish interpretive tradition, classical Reform rejected the authority of the *halakhah*. Orthodoxy denied the relevance of the new methodologies to traditional axioms. Conservative or positive-historical Judaism attempted to synthesize a commitment to the traditional normative tradition with an acceptance of the new historical critical methodologies. Later, and most radically, Reconstructionist Judaism posited a new theology, a Judaism without supernaturalism, clearly the sharpest departure from traditionalism of all the post-Enlightenment religious formulations.

Ideological and Stylistic Convergence

What is the current reality of these ideological positions that gave rise to Jewish denominations in the nineteenth and early twentieth centuries? Here, a distinction needs to be made between leadership of the movements and rank-and-file Jews. On both levels, dramatic changes have occurred within the ranks of denominational adherents. Leaders of the movements are more strongly assertive of the importance of denominational differentiations than are the Jews in the pews. But even among the leadership of the movements, significant evolution has taken place ideologically.

Perhaps most dramatically, Reform Judaism has moved from its earlier positions to embrace an evolving vocabulary and a transformed pattern of institutional life. Reform liturgy has become dramatically more Hebraic and participatory; the Reform synagogue service now frequently welcomes the wearing of the *tallit* and the *kippah*. Reform has become ardently Zionist and the movement supports Jewish day schools, once ideologically anathema. Even discussions of halakhah, appropriate norms for religious practice, have been taking place within the Reform movement for decades. These changes all represent a moving towards a kind of Jewish centrism from a formerly more radical position regarding Jewish tradition, at least behaviorally.

Reconstructionism no longer consistently embraces the humanistic theological formulation of Mordecai Kaplan that gave birth to it. Orthodoxy, at least in what has come to be known as modern Orthodoxy, no longer ignores issues of contemporary critical scholarship but seeks ways to find compatibility between contemporary scholarly approaches and unwavering adherence to halakhic scrupulosity. Conservative Judaism has sought to maintain its synthesis of critical scholarship and halakhic authority as well, but has moved in practice towards egalitarianism in the areas of women's ordination and participation.

As is always the case, the dynamics of these transformations have been forged in the dialogue between community and leadership and in the context of developments in the larger world. These positions have by-and-large been embraced by both leadership and adherents of the respective denominations and have been shaped by leaders of the respective denominations. For movement leaders, both lay and professional, denominational affiliation has remained of central significance. For the synagogue community in general, however, the significance of denominational association has declined substantially, with increasing numbers of Jews either identifying as "just Jews," or explicitly indicating that they reject denominational identification.

Despite the softening of ideological lines, differences of approach clearly persist, especially in the nexus of ideology and practice, particularly in such areas as women's participation, responses to intermarriage, and treatment of homosexuality and homosexuals. But here, too, distinct approaches often do not correspond to denominational labels.

Orthodoxy: A Special Case

In the context of the softening of ideological lines, Orthodox Judaism represents a special case and deserves special attention. As I suggested, a range of approaches to the challenges presented by modernity to formerly axiomatic beliefs has developed within each of the other denominations. The response within Orthodoxy has been the most palpably polar, with an increasingly clear divide between the "modern Orthodox" and traditionalist Orthodox groups. This should come as no surprise, since a group which chooses to identify as *ortho-dox*, or as teaching the "straight" or pure truth, faces special challenges in responding to challenges to those "straight" teachings. Though at some risk of oversimplification, I believe that it is fair to describe the traditionalist Orthodox as continuing to reject the validity of questions asked from historical and cross-cultural studies about claims to unique access to truth, the uniqueness of the divine revelation to the Jewish people, chosenness, and the impact of social and economic forces on the development of Jewish law. This translates into a continued insularity within the Jewish and larger religious communities and a disinclination to pursue "secular" studies except in connection with earning a livelihood. Modern Orthodoxy, on the other hand, has become far more open to the larger world of people and ideas, and while on some level it maintains its commitment to traditional formulations, in many ways it might better be described as *Orthoprax*, rather than Orthodox, emphasizing scrupulous adherence to traditional legal norms but representing a broad range of approaches on the authority of Scripture, the role of history in shaping tradition, and the place of Jews in the larger world. Modern Orthodox Jews are consequently far more open to relationships with non-Orthodox Jews and with the larger world as well, and they eagerly embrace intellectual pursuits beyond the disciplines of traditional Jewish study. One interesting exception to this polar construction is Chabad Hasidisim, which doctrinally can accurately be described as traditionalist but which reaches out to the larger Jewish community as emissaries of an exhilarating style of Jewish evangelism.

In my view, in recent years the divide between traditionalist Orthodoxy and modern Orthodoxy has grown, and I have no reason to think that it will not continue to intensify and grow in the foreseeable future.

In the dynamics of this moment, it is useful to reflect on the denominations' impressive achievements in American Jewish life. The creation of an extraordinary array of synagogues within the denominational framework is an achievement of the first rank. Each of the denominations has created impressive and productive institutions of higher learning and professional training and has nurtured generations of Jewish scholars, professionals, and lay leaders, accomplishing much of this before Jewish studies entered the American university and when the real possibility existed that extinction of Jewish scholarship in the world would result from the destruction of European Jewry. The denominations created institutional and organizational vehicles for professional and lay leaders to exercise roles that enriched their lives and the life of the community by bringing their talents to bear in Jewish communal life. Much of this active and creative role continues in the contemporary American Jewish community.

Crossover Institutions

Yet the changes earlier described have raised questions about the continued viability and vitality of the denominational structure as it presently exists. Are the denominational distinctions too sharply drawn in light of both Reform and Conservative Judaism's move to the center? Are the existing divisions wasteful of resources that could be better utilized in programming for a community that has a range of attractive options outside the Jewish community competing for their interest and engagement? With the softening of ideological distinctions and the declining interest of large numbers in the community in denominational labeling, are the far more subtle stylistic differences within the non-Orthodox denominations sufficient to sustain the elaborate and costly denominational structures that currently exist? And, finally, with the growth of synagogues, schools, communal institutions dealing with education, social and political action and rabbinical and cantorial schools that cross denominational lines, what policy should the community adopt with regard to denominations, and what is the prognosis for denominations in the coming decades?

The future of the denominations will be determined by the membership of the denominations themselves. If members of the denominations continue to identify strongly with their denominations, and support the institutions and initiatives of the respective denominations accordingly, the denominations will be sustained. On the whole, I see no role for the "community" outside the denominational structure to advocate neither the viability nor the dissolution of the denominations. Inevitably, however, the growth of transdenominational initiatives, as a response to the declining valence of denominational labels for many Jews, constitutes a challenge to denominations. It is clear to me that more rabbis, cantors, and educators will receive their training in institutions that cross denominational borders. This makes sense not only because it is cost effective, but also in the face of growing concerns over Jewish unity and the coherence of the Jewish community, it makes little sense to train leaders in a denominationally isolating fashion. Whatever an individual's personal theological and ideological position, the ability of a professional to function in a diverse Jewish community can only be enhanced by the experience of being trained in a diverse and pluralistic educational environment.

The expansion of transdenominational institutions is inevitable. There will be more communal as opposed to denominational day schools; adult learning programs and nonformal educational programs such as summer camps will increasingly be supported by the organized Jewish community and opt out of denominational labels, choosing instead programs that cross denominational lines. Other important transdenominational programs are already central on the Jewish communal agenda, including Hillel, Birthright Israel, and outreach programs to new populations. Denominational initiatives in these areas will have to find ways to compete effectively if they seek to sustain their independence and appeal to specific denominational adherents. They may succeed in some areas; it seems clear that in others, denominational initiatives should give way to transdenominational programs that can better serve the community and its interests.

A Deepening Divide

Donning the risky mantle of prognosticator, let me make a few predictions about the future of the denominations, individually and together. Each of the denominations brings to the twenty-first century rich resources and significant records of achievement; each faces new challenges beyond the general decline in denominational allegiance that I have described earlier. The Conservative movement has experienced the most serious decline in its ranks over the past several decades. This has been explained in contradictory ways. Advocates of the movement have suggested that the decline in numbers, with a membership shift from Conservative to Reform, is the result of the movement's success, inducing the Reform movement to adopt much of Conservative Judaism's agenda, making Reform an attractive and acceptable alternative address for Conservative Jews. Less sympathetic critics of Conservative Judaism have suggested that its institutions have demonstrated less vitality than those of other movements and that the leadership of Conservative Judaism has not responded aggressively and creatively to competitive challenges. There is some truth to both positions.

Inevitably, the centrist position, ideologically, theologically, or politically, is challenged by those to either side of the center, in this case Reform and modern Orthodoxy. The challenge has been reinforced by the move towards the center of Reform and the adoption of more communally oriented language by modern Orthodoxy. It may be that Conservative Judaism has lost its dominant position as the "moderate middle ground" to resurgent Reform. Whether it can regain that position and whether it is important that it do so remain open questions. Much will depend on the strength and vigor of Conservative Judaism's leadership and the clarification of the niche in Jewish life that it now seeks to occupy. In the area of normative behaviors, for example, with continued Orthodox adherence to traditional halakhah and the new concern for norms within Reform, articulating and communicating a distinct and appealing position to its adherents will be a major challenge, even at a time of diminished ideological focus.

Reform Judaism has grown rapidly in recent decades but faces its own challenges. Is the resurgence of Reform wider rather than deeper? Is Reform capable of generating genuine commitment and passion, embracing the spiritual and intellectual dimensions of Jewish tradition? Indications are promising and enormous resources are being invested in education, but the jury is still out. Again, much will depend on the creative energy of movement leaders in responding to challenges to denominational affiliation, even to the largest of the denominations, Reform.

My sense of contemporary Reconstructionist Judaism is that while it attempts to preserve the significance of the rational in the spiritual-intellectual dualism of Jewish tradition, its appeal is currently in the style of its worship services that emphasizes warmth, participation, and individual expression. While Reconstructionist synagogues are often attractive and impressive in their programs, it is hard to predict how Reconstructionism will fare in the competitive denominational environment and amid weakening commitment to denominational labeling. Were the movement to embrace more emphatically the theology of its founder, it would be easier to identify its specific niche in the denominational constellation, but that does not appear to be the direction in which the movement is heading.

Orthodoxy in America has made significant strides. It embraces a committed and frequently knowledgeable constituency, committed both to the synagogue and to traditional observance, and its continued focus on traditional education is impressive. It will continue to attract a significant minority of American Jews.

Its principal challenges relate to pressures from the "right," for increased insularity and a kind of competitive scrupulosity in observance. An example is the movement's navigation of women's participation. Some of the more interesting initiatives to expand women's role in public worship and in teaching have taken place in Orthodoxy. But resistance to these efforts has also intensified. Whether it will be possible for modern Orthodoxy to navigate the challenges from the right and continue to hold its constituency and attract adherents from the nonaffiliated and from other denominations remains to be seen.

Having risked predictive speculation on the individual movements, let me indulge in one further area of speculation: the possible realignment of the movements themselves. If we were to set aside organizational issues, and they are not easily set aside and are destined to have significant impact on any potential changes of the kind I am referring to, I would suggest that we are witnessing the emergence of a new set of forms of religious expression that could ultimately evolve into a new denominational structure. At the center would quite naturally be a centrist movement, formed from the Conservative movement's mainstream and Reform's more traditionalist expressions and some portion of Reconstructionism. To the left would emerge both a liberal group comprised of Reform's and Reconstructionism's more liberal components and a movement of Spiritual Judaism, bringing together those of all the aforementioned groups with a special focus on the Jewish spiritual and mystical tradition. To the right of the centrist group would be a traditionalist group consisting of Conservative Judaism's more traditional adherents and modern Orthodoxy's more liberal constituents. Finally, a group comprising fundamentalists and strict constructionists would round out the picture. How such a constellation of groupings would be organized and come into being is beyond the scope of this analysis, even if prophecy were possible. But the suggestion arises from a belief in the principle that "form follows function."

From these comments, it follows that I do not predict that the denominational structure of Jewish religious life in America is about to disappear. I predict that it will continue to occupy an important place for American Jews, but that its centrality will decline as transdenominational Judaism and its institutional expressions continue to grow.

A concluding observation: Synagogues, denominational or transdenominational, face a common challenge—to create inviting, exciting, life-enhancing, spiritually and intellectually rich institutions for Jews of all theological, ideological, and intellectual inclinations. No single response to this challenge is likely to provide any single effective result. The Jewish community requires many creative responses. They will emerge from denominational structures and from transdenominational structures as well. We should not look to domination by any form of expression. Rather, we need to find ways of preserving the creative energies of individual denominational and transdenominational groups and find ways of fostering communication between and among these groups to ensure a coherence and continued vitality to Jewish life in a richly diverse and pluralistic community.

CHAPTER 8

Postdenominational American Judaism
Reality or Illusion?

Rela Mintz Geffen

Over the last few years speculation has been rife in some educational and religious leadership circles about a developing twenty-
first century post-Reform, Conservative, and Reconstructionist
amalgamation of American Judaism. While greater adherence to
observance by those from the more progressive movements is one
aspect of this vision, with the exception of a few well-known individuals, Orthodoxy, even in its most modern iterations, is not
usually part of the projected new grouping. Synagogue revitalization efforts such as Synagogue 3000 (formerly Synagogue 2000),
or S3K, which was billed as a transdenominational project, and
Project STAR's (Synagogues: Transformation and Renewal)[1] Syn-
aplex, which aimed to revitalize Shabbat at pilot congregations
across the country, have not taken aim at the movements per se but
have sought to equip lay and professional leaders with new skills
and approaches to meet the needs of congregants more effectively.
Their goal was to enable the creation of strong spiritual and social
communities based in synagogues. One could say that they were
transideological or perhaps nonideological, focused on the means
that could be adapted to the ends of a variety of synagogues. Some
"neutral" ingredients added to the mix of leadership training are
spirituality, social action, adult study, and cultural happenings
ranging from kitsch (Matisyahu) to highbrow (commissioning
new music or art).

Before further comment on the potential for success of the
possible new amalgam, some terminology needs to be clarified.

Denomination may be a misnomer. Leaders of and spokespeople for the various institutions representing the variety of philosophies within American Jewish religious life have never called themselves denominations. They have preferred the term *movement*, which is probably more accurate, though the expressions postmovement, transmovement, and nonmovement have an awkward ring.[2] So, do those who tout the development of postdenominationalism really mean that a nascent movement in American Judaism will bridge and subsume them or create a new mix? Is this new grouping meant to succeed them all? Or, perhaps, like Project STAR or S3K, their vision is of a nondenominational amalgam—a grouping of individuals with a wide variety of Jewish commitments who want to pray, study, and celebrate with a multicultural mix of Jews; a group to which they will all contribute.[3] Each group would learn about the other but not be pushed into some new form that would emerge from the interaction of differing ideologies and institutional culture.

The Context—Jewish America in 2008

In my opinion, the American Jewish Community hasn't experienced an era of creativity like this since the period between 1970 and 1985.[4] Fin de siècle boredom has given way to Jewish bike rides, Jewish reggae, the Jewish TV Network, and the Nextbook Judaica series. One need only point his or her browser to the website of Slingshot to find "A Resource Guide to Jewish Innovation" with its third annual inventory of innovative happenings. According to its founders:

> *Slingshot, A Resource Guide to Jewish Innovation*, is an annual compilation of the 50 most inspiring and innovative organizations, projects, and programs in the North American Jewish community today. First published in 2005, and now in its third edition, *Slingshot* continues to highlight those organizations in Jewish life with particular resonance among the next generation. The Slingshot Fund is designed to highlight, encourage and provide support for a subset of the undercapitalized organizations

featured in *Slingshot*. Founded by Jews in their 20s and 30s, the Fund aims to provide a new model for raising and distributing grants by engaging people in Jewish philanthropy who would otherwise not be involved.[5]

The 2007–2008 listing ranges from what by now are thought of as quasi-establishment groups, from MAZON, Birthright Israel, the Drisha Institute for Jewish Education, and *Lilith* magazine to the more recently founded congregations, Hadar in New York and IKAR in Los Angeles, the Jewish Orthodox Feminist Alliance (JOFA), Hazon, and Limmud. Some of these institutions, such as JOFA, are linked to particular religious points of view while others, though related to synagogue life, appear to have made a commitment to a new pluralist postdenominational identity. Clearly, the soil is fertile at this time in the United States for experimentation and the development of new ideas and institutions to support their implementation. An evolution is in the making even if it is not a revolution.

These opportunities are also occurring at a time when a significant percentage of Jews and potential Jews (especially grown children of interfaith marriages) are marginally or not at all affiliated with the Jewish community, although their individual Jewish identities may be strong or even central to who they are.

Another large undefined group consists of those who sporadically enter into Jewish life—sometimes at a critical life-cycle moment and more often for a cultural or political or social action cause or event that touches them. They often do not define themselves in terms of any movement affiliation. However, that does not make them part of a postdenominational or transdenominational group or likely initiators of any new trend in Judaism. Confusing them with or arbitrarily counting them into the new postdenominational flock is not only wrong, but it also does a disservice to those who really are trying to reshape the institutions of American Judaism.

Exciting innovation often has a trickle-down effect that economists call a bandwagon effect. *Havurot*, which began as campus living groups similar to communes in the 1960s, became an instrument for strengthening synagogue life in the 1970s and 1980s. The Limmud program of New York, the Me'ah and Melton adult classes around the country, and Birthright Israel are certainly examples of programs that began with a few people and have had an ongoing impact on tens of thousands of Jews. Is being trans-denominational an exciting concept that might enable elites to energize masses of Jews? I don't know the answer to that, but I do know that a large percentage of U.S. Jews identify with one of the major movements. And, even if they don't live up to the official standards of that movement, the fact that they declare themselves a part of it affects their responses to Jewish life.

Is Movement "Membership" Meaningful Today? A Few Examples from National Jewish Population Survey 2002

When one asks an Israeli Jew about his or her Judaism she or he may identify as *hiloni* (secular), *masorti* (traditional), or *dati* (religious). Some will say *haredi* (ultraorthodox) or perhaps the new term *hardal* (a contraction of *haredi leumi* meaning ultraorthodox with a nationalistic bent). Hasidim may identify using the name of the rebbe of the sect to which they belong or the name of the town in Eastern Europe where the group originated. Many American Jews modify the words *Jew* or *Jewish* with the name of a movement. They may say, I am a Reform Jew or an Orthodox Jew—most do not say I am "just Jewish." Whether or not they belong to a synagogue at any given moment, they still qualify the word *Jewish* with the name of a movement.

As sociologist Steven M. Cohen has noted, "the number of adult Jews who decline to identify with a major denomination rose from 20 to 27 percent over the ten year period."[6] Looking at it another way, about three-quarters of American Jews continue to identify themselves with one of the major "denominational choices," as he chooses to call them.[7] Moreover, those who do identify with one of the movements are more connected to Jewish life and are much less likely to be intermarried or to be the children of interfaith marriage and much more likely to be affiliated with a synagogue. Those who don't identify with a movement "score far lower on all measures of conventional Jewish engagement than do any of the denominationally identified, be they Orthodox, Conservative, Reform or Reconstructionists" (Of the four denominations, self-declared adherents of the latter two denominations report the lowest average levels of ritual observance, communal affiliation, and subjective importance of being Jewish, but even they substantially outscore the nondenominational in these categories).[8]

Let's take a moment to consider the term *self-declared*. I did an analysis of National Jewish Population Survey (NJPS) data on movement affiliation to see if there was an independent effect of calling oneself a movement member regardless of current synagogue affiliation or otherwise living up to a particular movement's theoretical ritual standards of behavior. In every case, the fact that people designated themselves as part of a particular movement made a significant difference in their attitudes.[9]

Table 1
How important is religion in your life today?

	Orthodox	Conservative	Reform	Secular
Very	81%	41%	24%	14%
Somewhat	16	50	52	36
Not very	2	8	20	30
Not at all	1	1	4	20

Table 2
How important is being Jewish in your life?

	Orthodox	Conservative	Reform	Secular
Very	90%	69%	45%	33%
Somewhat	8	27	44	41
Not very	2	3	10	17
Not at all	–	–	12	10

Table 3
I look to Judaism for guidance in important life decisions.

	Orthodox	Conservative	Reform	Secular
Strongly agree	72%	32%	14%	10%
Somewhat agree	19	40	40	24
Somewhat disagree	4	18	24	23
Strongly disagree	5	8	19	40
Neither	0	2	2	3

In addition to religion, being Jewish clearly involves ethnicity, food, music, art, and relationships to Israel. As a result, the differentiation by movement is more pronounced in table 1, which records responses to a question that specifies the importance of religion in the person's life. Of those terming themselves secular, a significantly higher percentage rate being *Jewish* as very important in their lives compared to those saying *religion* is very important in their lives. (Indeed, it would be very surprising to find many secular Jews who rate religion highly for their own lives.) Still, for our purposes, an important point is illustrated in both of these tables. Names are powerful. Describing oneself by a name or the name of a movement has significance.

Seeking to check out responses to more behavioral items from the NJPS (though not ritual behaviors), I looked at the responses by self-identified movement affiliation to see whether the respondents look to Judaism for guidance in important life decisions. The responses to this item are shown in table 3 above.

Again it is clear that movement consciousness is related to the centrality of Judaism in the respondents' lives.

Another behavioral measure of differentiation by self-identification is the networks or close friendship circles of the respondents. More than half (54 percent) of those who self-identified as Orthodox reported that most or all of their close friends were Jewish at the time of the survey. The figure for Conservative identifiers was

33 percent, for Reform 26 percent, and for those calling themselves secular it was 19 percent. Jewish social circles may construct identity as much as synagogues do. Maintaining a countercultural way of life in American society is very difficult. When this is combined with the "groupie" nature of following the *mitzvot*, one can see how important a friendship network is to maintenance of a Jewish way of life. Observance of the Jewish calendar and life cycle rituals requires commitment and a support system. It is difficult to imagine individuals continuing observance of rituals such as Shabbat meals, Passover Seder, sitting *shivah*, or lighting Hanukkah candles absent a community. For this essay, what is most salient is yet another confirmation of a differential by movement identification.

Given the findings noted above, it is apparent that though movement labels are rejected by a quarter of U.S. Jews who are minimally affiliated, and eschewed by a small elite of perhaps ten thousand who are seriously committed to Jewish life, the movements still have the potential to influence a majority of Jewish people in the United States. Until now, much of this influence has been mediated through synagogue life. Even though fewer than half of U.S. Jews belong to synagogues at any one point in time, more than 80 percent affiliate for a number of years in the course of their lives. Finally, even when they are not dues-paying members of a synagogue, we have seen that Jewish Americans identify with the movements and are affected by that identification. The two great cycles of Jewish life, that of the *luach* (Shabbat and holiday calendar) and of the life cycle from birth through death and mourning, generate yearning within many Jews to connect with their tradition. In North America, the synagogue has been the grassroots institution best positioned to satisfy these needs.[10]

One cannot escape the conclusion that as in the nucleus of an atom, great potential power is stored in the overgrown movement bureaucracies and in a reservoir of goodwill among the grassroots laity. Harnessing, or perhaps more precisely, releasing this power and energy is the task of this decade. In some of the movements, leadership transitions to a new generation are now occurring or have already taken place since the start of the new century. For example, in the Conservative movement, by 2010 the executive leadership of four major organizational segments will have transitioned—the posts of chancellor of the Jewish Theological Seminary and the executive director of the Women's League for Conservative Judaism have already transitioned, and the executive vice presidents of the United Synagogue of Conservative Judaism and of the Rabbinical Assembly will turnover in 2009.

A Note on What the Future May Bring

This essay has analyzed several different groups. They will have differing impacts on the shape and substance of North American Jewry of 2020. Of the one-fourth of adult Jews termed nondenominational and who designated themselves as secular or "just Jewish" in the 2002 NJPS, many will no longer be part of the Jewish community. If their proportion within the overall Jewish population stays the same, it will be due to a further increase of interfaith marriage partners providing replacements for those who have passed on. Many of their children will identify with mainline Christian denominations while others will consider themselves secular Jews or, perhaps, half Jews. Probably all will be proud of their Jewish antecedents and may have some symbolic art, books, and ritual objects on display in their homes.

Assuming that the seriously committed postdenominational group becomes institutionalized, its path may follow that of the founders of the Havurah movement in the 1970s. Some will continue in alternative *minyanim* and as models and catalysts for reenergized social action on the part of all North American Jewry. Like the National Havurah Committee today and the Jewish Renewal movement, they will develop their own national structures, rules for leadership succession, paid professionals, and the like. This follows the paradigm of charisma and its routinization developed by the sociologist Max Weber, who noted that in the second generation of a charismatic movement's development, issues of leadership succession and program maintenance must be addressed. Either rational-legal or traditional authority along with bureaucratic organizational structures must be put into place to ensure that the group will continue. One can't count on charisma once the charismatic founder or founders are no longer alive.[11] Perhaps even more significant than the "official" groups, which will remain a small elite, will be the impact the postdenominational groups' emphases have on the vibrancy of the established movements. Their spirit of civility amid pluralism, synergy of spirituality and the social action imperative, together with an emphasis on community building will trickle down, particularly within the Reform and Conservative movements.

Finally, what about the future of those established movements? They will continue to exist and to have distinctive identities and substantive commitments related to what it means to live a Jewish life. Orthodoxy's various segments will continue to grow and make up a fifth of the Jewish community. The high level of congruity of practice among the vast majority of centrist and more fervent Orthodox Jews will make them seem like an even larger proportion of organized Jewish life. Sensitivity to tradition will be heightened throughout the community at large as their presence is strengthened in community affairs.

The Reform movement will be smaller in the next generation as most of the attrition to nondenominational and secular will come from their ranks. However, the Reform movement that remains (and it may still be the largest group in terms of sheer numbers) will have a stronger committed core dominated by graduates of their day schools, camping system, youth movement, Israel programs, and the schools of Hebrew Union College–Jewish Institute of Religion.

Reconstuctionists will remain 2 to 3 percent of U.S. Jewry and a lesser percentage of Canadian Jewry. They will continue to partner with the Union for Reform Judaism (URJ) in worldwide institutions of progressive Judaism. Their alliance with Reform may broaden so that they become one progressive movement within the United States, much as they are abroad. They will enhance their rabbinical school, the Reconstructionist Rabbinical College, and their youth movement and summer camp will expand.

The Conservative/Masorti movement has already suffered its greatest numerical losses and will probably stabilize at its current size. The challenge before it is to regain its esprit de corps. Leaders and congregants must have confidence in its message that tradition and change cannot only be pursued simultaneously but also yield positive synergy. It is always difficult to be passionate about moderation. Yet this is what the Conservative movement must accomplish in order to remain vital. Impending leadership transitions together with the influence of postdenominational communities, such as Hadar and IKAR, that emanate from and are led by Jewish Theological Seminary graduates and the growth of Schechter elementary and high schools, Camps Ramah, and adult learning programs engender an attitude of hope for the future. The keys to regaining passion and momentum are charismatic leadership and willingness on the part of those leaders to make demands on themselves and, at the same time, to risk requiring commitments from their constituents. The movement also has to be open to changes in the role of professional leaders, their relationship to the laity and to the structure of institutions that had a history of success in the movement's glory days.

While there is no sure way to predict the future, it is safe to say that twentieth-century Jewish movements in the United States and Canada will persist long into the twenty-first century. America is a society in which religion is pervasive. Often the most comfortable way for Jews, as individuals, to participate in the multicultural mix is as part of a religious group. Transdenominational spiritual and social action efforts and institutions will have an important impact on the movements' adherents and by example on all of American Jewish life, but they will not be the normative mode in the decades to come.

PART 3

Prescriptions

CHAPTER 9

Synagogue Renewal in an Age of Extreme Choice
Anything, Anyone, Anytime, Anywhere

Hayim Herring

At this moment in Jewish history, philanthropists are investing significant funds in search of the next "big idea," the concept that will ensure the vitality of the Jewish people for decades to come. This search is well intentioned and will certainly produce multiple, meaningful innovative programs, which will deepen connections between Jews and the Jewish community—a significant accomplishment. However, there is a difference between big ideas and big programs. As Mordecai Kaplan astutely observed more than seven decades after he first stated it, Judaism is a religious civilization.[1] Since shortly after the Emancipation and continuing to our own day, other expressions of Jewish life have entered and then exited the scene, some leaving a permanent influence and others flourishing briefly, barely leaving a trace. In the end, the big idea of Judaism must focus on understandings of God, Torah, and Israel, however broadly defined, as the sources that renew and reenergize Judaism.

In the United States, since the nineteenth century, denominational synagogues—that is, those affiliated with a denominational movement—have been the repositories and often the incubators of Jewish religious life.[2] The denominational synagogue is being challenged by spiritual and secular alternatives and is frequently faulted for its inability to capture the spiritual imagination of American Jewry. This essay will explore the possibilities denominational synagogues have to lead a religious renaissance and suggest a reorienting framework for them to achieve this goal.

111

The thesis of this chapter is that synagogue-based Judaism must engage in a radical reorientation if American Jews, and the many constellations in which they come, are to perceive the Jewish religion as responsive to real-life issues. By understanding how Judaism can help people meaningfully navigate these issues; by developing leaders who use the language of Jewish values to speak in ways that motivate and engage them; and by changing the organizational thinking and culture of synagogues so that they can develop into authentic communities, or what urban sociologists call "third places," more synagogues can become communities of inspiration and individual Jewish character formation.

Some parts of this reorientation are happening already on the local level. While some synagogues are informally engaged in this kind of adaptation, the leadership of their denominational movements will have to play an active role in catalyzing and scaling local successes and framing them into a compelling narrative of Jewish religious and spiritual life. So far, they have been unable to play this role. However, if the liberal denominations were to create a strong alliance, because they have more in common than they do that separates them, it might be possible for them to lead a spiritual renaissance.

Although some of the more intriguing denominational developments are actually occurring within Orthodoxy, I do not treat them here because of a fundamental theological divide between liberal and orthodox expressions of Judaism. However, this chapter does acknowledge the work of Orthodoxy in mobilizing significant interest in Jewish educational and spiritual life. Liberal denominations can learn from Orthodox outreach efforts and replicate their successes.

Anything, Anyone, Anytime, Anywhere— Understanding Denominational Challenges

We live in a time of tremendous societal upheaval. While history is often cyclical, showing both change and continuity, there are times when change is so systemic and deep that we enter a fundamentally new era. These changes are of such profound magnitude that they are redefining how life is lived in many areas we assumed were unyielding givens. In broad terms, we might think about boundary shifting, permeability, and cross-religious and cultural appropriation as the motifs that characterize this age. Culture, economics, history, biology, technology—all areas of life are up for reassessment or revision because of these forces. Whether we in the Jewish community view our current era as essentially more of the same or fundamentally different is not a moot issue. Rather, it influences whether we apply current models of thinking about all aspects of our world or if we need different ones.

For shorthand, I refer to our contemporary era as the Age of Four A's: anything, anyone, anytime, anywhere. It is in this crucible that Jewish life is being recast today. This shorthand description of our times captures well-described attributes of daily life, if not precisely for boomers, than increasingly so for Gen Xers and Millennials:

- *Anything* (almost)—products or services—can be can be modified, or if nonexistent, can be created with relative ease.
- *Anyone*, regardless of credentials or pedigree, can be their own expert in many fields that were typically reserved for specialists (for example, we can be our own stock brokers, financial planners, publishing houses, filmmakers, business consultants, and educators).
- *Anytime*; we increasingly demand that goods and services be available to us at our convenience.
- *Anywhere*, in real time or virtually, at home or abroad, we can experience different cultures on a global scale.

A brief review of the entertainment industry will illustrate how these four dynamics can reshape an entire industry and, in so doing, how we experience one aspect of life.

In both the old Hollywood of the 1920s, '30s, and '40s, as invented by rags-to-riches Eastern European Jewish immigrants, and the new Hollywood of our day, recast by the CEOs of global conglomerates—Disney, General Electric, News Corporation, Sony, Time Warner, and Viacom—hardly more than a handful of moguls at any time have controlled the preeminent forms of entertainment: film and television. They have determined how movies and shows are created and have dictated when, where, and how we can consume them. Want to see a new movie? You have to line up at the multiplex for its 7:15 or 9:30 p.m. show, or wait for months until you can buy the DVD or see it on cable. Like a TV show? It airs only on Tuesdays at 8:00.

That's over, or will be soon: In the new Hollywood of the digital era, no one will be in control—except, in a way, all of us will be. The oligarchy of the moguls is falling to the democracy of the consumers. A small cadre of corporate chiefs could control the cinemas, the airwaves, and the shelf space in the DVD aisles at Blockbuster and Wal-Mart, but no one can control the Internet. Transmitting video files to consumers over digital broadband connections—whether via cable, phone, satellite, or wireless WiMAX—changes the whole equation.[3]

The radical transformation of Hollywood's entertainment industry provides a snapshot of these forces at work both individually and interactively. In a relatively brief period, a small group of individuals lost control over an entire industry. Anyone can make and distribute their own movie relatively inexpensively and achieve recognition, thanks to digital recording and editing technologies and sites like YouTube and Google. The content of that movie may be about any imaginable subject and is available on demand. Just as mainstream television and movie theaters were challenged by cable and satellite television, cable and satellite entertainment—still relatively new themselves—are already being challenged by these new technologies. What is clear is that a basic industry in American life and culture has been changed, and that is only one of many.

Key Challenges for Liberal Denominations

This illustration about radical change in creating and distributing forms of entertainment is being replayed across every industry and business—and that includes religion. "Anything, anyone, anytime, anywhere" is an environment that runs counter to the synagogue milieu, which might be described as "some things, some people, sometimes, and some places." In other words, only some things are open to innovation, only some people get to decide what is in and what is out, only sometimes are synagogue resources available, and only some cultures like Israel and Jewish Diaspora communities are places of interest. If the gap between contemporary society and the current synagogue model is not closed, liberal denominational synagogues will play an increasingly marginal role in setting the tone of Jewish spiritual life in twenty-first-century America. What fresh concepts can help mediate between the general culture of instantaneous expectations and the synagogue environment of uneven, sometimes mediocre, and gradual change?

I will focus on three central concepts that are key to enabling synagogues to be places of inspiration:

- Revising institutional *views* about the synagogue
- Reinterpreting Jewish *values*
- Reimagining the *venue* of the synagogue

By unshackling synagogues from leftover views about how they do their work, by creating stronger points of connection between Jewish values and the real life concerns of individuals, and by reimagining the synagogue as a venue where people are empowered to find and create community on their terms, synagogues may become places of greater vision, inspiration, and relevance.

Institutional Views: Then and Now

As noted earlier, Jewish religious life in the United States has expressed itself primarily through denominational structures. But the denominations originated in a fundamentally different time and place—mid-nineteenth-century Germany. The contemporary synagogue emerged toward the beginning of the Emancipation era while today's Jewish descendants are living at the end of this age—or perhaps have entered a new one. A few contrasting examples between then and now illustrate just how different some of the issues are.

Recent ancestors of Jewish Americans had to make a bargain with modernity. In order to enjoy new personal freedoms, won at great cost, they had to give up their corporate identity and pledge their loyalty to the nation-state. That often meant rapid assimilation into the majority culture and, in some cases, even conversion to Christianity, to ensure a more integrated fit with the majority. Denominational Judaism arose to meet those challenges.

Reform, Orthodox, and Conservative Judaism attempted to craft approaches to Jewish life that would enable Jews both to retain their Jewish allegiances and also to enjoy the emerging civic, educational, and professional opportunities as citizens of their nations. They did so by trying to limit, balance, compartmentalize, or harmonize Judaism and Emancipation. The synagogue was a mediating institution, tasked both with being the venue that would help Jews retain their Jewish loyalties and showcase to the non-Jewish world that Judaism was every bit as sophisticated as the then-current majority Protestant religion of Germany.[4]

The synagogue, as the public stage of Judaism, had the paradoxical task of opening itself to the broader community, which was still suspicious of Jews, but trying to limit the parts of modernity deemed inimical to Jewish communal survival—a very delicate balancing act.

What were some of the worldviews that shaped the synagogue as an institution at this early stage of Emancipation? The worldview of Jewish denominationalism's pioneers included concerns for tribalism while still espousing universalism, exclusivity, authority, rationality, hierarchy, subservience of the individual to the community, homogeneity, suspicion of the other, and insecurity of self. These views were incorporated into how the synagogue functioned as an institution.

However, today the Jewish community is so far beyond the early stages of Emancipation that it is often oblivious to Emancipation's major struggles. Yesterday's Jews shed their Hebrew names—today, they have the option to reclaim them. They had to hide symbols of Jewish identification, today even non-Jews claim them. Being Jewish is generally not a barrier to acceptance into politics, education, or professions, including law, medicine, and accounting, nor is the issue of Jewish loyalty to America.

For simplicity's sake, the chart below provides an accessible way to contrast the worldview of synagogues born in another era with the fundamentally different times in which we live.

Yesterday's Views of the World	Today's Views of the World
Authoritarian	Democratic
Hierarchical	Less structured, more participatory
Pedigreed experts make changes	Expertise determined by ability, interest
Closed system; closed source	Open system; open source
Institutionally focused	Individually focused
Stand-alone institution	Linked with Jewish, non-Jewish, and secular institutions
Denominational	Pluralistic, open to all
Fearful	Hopeful, celebratory
Somber, formal	Warm, informal
Tribal, ethnic	Global
Scarcity oriented	Abundance oriented
Intellectual, rational	Spiritual
Insecure, defensive	Secure, proud

The problem today for many synagogues is that much of American Jewry finds itself living their lives in the right-hand column, "Today's Views of the World,"[5] while they perceive that the leadership of many synagogues is still viewing the world through the left-hand column, "Yesterday's Views of the World." Synagogue leadership is certainly aware that Jewish life in America in 2009 is radically different from Jewish life in Germany in 1870, and synagogues certainly do change. However, by their nature, they change slowly. Their primary task is preservation, transmission, and evolutionary adaptation, balancing the needs of the hour with their mission of remaining true to a historic tradition and a denominational and congregational heritage.

This defense mechanism of synagogues that provides needed sensitivity toward the past has now become one of the contributing causes to alienation between the vast majority of American Jews today and the synagogue. Low rates of affiliation, participation, and funding of mainstream synagogues suggest that synagogues will capture the attention and involvement of more individuals in a post-Emancipation era only if they more closely align their organizational worldviews to the contemporary reality of American life as most of the Jewish community lives it.

The Urgent Need for a Contemporary Restatement of Jewish Values

The good news is that the age of anything, anyone, anytime, anywhere raises profound issues of meaning, making existential questions about life more insistent:

- If I live in an age when I can get whatever I want, how do I decide what is ultimately most important?
- If I have unlimited control over my life, how do I exercise it wisely?
- If I can choose to be a part of any community, which one is more desirable for me to join?
- If I live in world that is always "on," how can I ensure that I find ways to disconnect so that I do not lose my soul?
- If I live in an age of unlimited power, how do I remain humble, not exploit others, and work to ensure that that all people are treated with basic human dignity?
- If I live in a world where I can keep taking, do I have a responsibility to give something back?

These big questions—which most people eventually have to face—are exciting for those who believe that the religious core of Judaism provides an invaluable resource for grappling with them. While individuals have maximized their ability to choose, they often have doubts about their ability to choose wisely. They are therefore open to seeking guidance from religious traditions of all kinds, provided that they do not lose control over how they live their lives. In this environment, religion loses its ability to coerce (a good thing) but gains an opportunity to influence (also a good thing)—if it is relevant.

Judaism is well-suited to deal with issues of personal meaning and help people explore them with a community that also struggles with them. While frequent references to *halakhah* leave an impression of its preeminence, Judaism has an equally rich tradition that emphasizes timeless values about what is ultimately important in life. This tradition is found both in ancient and contemporary Jewish philosophical literature, which seeks to identify underlying values[6] of halakhah, classical *midrashic* literature, and contemporary works on Jewish values that explore a wide range of topics, from biomedical ethics to everyday relationships.[7] Byron Sherwin and Seymour M. Cohen summarize the role of Jewish ethics and values beautifully when they wrote:

> The works that comprise Jewish ethical literature are self-help manuals in the art form of life. Their primary goal is not to inform but to transform. . . . Their agenda addresses the ultimate and the most intimate problems of human experience. They deal with the nature and expression of basic human emotions such as joy and love, anger and envy . . . and prescribe fundamental humane values such as humility and compassion. They address visceral human drives such as acquisitiveness and lust. They discuss and analyze social issues such as interpersonal communication and the employment of wealth. No human emotion, no human conflict, no moral problem eludes their grasp.[8]

Today, these values are often encrusted in language that obscures their meaning and inhibits their potential to influence and inspire. For example, the category of *mitzvah*, often translated as a "sacred obligation" or "commandment," clashes with the notion of personal autonomy. However, what happens when we speak about committing ourselves to a higher purpose in life, which is one potential way of reframing the category of mitzvah? Another example: in a world that is always "on," what will resonate with individuals on a personal level, observing Shabbat and holidays or resting and renewing one's body, spirit, and mind?

Jewish Value	English Translation
ahavat yisrael; klal yisrael	Loving all Jewish people; pluralism
bechirat chayyim	Making life-affirming choices
breeyot	Promoting mental and physical health
brit	Creating lasting, ongoing relationships
b'tzelem Elokim	Categorical human dignity for each person
darchei shalom	Seeking peace
emet, shelaymut	Living truthfully, decently, and with integrity
hiddur mitzvah	Appreciating and promoting beauty
hodayah	Displaying gratitude
kedusha	Pursuing holiness, spirituality
kehillah	Community
keruv	Drawing people near to beauty of Judaism
k'vod ha-briot	Honoring the dignity, equality, uniqueness of all people
limud Torah	Acquiring Jewish wisdom
menucha	Resting and renewing one's spirit
mitzvah	Committing to a higher life purpose
n'davah	Respecting gifts of volunteers
oneg, ha'na'ah	Enjoying worldly pleasures
p'ru u'revu	Fertility, abundance
rachmanut, hesed	Acting with compassion and kindness
shemirat ha-adamah, ba'al taschit	Caring for the planet
shemirat ha-lashon	Speaking and acting ethically
shiv'im panim la-torah	Expressing Judaism in multiple, valid ways
shutafut	Partnerships, collaborations
simcha shel mitzvah	Living joyfully
tikkun olam; avodah	Improving the world; service
tzneut lekhet, anevut	Humility
yirat shamayim	Living with awe, appreciation

The language used to describe these values can either motivate people to participate in the Jewish enterprise or push them to look for sources of meaning outside of the Jewish community. And self-described secular or nonreligious Jews are spiritually hungry.[9] You can find them in Chabad houses, in adult learning classes (again, more often than not, offered under Orthodox auspices, or to our great loss, Buddhist centers, Christian worship spaces, and Baha'i temples, to name a few options outside the Jewish community).

The chart on page 120 represents one sample effort to reframe authentic, classical Jewish values in contemporary terms.[10] This chart is not meant to serve as a definitive list of reframed values, but as an illustration of the process of enabling "Torah to speak in contemporary terms," a recommendation already espoused by the classical rabbis.[11]

Filtering Enduring Jewish Values through Fresh Organizational Thinking

A significant connection exists between understanding yesterday's organizational views about synagogues and today's realities about the values that resonate with people in this age of anything, anyone, anytime, anywhere. Organizational thinking serves as a filter for determining how values are articulated and lived in the life of a congregation. The chart below illustrates how organizational views determine the overall orientation of a congregation.

Of course, many synagogues have intuitively or consciously moved in the direction of making their congregations more participatory, open, and better connected to their Jewish and broader communities. However, it is unclear how many have done so as a result of a systematic process or as a scattershot response to changing conditions. The Reconstructionist movement has emphasized the role of values in the decision-making process of their congregations, but even here decisions in the life of a congregation are typically made on an as-needed basis.[12] Undertaking a broader review of values and the role that they can play in every aspect of the congregation, from staff hiring and job descriptions to worship, takes a tremendous amount of energy, vision, and lay and professional commitment.

Enduring Jewish Value	Yesterday's Views	Today's Views
Dignity of all people	Applied mostly to Jews; suspicion of non-Jews; unwelcoming attitude in community	Applied to all people; appreciation and welcoming for non-Jews who participate in life of community
Worship	Formal, pulpit centered, performance oriented; prayer tended toward either traditional or all modern	Informal, participatory, musical, creative; innovative while respectful of tradition
Compassion, kindness	Focus on the vulnerable within Jewish community	Focus on all vulnerable people—locally, nationally, globally—with Jewish intention
Torah study	Subjects chosen and led by clergy	Subjects determined and led by anyone knowledgeable

Rethinking the Synagogue as Venue for Meaning

Many synagogues have developed mission, vision, and values statements that try to capture why they are in business and what their desired picture of the Jewish future is. Not surprisingly, given their shared missions, they often sound similar regardless of denominational affiliation.[13] Mission statements often refer to synagogues as a "home," a "family," a "warm, welcoming, spiritual community," an "inclusive community," a "learning community," and a "sacred community." Yet, a frequent critique of synagogues is that they are cold and cliquish. What accounts for this gap between the warm, inclusive community that the synagogue aspires to be and the often-felt reality of its being a sterile environment?

Rather than only analyze why the synagogue as a venue is broken for many, it is more useful to examine other venues that are experiencing success and ask what we can apply from them to synagogues. Urban sociology literature has a concept called the "third place."[14] The first place is home and the second place is work. Then there are venues called the third place. According to sociologist Ray Oldenburg, third places "host the regular, voluntary, informal, and happily anticipated gatherings of individuals beyond the realms of home and work." Oldenburg suggests that main streets, coffeehouses, and other third places are the heart of a community's social vitality and the foundation of a functioning democracy. They promote social equality by leveling the status of guests, create habits of public association, and offer psychological support to individuals and communities."[15]

More simply conceived, the third place is the informal public space between home and work that connects people to each other, allows them to recharge, pause, and then reengage the world. They are places in which participants feel strong, positive emotional ties because they creating rewarding, meaningful social experiences and a warm community environment. That is why successful third places do not have to engage in gimmicks to stimulate participation; they are places that individuals voluntarily choose to visit.

Starbucks is an example of a highly successful corporation that recognized the vacuum of third places in American culture. They modeled their coffeehouses after the traditional European coffee shop as a third place between home and office, one that leveled class and economic differences. Though Starbucks has lost some of its luster, initially consumers perceived the third place nature of Starbucks, viewing it as a place for individuals to relax between a hectic work schedule and a frenzied home life and to connect with people who sought these same goals.[16] Starbucks did not invent coffee, but reinvented the experience of drinking coffee by providing relaxation, wisdom in a cup,[17] and culture.

They also joined the effort to provide fair trade coffee (making a values statement about the environment), and they invested heavily in training and benefits for their employees (making a values statement that they care most about the people who create the experience for customers). Whoever thought a venue that sells a stimulant at a price few could not long ago imagine as sustainable could come to symbolize relaxation?[18] As the Starbucks experience shows, even a for-profit corporation can leverage a social vacuum and become relevant by selling not just products and services, but also values and meaning. Smart corporations recognize that products and services will evolve, but if customers feel an emotional loyalty to the venue and what it embodies, it will thrive through these natural changes.[19]

The synagogue has a history that is more than two thousand years old—a rather impressive track record for an institution![20] However, its origins are also sources of its current weakness. As a venue, it derives some of its functions and inspiration from the Second Temple period. On a local level, the synagogue was supposed to replicate some of those functions (a centralized location with prayer and study as replacements for sacrifice; a place to which people were supposed to show lifetime allegiance through ongoing financial contributions and visits, supporting a greater religious and national cause, sustained by a class of professionals that attended to its ongoing business). The values of this venue, which still express themselves in today's synagogues, are in conflict with the notion of third places in that third places are spaces where individuals can find community on their terms and receive individual benefits for their participation. A new mental map of the synagogue as a third place would be much more in tune with the age of anything, anyone, anytime, anywhere in which individuals focus on personal meaning, autonomy, and a search for community on personal terms.

If synagogues would reconceptualize their venue as a third place, they would feel more like a welcoming home in all aspects of their operations.[21] Reenvisioning the synagogue venue in this way is not a far stretch in imagination, as "home," or *bayit*, precedes the three primary functions of synagogues (*beit kenesset, beit midrash, beit tefillah*). This shift in thinking can cause profound changes in how synagogues relate to people on an individual level, how they approach the diversity of today's Jewish community, and how they seek to relate to their broader environment. For example, in contrast to the above mission and vision statements, a synagogue that sees itself as third place might have the following mission and vision:

> The mission of Temple XX is to enable members and seekers to experience Judaism in a community that offers compelling meaning to today's big and small questions of life from a Jewish perspective.

Temple XX broadens and deepens opportunities for all—young and old, Jewish and non-Jewish, religious and secular, learned and just learning, committed and seeking—to find and create a welcoming home. By realigning outdated organizational thinking with relevant frameworks for building Jewish community, Temple XX's initiatives reach out to those beyond the core synagogue community.

A synagogue that reenvisions itself as a third place might have a vision statement that reads:

Our synagogue aspires to become a place of relevance, where people will want to experience the joy of community and be inspired by enduring Jewish values. Between a hectic home life and a pressured work environment, our synagogue will be the Jewish place where people renew their minds and spirits and create rewarding Jewish connections.

Metaphors of the synagogue as Temple-replacement and a Jewish version of a nineteenth-century Protestant church, which imply hierarchy, control, and insecurity, will limit the creative thinking required of synagogue leadership for synagogue revitalization. Leaders can find ways to still honor the roots and subsequent developments of the synagogue, but expanded thinking about the venue of the synagogue will make the task of refreshing organizational views and values flow more organically.

The Role of Denominations in Driving a Jewish Spiritual Renaissance

The purpose of exploring the synagogue's origins is to make sure that the venue has historical continuity and is also conducive to the fresh organizational thinking and a rearticulation of values described earlier. Organizational views, values, and venues must be mutually compatible and supportive in creating synagogues that will inspire people with an authentic Jewish vision of how the world should be. This threefold process can accelerate the shift for congregations from an antiquated Emancipation mindset to a relevant post-Emancipation environment, one better suited to the age of anything, anyone, anytime, anywhere. Some synagogues have taken strides toward this reimagination of views, values, and venues. But their resources are limited and they are tasked with focusing on their local community. This reimagination is the kind of large project that requires the full resources of all of the liberal movements, working together both to strengthen their own constituencies and to work on behalf of the greater good of the Jewish people. Are the denominations up to this task?

In theory, the answer is yes. Denominational Judaism, with its network of schools, camps, and professional organizations, represents a tremendous amount of social, intellectual, and physical capital. Compared with other alternatives, denominational structures also provide a level of quality assurance not automatically found in less-structured organizations. With their regional structures, they can know what experiments are happening on the local synagogue level and help to catalyze them into something more significant. However, while denominations have the apparatuses to have a much broader and deeper reach, are they likely to become a leading force for renewing the Jewish religious spirit in America?[22] Based on my interpretation of current data, it appears that the answer is no. But this is not an inevitable conclusion, and the denominations still have the opportunity to rise to the challenges of our day. My concern about their ability to seize this opportunity is based on the following three observations: (1) The convergence of liberal denominational practice and belief intensifies competition for an increasingly limited pool of people interested in denominational synagogues; (2) options for services outside of denominations are increasing; (3) the disconnect between synagogue-affiliated Jews and those who do not affiliate with synagogues is growing.

Intensified Competition for a Limited Pool

During the past approximately two decades, denominational leaders have undertaken different types of processes designed to clearly articulate their unique approaches to Judaism.[23] Additionally, the spate of liturgical publications within each movement indicates the attention they are giving to self-definition, as liturgy is a highly public expression of a denomination's theology and ideology. Though certainly not intended, while attempting to respectively clarify their denominational uniqueness, the liberal denominations have moved increasingly closer in key areas of practice and belief.[24]

Specifically, seven major fault lines used to distinguish the liberal movements from one another, five related to Jewish personal status and inclusion and two related to theology. They were

1. Acceptance of patrilineal descent;
2. Sanctification of interfaith marriages;
3. Requiring a Jewish divorce (*get*) for remarriage;
4. Sanctification of same-sex unions and acceptance of gay and lesbian Jews in leadership roles;
5. Full acceptance of women in all aspects of Jewish leadership, scholarship, and religious life;
6. Belief in Jewish law as God given; and
7. Belief that Jewish law is in principle binding on individuals.

The trend line on these issues has been toward a convergence of viewpoints, as the following chart clearly illustrates:

Issue	Conservative	Reconstructionist	Reform
Patrilineal descent	-	+	+
Rabbinic officiation at interfaith marriages	-	+	+
Requirement of Jewish divorce for remarriage	+	+/-	+/-
Inclusion of gays and lesbians	+/-	+	+
Inclusion of women	+	+	+
Law considered literal word of God	+/-	-	-
Law viewed as binding	+/-	-	-

A plus (+) indicates that the position is operative within the movement, a minus (-) indicates a rejection, and a combination of plus and minus (+/-) indicates that both views operate officially or functionally.

The official positions of Conservative, Reconstructionist, and Reform Judaism on these seven issues used to be more easily distinguishable from each other. The two clear differences that remain, patrilineal descent and sanctification of interfaith marriages, are significant, but it appears that the trend toward convergence will continue. The recent ruling of the Conservative movement's Committee on Jewish Law and Standards (CJLS) has opened the door for liberalization in other halakhic issues that may decrease distinctiveness from the Reform and Reconstructionist movements. For example, Conservative-affiliated congregants, following one of the rulings of the CJLS on gay and lesbian inclusion, may request rabbinic officiation at commitment ceremonies for interfaith couples.

In addition to theology and practice moving into greater alignment, a number of the liturgical distinctions and styles that separated one movement from another have vanished, as the following chart suggests.

Issue	Conservative	Reconstructionist	Reform
Significant use of Hebrew	+	+	+
Increasing use of instrumentation	+	+	+
Innovation in tefillah	+	+	+
Use of creative rituals	+	+	+
Zionist in orientation	+	+	+
Open to new forms of spiritual expression	+	+	+
Serious emphasis on Torah study	+	+	+

Here we see a case of total convergence. That is why laypeople who attend different kinds of religious services will often comment on similarity of liturgical styles, despite the denominational difference. What is further confusing is the great variety of styles within the same denomination, leading laypeople to remark on the difficulty of understanding how such radically different options can exist within the same movement.

Finally, a de facto cluster of ritual behaviors of synagogue-affiliated Jews, regardless of denomination, has emerged and been documented repeatedly for at least twenty-five years in national and local demographic studies.[25] Well over 50 percent of synagogue-affiliated Jews

- light Hanukkah candles;
- fast on Yom Kippur; and
- attend a Passover Seder.

To a lesser degree, they also:

- give *tzedakah* to a Jewish cause;
- light Shabbat candles;
- attend synagogue monthly;
- visit Israel;
- provide a Jewish education for children;
- volunteer for a Jewish cause; and
- engage in adult learning.

Increasing similarity of liturgical styles, convergence of denominational ideology and practice, and a documented pattern of core ritual observance among denominational Jews all put continued pressure on denominational partisans to expend additional efforts toward justifying the need for separate denominational structures, especially in view of the liberal movements' inability to engage greater numbers of Jews.[26] Indeed, it is tantalizing to imagine what the liberal denominations could accomplish together if they really used their imaginations and resources to catalyze a spiritual revolution, with the synagogue as its home base and launching pad.

Currently, with the exception of Orthodox outreach movements, unaffiliated Jews have been generally neglected by the national denominations and their local affiliates, except under the rubric of growing membership. While this is a worthy goal, the liberal movements have been unable to decouple the issues of outreach to the unaffiliated from congregational membership. As a result,

they aim toward an immediate commitment that many unaffiliated are unready to make, instead of first developing an uncondi-
tional relationship with them. Aside from a few programs, the liberal denominations have placed sparse resources into the general
category of outreach. On the local level, while congregations are
working on reaching out to members who have felt marginalized
(for example, gay and lesbian Jews, interfaith couples and families,
and biracial families), how many congregations have standing outreach committees actively targeting nonsynagogue members, not
with the goal of having them affiliate but with the hope of initially
just gaining their involvement in the congregation?

Increasing Options for Services Outside Denominations

Currently, the denominational schools, congregational organizations, and professional associations of clergy and Jewish educators
form an interdependent triad. Through this triad, congregations
can access high-quality educational resources and programs, administrative and marketing support, and youth services and programs. Rabbis and cantors are placed in congregations through
their respective professional organizations, and denominational
congregations often turn to candidates whose education matches
their ideology. When one speaks informally with some congregational leaders, they especially highlight the benefits of youth
services (youth groups, camps, Israel experiences) and rabbinic
placement. However, some of these leaders are unhappy with the
placement process and dislike the feeling of being held hostage
by denominational membership dues simply to assure their youth
programs and placement. It does cost money for national movements to provide these and other services, and feelings of unhappi-
ness from local organizations toward their national headquarters
are common. Anecdotally, these feelings seem to be increasing.

Why is this a concern for denominational movements? As we
review this summary list of denominational services and resources,
we note that alternatives exist in each area and are only likely to
increase. A few examples will suffice.

- Several nondenominational or transdenominational rabbinical programs already exist, including ones at the Academy for Jewish Religion in New York and more recently the Academy for Jewish Religion in Los Angeles, ALEPH: Alliance for Jewish Renewal, and the Rabbinical School of Hebrew College. Additionally, the first online ordination program, the Jerusalem-based Shulchan Aruch Learning Program of Pirchei Shoshanim, ordained three rabbis in January 2007, and we can anticipate that other virtual rabbinical ordination programs will arise in the near future. Some suspect schools have been advertising rabbinical ordination programs and it appears that individual *semikha* is on the rise. Even now, denominational rabbinical programs are no longer the only options available, and a steady stream of individuals who use the title "rabbi," legitimately or not, may be perceived as such by parts of the Jewish community.
- In a related vein, the number of nondenominational *minyanim* and synagogues is increasing.[27] For a variety of reasons, it seems that more congregations and communities are resisting denominational labels and can support themselves through their own knowledgeable volunteer base and through nondenominational professional services and resources.
- There are also alternatives to educational and administrative resources and services that support congregational life. Curricular resources for synagogue preschools and supplemental schools exist in abundance. Nondenominational administrative materials and services are equally available through local and national nonprofit organizations, with an incredible wealth of resources readily available through the Internet. Nondenominational youth groups, like BBYO, offer an alternative to denominational youth groups, and many nondenominational Israel experiences are also available.

These observations suggest that congregations have a robust set of support options available outside of the denominations that will only grow stronger in the years ahead. Congregations are also very local entities and value their independence. Typical of many membership service organizations today, denominational synagogues often complain about the financial cost of denominational affiliation versus the perceived value. In fact, if a synagogue can secure a rabbi, involve its youth in youth programs, locate educators and educational materials, and find help in administration and management outside of the denominations, why does it need to belong to a denomination? That question will likely drive denominations to put greater attention into membership retention and cultivation by creating more value-added services and to limit their vision to growing their denomination.

The Affiliated and Unaffiliated: A Growing Disconnect

The Jewish community has seen an abundance of innovation since about the mid-1990s.[28] By that time, the impact of the 1990 National Jewish Population Survey (NJPS) had begun to percolate through the Jewish community and galvanize a few federations and some major philanthropists to devise serious responses to a community snapshot that only showed the community's decline.[29] Also, as technology has better allowed individuals and nondenominational groups to organize, organic growth and development at the local level have engaged more Jews in Jewish life outside of synagogues.

The following analogy can help underscore the disconnect between the denominations and much of the Jewish community. Imagine that the denominations were in the television business today. Their behavior would be akin to competing against each other over using a Betamax or a VHS videotape format to deliver *Leave It to Beaver* or *Gilligan's Island*–type programming, while *amcha* were independently creating their own niche programming or getting their content on demand through streaming video, digital cable, or podcasts. Denominational format and content have missed the mark for much of the Jewish community and are out of touch with the interests of members and potential members.[30] The blossoming of religious and nonreligious forms of Jewish expression suggests that energy and creativity are bypassing the denominational movements because those involved in funding and creating these new endeavors do not believe the synagogue has the capacity to incubate, develop, and house them.

Denominational leaders are aware of these new conditions and, indeed, deal with them on a daily basis. However, they have not responded to them systematically because their fundamental orientation is anchored in an outdated mind-set of organizational thinking and a value set that speaks to a limited segment of the Jewish community. Therefore, we find denominations addressing issues that have little or episodic relevance to the daily lives of most American Jews.

During the past two decades, the denominational movements have not expressed their potential in leading a spiritual rebirth. This is evident on multiple levels:

- The rate at which American Jews identify as "secular" or "cultural"[31] suggests that the term *religious* carries negative connotations.
- The emergence of non-, trans-, and postdenominational minyanim suggests that people hunger spiritually but that denominations are not feeding that hunger.
- Chabad, Aish HaTorah, and the Kollel movements have found ways to welcome and make Judaism appealing for many Jews who are not Orthodox and will never identify as Orthodox. Some of them have left the liberal denominations or were not attracted to them in the first place. At the same time, as liberal national denominational movements struggle with budget issues to retain existing services, their ability to reach out aggressively beyond their current constituents remains in doubt.
- The outflow of Conservative Jews to Reform, Orthodox, and nondenominational minyanim also indicates that ideology does not provide a compelling reason to affiliate, sometimes even for adherents of a denomination, let alone the unaffiliated.
- If researchers are correct about the undercounting of the Jewish population by NJPS 2000–01, then affiliation rates with synagogues are likely lower than NJPS findings report.[32]
- Gen X blogs, such as Jewschool, Jewlicious, and JSpot,[33] and ongoing reportage on Gen X Jews[34] regularly vent

about the inadequacy of the current denominational "labeling" system and reveal a hunger for a more permeable community that allows for easier participation than the current structure permits.

The majority of American Jews who do not affiliate with synagogues but care about their spiritual lives have been creating their own versions of Judaism. These new expressions incorporate a more contemporary value set and are very different from the organizational framework in which denominations operate. One founder of an independent minyan, Beth Tritter, captured the inadequacy of denominational labels and structures.

> Labels are hard because they offend people. If you say, "traditional," what do you mean, whose tradition are you talking about? We really view ourselves as post-denominational. We don't really feel that we need to be beholden to a movement to tell us how to conduct our services, what kind of scholarship we should be following or what sorts of discussions we should be having. We feel empowered to look at the options that are out there, to set our own boundaries, and to consult the people we want to consult to help us set those parameters. We also don't feel like we have to have a spiritual head, a certain rabbi who we go to all the time. Sometimes when we describe ourselves we say conservadox but that's a horrible word.[35]

If a Jewish religious renaissance occurs and if the denominations are unlikely to play a more robust role in generating one, from where is that religious renaissance likely to come?

Conclusion and Policy Recommendations

If more American Jews and the many constellations in which they come are to perceive the Jewish religion as responsive to real-life issues, synagogue-based Judaism will require a radical reorientation program. Synagogues will need to reframe their work so that they move from asking questions that were fitting for early stages of modernity and begin with the premise that we are living in an age of anything, anytime, anyone, and anywhere. A rethinking of organizational views about synagogues, a rearticulation of enduring Jewish values, and a reimagination of venue can lead to synagogues that will produce incredibly inspiring and motivating visions of what it means to be Jewish.

As some of the innovations in Jewish life suggest, and as a few synagogues have shown, the Jewish community has abundant talent that can help with a spiritual renaissance.[36] Additionally, the achievement level of American Jews in education, the professions, the arts, the entertainment industry, politics, and business has no parallel in Jewish history. Yet, the leaders of the Jewish religious community have not communicated to them that the Jewish tradition in all its breadth and depth is their inheritance to explore on their terms, rather than in categories and concerns defined by denominational label. As a result, the leadership has not even begun to unleash this most potent asset—potential volunteers with unmatched talent—and involve more of them in the task of reimagining Judaism.

From where will significant energy for synagogue change likely occur? One possibility is that the *denominational leadership* will step forward and meet the challenges of adapting the outdated views, values, and venues embodied in the synagogue to contemporary Jewish life. In fact, with an overall trend toward convergence of practice and belief, and positive personal relationships between the heads of the two largest liberal seminaries, that potential has never been greater. Yet, it appears that too many and varied institutional obstacles exist to realize this expectation. These obstacles include internal challenges facing each movement and a broader inability of movement leadership to seize the opportunity for the fundamental and necessary reorientation that will enable Judaism to speak meaningfully to the average American Jew. There is much creativity and vibrancy on the local congregational level. The question is whether the denominations can better catalyze this energy into something greater and lead their member congregations and the broader Jewish community with greater vision.

A second possibility is that it will come from the *grassroots level*. As noted earlier, this level has scattered examples of vibrant creativity: in arts and culture, in service (*tikkun olam*), in spirituality, and even in a few synagogues. The problem is that these ventures often lack basic resources, making even short-term sustainability a challenge. Additionally, these pockets of innovation have no overarching infrastructure that can be leveraged for the benefit of the broader community. Understandably, their interest is in basic viability at the local level.

Ultimately, a multipronged strategy to accelerate a renewal of Jewish life in America is required. The tracks to this strategy will need to include:

- Strengthening grassroots and independent minyanim so that they are sustainable and fostering respectful partnerships with denominational synagogues;
- Investing in training programs for rabbis and other synagogue professionals and for synagogue lay leaders that foster the fresh thinking about synagogues described earlier. Training should jointly involve teams of professional leaders, key staff, and lay leaders, and some of the lay leaders should be tapped from the top echelons of corporations that have a track record of successful adaptation and innovation (programs like the Wexner Heritage Program) can provide one stream for locating such leaders);
- Promoting multidenominational collaborative learning beginning in the various rabbinical, cantorial, and educational schools of the seminaries;
- Promoting multidenominational collaborative action among lay leaders on the local and national levels. In some communities, federations can be the key catalyst for convening and facilitating such collaboration;
- Seeding in major Jewish communities new synagogues that model the principles and values of the successful ones that exist;
- Connecting grassroots Jewish creativity with mainstream congregations so that each can benefit from the strengths of the other, while still retaining their independence;
- Supporting with financial and organizational resources synagogues that are moving in this direction so that they

progress to the next level, helping to replicate models of such synagogues across the country;

- Removing structural barriers to participation, including high financial hurdles and cumbersome membership processes, as some synagogues have done and successfully replicated for other synagogues;[37] and
- Teaching every synagogue how to truly respect the unique talents of their members by creating people and systems that routinely catalogue, utilize, and recognize that the greatest asset of a congregation is its members.

Currently, only a handful of major philanthropists and federations have shown a willingness to fund synagogues and emerging spiritual organizations. These funders bring powerful financial resources, vision that transcends parochial agendas, and a drive to accomplish measurable change. Without their ongoing involvement and an expanded list of contributors, it is difficult to envision a spiritual and religious renaissance that can lead to a deeper, sustainable renewal of the Jewish community.

In some ways, this agenda of broad synagogue transformation sounds daunting. However, without minimizing its many challenges, we in the Jewish religious community need to look at ourselves honestly and ask why, outside of Orthodox outreach movements, so few examples of dynamic synagogue communities exist. When Jews are in danger physically, we expend every effort to bring them to safety. When Jews in far-flung places hunger, we quickly determine how to feed them. Yet, though many Jews in our community hunger for a relevant Judaism and Jewish spiritual meaning, we have outsourced those holy tasks to others within and outside of the Jewish community.

By understanding what people seek today that can help them navigate work and home; by developing leaders who use the language of Jewish values to speak in ways that inspire and engage them; by changing the organizational thinking of synagogues so that they can develop into a third place—we can turn more synagogues into venues of relevance, inspiration, and Jewish character formation.

Synagogue programs and initiatives will continue to change, as they always have. But with a more compelling and clearly articulated set of values and a broad vision of the Jewish community, congregations and emerging minyanim can help Jewish spiritual life flourish. Compared to other initiatives, this project need not require a massive allocation of new resources, for the raison d'être of synagogues is to offer a vibrant place for Jewish religious expression and exploration, and synagogues have the building blocks to create this new foundation. (At the same time, the community should think generously about the financial needs for increasing and sustaining participation in synagogues and not stint on needed resources.) The greatest challenge will be identifying and cultivating thousands of people who think boldly about the possibilities of a true Jewish spiritual renaissance and are willing to put themselves on the line to bring those possibilities to fruition.[38]

CHAPTER 10

Jewish Education
Postdenominationalism and the Continuing Influence of Denominations

Jonathan Woocher

Jews have debated how to understand their shared tradition since the time that Moses and Korach clashed over what it means to be a "holy people."[1] Today's "denominations"—Orthodox, Conservative, Reform, Reconstructionist, and so forth—are thoroughly modern phenomena, born in the nineteenth and twentieth centuries. Yet, divisions in Jewish life are hardly new. Arguments between priests and prophets, Pharisees and Sadducees, Rabbanites and Karaites, mystics and rationalists, *hasidim* and *mitnagdim*, enlighteners and traditionalists, Zionists and anti-Zionists fill the pages of Jewish history. Such differences, echoed in the disagreements among contemporary denominations, appear in new forms in successive generations. But division seems as much a part of Jewish reality as unity is of Jewish aspiration.

This does not mean, however, that the present is merely a continuation of the past. The overall context within which Jewish denominations operate today—including their relationship to the enterprise of Jewish education—is clearly changing. For the better part of a century, denominations have been the fundamental organizing framework for Jewish religious and educational life in North America. Now, many observers see signs that this dominance is eroding. Fewer Jews identify with any of the major denominational movements.[2] Even those that do may do so more as a matter of convenience than conviction. A growing number of younger Jews label themselves "postdenominational." And, in the educational arena, various avowedly nondenominational and pluralistic options are asserting themselves, perhaps turning the American Jewish community back toward the days early in the twentieth century when communal Jewish education was seen as the norm.

It is far too early to pronounce the demise of denominationally sponsored Jewish education. Indeed, there are countertrends to those cited above, especially in the Orthodox community, that argue for a strengthening of denominational influence on Jewish education both ideologically and behaviorally. Nevertheless, it as an appropriate moment to revisit the questions of how Jewish education and American Jewish denominationalism relate to one another, and what the future may hold for this historically important, but perhaps increasingly problematic relationship.

How We Got Here

Jewish education is inherently ideological. Every program of study reflects a particular view of what is to be taught and of how what *is* taught should be interpreted and understood. In American Jewish history, educational programs and activities have been guided by a wide range of ideological perspectives. Often, these perspectives have emanated from or been associated with the religious movements that we call denominations. In the twentieth century this association became especially close. Thus, though the intimate relationship of education and denominationalism constitutes but one chapter in the history of American Jewish education, it is a uniquely significant one.

Elements of this chapter have been recounted elsewhere.[3] For the purposes of this chapter, it is sufficient to note that beginning toward the end of the first quarter of the twentieth century, and with increasing momentum thereafter, synagogues became the dominant providers of Jewish education for the vast majority of young people and families. This opened the door for the denominational movements, of which these congregations were a part, to become the most far-reaching organizing frameworks for Jewish education in

North America. During the course of the twentieth century, the denominational movements took on the roles not only of educational support systems for their affiliated synagogues—providing curriculum, training educators, running conferences, and, where feasible, setting standards—but also of catalysts for and sponsors of new educational endeavors, only some of which were synagogue based, including youth movements, adult learning programs, summer camps, and day schools. For the Orthodox, the last of these almost entirely eclipsed synagogue schools, and now constitutes the normative educational framework for most traditional families. It is fair to say that for most American Jews, Jewish education became both an integral, perhaps even central, part of their religious lives. Further, these religious lives were in turn framed within the institutions and ideology of one or another of the denominational movements.

This ascendance of denominationally based Jewish education did not mean that the denominational movements themselves ran or had monopolistic control of Jewish education. American Jewish education, like American Jewish life as a whole, has historically been highly local and voluntary. Each synagogue and school retains ultimate autonomy. The educational infrastructures of the movements remained weak in many respects, unable to force compliance with national norms or compel use of their curricula. They also compete with alternative sources of guidance and support for educational programs and educators, ranging from local central agencies for Jewish education to commercial publishers. Alternatives to denominationally linked programs and institutions never vanished, especially in the arena of informal Jewish education (youth movements and camping). Nonetheless, in its heyday—during the period from the 1950s through the 1970s when baby boomers were filling Jewish schools and camps—denominationally sponsored Jewish education was unquestionably the preeminent form of Jewish education in North America.

Five Dimensions of a Denomination

What did this preeminence of denominational sponsorship mean for Jewish education itself, and how might this relationship be changing today? This is a more complex story to uncover and re-

count. It leads to a wider consideration of the place of denominational movements in American Jewish life as a whole. It is useful,
perhaps, to step back then and to ask: what does *denomination* or
denominational movement mean in the context of American Judaism, and how do the several dimensions of a denomination relate
to Jewish education?

At least five dimensions of a denomination come into play when we
consider how denominations and Jewish education are intertwined.

Ideology

The first dimension is, of course, the denomination's ideology:
what it stands for, its particular understanding of Judaism and all
of the concepts connected thereto. No denomination today has a
single coherent ideology (though some come closer than others).
We can, nonetheless, speak of *a family of ideologies* that share certain common vocabularies, concerns, and conclusions. All forms
of Orthodox ideology consider Torah to be divinely revealed and
halakhah to be binding. All forms of Reform ideology call for informed choice in decision making and affirm the value of contemporary religious creativity. All forms of Conservative ideology
seek to balance respect for and fidelity to traditional thought and
practice with an openness to contemporary norms and values.

Beyond these basics, however, lie many and varied details
of belief and prescription. One of the persistent challenges for
denominational institutions is how to translate these ideological frameworks into educational curricula. Suffice to say that the
responses are even more varied than the ideologies themselves.
In some cases, curricula are designed to reflect very specific
ideological perspectives, but in many others, the connection is
far looser, especially since so much of the raw material for Jewish teaching—texts, historical personages and events, customs and
traditions—precedes or developed entirely outside the context of
modern denominations. Thus, while one is unlikely to mistake a
Reform educational program for an Orthodox one, it is far more
difficult, even with the movements' curricular efforts, to predict what the specific stance and content of a given institution's
educational offerings will be merely on the basis of its denominational identity.

Program

Denominations are, though, more than their ideologies. Typically, they also embrace a *program*, meaning in this instance a set of action areas that are emphasized in practice and communicated as priorities to their adherents. These programs are much narrower and focused than the movements' total ideologies, but they are critically important in shaping the denomination's brand and culture. To cite a few examples: For years, the Reform movement has emphasized social action and social justice in its program. More recently, it has added parallel emphases on lifelong Jewish learning and spirituality. Orthodoxy has successfully focused great attention on intensive Jewish learning as a signature program emphasis, as expressed in the now near-universal matriculation of Orthodox youth in day schools, the rapid growth of yeshiva learning in Israel after high school as a norm, and significant participation in Daf Yomi and other forms of intensive adult Jewish learning. (Tellingly, it is more difficult to identify a major program thrust identified with the Conservative movement, unless it is Shabbat and *kashrut* observance, neither of which has captured the imagination of large proportions of the movement's nominal constituency.) The denominations' program emphases are not abstract ideals; they are embodied in each movement's institutions and programming (in the more traditional sense), including its educational activities. Of course, not every constituent actively embraces the movement's program, but often it is the program, even more than the ideology, that captures the enthusiasm and loyalty of its youth.

Institutions

Third, denominations are sets of institutions. Each of the major denominations in American Jewish life today has a well-elaborated institutional framework including congregations, national synagogue confederations, academic institutions, rabbinic organizations, schools, camps, youth movements, Zionist groups (except for the *haredim*), and others. From a practical standpoint, these institutions *are* in many respects the movement, far more than ideologies or even programs. The denominational infrastructures for

Jewish education are substantial, but, as noted above, they are also loosely coupled, exist alongside parallel (and occasionally competing) infrastructures, are often underresourced, and are not necessarily seen as embodying cutting-edge thinking or state-of-the-art skills. As a result, it is unclear to what extent the education delivered on the front lines by a given school, camp, or congregation is substantially affected by its position within a denominational institutional framework. In some instances, particularly where the national movement has significant control, the influence is undoubtedly considerable. In others, it is virtually nonexistent. Still, large numbers of educating institutions are and regard themselves as being connected to other institutions in networks of reciprocal influence. This connection injects an element of, or at least the potential for, coherence in what is an otherwise quasi-anarchic Jewish educational system. These relationships also have the potential to link Jewish learning to Jewish living, mitigating one of American Jewish education's notable weaknesses: the frequent disconnect between what is taught and what is practiced and observed.

People

The institutions that comprise denominations are made up of people. There is a familiar old joke: Cohen asks Schwartz, a well-known atheist, "Why do you go to *shul*? Are you starting to talk to God?" "No," replies Schwartz. "Greenberg goes to shul to talk to God; I go to shul to talk to Greenberg." Personal connections—who we know, who we like, who we see ourselves as being like—unquestionably shape denominational choices and educational decision making. Relationships can both enhance and undercut an institution's efforts to forge and deliver a coherent educational vision. When such a vision is joined to a community of people who are deeply connected to one another, who share not only values but also life events, the impact can be extraordinary.

Yet, personal factors are not always aligned with ideological ones. We know anecdotally that people often join synagogues (or fail to, or leave one they have already joined) because of their reactions to the rabbi, the *hazzan*, or other people they encounter there, not the synagogue's ideology. Sometimes they go where friends go; sometimes the friends they make (for example, among fellow parents in an early childhood program) become the core of their social network. For those who go to camp or on a trip to Israel, enduring friendships may keep one connected to a movement throughout life, even when one's Jewish views have drifted away from its norms. So, the fact that denominations consist of real people, and diverse ones, can affect the educational dynamic of the movement and the educational experience of its constituents in multiple and potentially cross-cutting ways.

Style

Finally, denominations have cultural styles. *Style* means the confluence of aesthetic, behavioral, environmental, and other factors that gives a religious or educational experience its particular feel—formal and serious, warm and welcoming, energized and engaging, open and experimental. Although what goes into making a specific style is somewhat elusive to pin down, the overall impact of an educational experience is often more a product of that style than of the content being taught. (Think about the different styles of the typical Hebrew school and the typical summer camp.) The correspondence between denomination and style is perhaps the loosest among the five dimensions we are looking at here. No denominational movement has just a single style, and styles of both worship and educational activity cut across the various movements (for example, the transdenominational popularity of Carlebach-style services and *hevruta* learning). Nonetheless, cultural style, particularly as reflected in pedagogy, does constitute one additional variable along which denominations may differentiate themselves. Differences in style seem especially salient today for distinguishing Orthodoxy from the other movements (for example, much Orthodox learning relies heavily on formal *shiurim* [lectures] and intensive text study; non-Orthodox education appears to be placing increasing emphasis on constructivist discussion and learning through doing).

This brief review of the several dimensions of denominationalism illustrates why organizing Jewish education within the frameworks of religious movements makes sense. The movements provide not only ideological guidance and focus for decisions regarding what to teach, but a social framework for educational activity that is equally, if not more, important in shaping Jewish identity and commitment. Education is not an abstract intellectual pursuit. Effective education stimulates emotions, shapes memories, and fosters connections and community. At its best, denominationally sponsored Jewish education does this extremely well. The synagogue, the school, the summer camp, the youth group, the friends one makes and the teachers one encounters all become elements of an experience of Jewishness that is holistic and life shaping, one that is far deeper and more powerful than the ideological content of that experience alone. Precisely because denominations are multidimensional, they have the potential to align ideology, program, institutions, people, and styles of behavior to fashion a coherent educational package. The educational experience one receives in a synagogue or denominationally affiliated day school— or even better, in multiple denominational settings—can ground the individual in a living community where learning is reinforced by visible practice. This is why the leaders and core members of each religious movement, despite their evident differences, manifest similarly high levels of enthusiasm and commitment to their respective understandings of how to be affirmatively Jewish in the contemporary world.

Denominationalism and Its Alternatives

The picture, though, is not quite so simple. Although denominations and their institutions remain prominent loci for and sponsors of Jewish educational activity, they have far from an exclusive franchise. Indeed, many of the most exciting developments in Jewish education today are taking place in settings and under auspices that are explicitly nondenominational, transdenominational, communal, or pluralistic. These include:

- The expansion of Jewish education in Jewish community centers, especially early childhood education and camping;
- The growing numbers of community day schools at both the elementary and high school levels;

- New programs for teenagers, such as March of the Living and PANIM, that complement traditional youth groups and movements (themselves a mix of denominationally affiliated and nonaffiliated frameworks);
- The renaissance of Hillels on college campuses, not only in North America, but around the world, and the dramatic growth of university-level academic Jewish studies.
- The rapid spread of intensive adult Jewish learning programs, such as the Wexner Heritage Program, the Florence Melton Adult Mini-School, and Me'ah and of outreach learning programs sponsored by organizations such as Aish HaTorah or Chabad.
- Large-scale learning gatherings like Limmud, now an international phenomenon;
- The emergence and spread of alternative forms of part-time Jewish education, until recently the nearly exclusive provenance of synagogues and the religious movements.

As noted earlier, there has never been a time when denominational frameworks exercised monopoly control over Jewish educational activity. Still, the argument can be made that what is taking place today represents a significant shift, even a reversal, in the trend toward denominational dominance that began nearly a century ago. According to this reading, the role of religious movements and their affiliated institutions in Jewish education is now declining and likely to continue doing so.

Denominational Decline?

The evidence for this proposition, cited above as increased educational activity outside the domains of the religious movements and their affiliated institutions, can be buttressed by studies showing that American Jews in general, and especially younger Jews, are becoming less denominational.[4] We need to be careful in interpreting both survey results showing declines in denominational identification and anecdotal evidence of trans- or postdenominationalism. On the one hand, surveys showing growing numbers of "secular" or "just" Jews do not in themselves reliably depict the population participating in Jewish education, which tends to be drawn much more from those segments that *do* maintain active identification with one or another of the religious movements than from those Jews with weak or no denominational identity. The phenomenon of postdenominational Judaism, on the other hand, seems centered on a particular segment of a particular age group—young adults with relatively strong Jewish identities (often from Conservative Jewish backgrounds), but high levels of dissatisfaction with available institutional options. The question there is whether these individuals will maintain postdenominational identities as they age and settle into family rearing and educating their own children, or will they find themselves returning to one or another denominational fold, albeit with some reluctance.

Despite these cautionary notes, and despite continuing differences in typical educational behaviors between the population segments that identify with the several religious movements,[5] denominations per se, in both their ideological and institutional dimensions, do appear to be becoming less salient to a growing number of younger Jews. (The exception here is the Orthodox movement, which is on the whole growing younger through a combination of high birthrates and intensive day school education, leading to reduced attrition than in previous generations.) Recent research by Jack Wertheimer and his colleagues shows that the bases for educational decision-making by parents have become more personalized (what is right for my child and our family) along with other critical dimensions of Jewish identity.[6] Thus, even within one family, different children may be educated in settings with different denominational affiliations. Clearly, a large proportion of Jews continue to identify with and to educate their children and themselves within movement-affiliated synagogues, schools, and camps. But the extent and depth of their loyalty to a specific denomination, certainly on the ideological level, and the role that denominational identity plays in relation to other factors in shaping their educational journeys, varies widely. In a sense, this has always been so in American Jewish life—denominational "defections" and switching may even have been greater in the past than they are today. But it is incontestable that the overall culture of American Jewish life has changed dramatically over the past quarter century or so from one that was bounded in numerous ways, both externally and internally, to one that is far more open and more individually driven. In such a situation, denomination, like nearly every other dimension of Jewish life, becomes a utilitarian category, subject to choosing and rechoosing, defining and redefining on an almost continuous basis. Within the realm of Jewish education, the process of weakening denominational ties becomes self-reinforcing: As the number of educational options that operate outside the traditional denominational frameworks, ideologically and institutionally, grows, this itself further weakens the hold of denominations on consumer loyalty—supply (of alternatives) generates demand for them.

The Open Marketplace

Taking all the evidence into account, it may be most accurate to speak neither of a continuing dominant role for denominations in Jewish education nor of an inexorable or precipitous overturning of that dominance, but rather of the emergence of an *open marketplace* in Jewish education. In the new marketplace, denominationally linked and nondenominational options exist alongside one another, with neither having presumptive momentum on their side. All compete on the same playing field: seeking to convince individual Jews that they provide an appropriate, congenial, high-quality setting for Jewish self-expression and exploration for the individual and family, and for transmitting a positive Jewish identity to the next generation. For some Jews, the denominational identity of the setting will be a significant, even decisive, factor in choosing where to engage educationally; for others, denomination will be irrelevant or only one among a number of factors that need to be balanced in making educational choices.

In this new educational marketplace, denominationally sponsored or affiliated programs have a number of advantages. Earlier, I noted that in principle the confluence of ideology, program, institutions, people, and cultural style makes denominations potentially powerful contexts for educational activity. Another factor that strengthens the positioning of denominationally affiliated Jewish education is that, especially for non-Orthodox Jews, Jewish education remains closely tied to life-cycle events, particularly bar and bat mitzvah. Such life-cycle events remain largely the province of synagogues, and the vast majority of synagogues have a denominational affiliation. Families seek out synagogues as educational providers in order to ensure that their children have a traditional bar or bat mitzvah. The denominational connection comes with this, whether or not it is explicitly sought.

A different factor is at play in the Orthodox community, which makes denominationally based Jewish education the overwhelming norm there. Most Orthodox families will only educate their children in settings that maintain traditional patterns of halakhic observance, and the vast majority of these are under Orthodox auspices. The marketplace of Orthodox educational options is certainly diverse—the difference between a modern Orthodox day school and a "black hat" yeshiva is probably greater than that between the typical Conservative and Reform synagogue schools—but it is a bounded marketplace and few families go outside it.

The connection between childhood education and bar or bat mitzvah is a boon for denominational education, though not necessarily for Jewish education generally. Critics have noted that although the desire for one's children to become bar or bat mitzvah undoubtedly draws numerous families into Jewish education who might otherwise pass on the opportunity, it also serves as an endpoint to that education for far too many children. Perhaps equally deleterious is the fact that the focus on bar and bat mitzvah may distort the content and process of learning itself, encouraging an undue emphasis on rote reading (decoding) skills and preparation for participation in synagogue services, rather than fostering a more holistic appreciation of the multiple dimensions of Jewish life. Many observers of so-called supplementary education view the connection to bar and bat mitzvah as one of the primary causes of that domain's persistent mediocrity. By buying into this arrangement (verbal protestations to the contrary notwithstanding), synagogues and the denominational movements are, in this view, complicit in ensuring that many children receive an education that is ineffective and in the long run unsatisfying.

Jewish Education without Denominational Labels?

This critique of elementary synagogue education (which, it must be noted, overlooks many synagogues that have successfully transcended this parochial vision of Jewish education) is a microcosm of a larger critique of denominational education as a whole: that it no longer represents the best framework within which to explore and transmit the ideas, values, and behaviors that will serve as building blocks for contemporary Jews as they forge meaningful Jewish identities and vibrant Jewish communities. This critique, which implicitly or explicitly underlies much of the expanding universe of alternative educational settings and programs noted above, has several dimensions. But what they all boil down to is skepticism about the continuing value of organizing educational activity (and other forms of Jewish activity) solely or even substantially within the frameworks that current religious movements provide.

For some critics, the problem is simply that denominational labels feel uncomfortable and inaccurate as descriptors of what denominations believe, how they practice, who they associate with, and what they aspire to Jewishly. So, applying these same labels to the Jewish education they seek, participate in, or help to deliver seems limiting and even irrelevant. Today's major religious movements all developed initially in the nineteenth century. The sets of questions the movements respond to and the answers they offer are, at least for some contemporary Jews, not those of greatest concern for people who struggle with what being Jewish means in their lives. This mismatch has spawned the emergence of new movements like Jewish Renewal as well as active communities of Jews who come together around issues of social justice or contemporary expressions of Jewish culture. For many of these Jews, the traditional denominations are largely irrelevant, not only ideologically, but also as a source of and framework for the social connections they value—the people dimension of denominational life. Denominationally based communities like the conventional synagogue feel artificial and overinstitutionalized. Although they are not necessarily hostile to denominational Judaism, individuals who feel this way have no reason to seek out particular denominational sponsorship or content in the Jewish education they pursue.

Even among individuals who do locate themselves within one of the historically dominant denominational movements or institutions, there are those who chafe at the notion that their Jewish learning and teaching is defined and circumscribed by that affiliation. Unquestionably, there are educators and students who perceive Reform, Conservative, or Orthodox education as embodying unique perspectives and positions and who value these distinctions. However, what appears to be a growing number of educators and learners alike see many of these distinctions as contrived and at best secondary. They want to be able to draw on wisdom wherever they find it and to encounter the raw materials of Jewish learning unencumbered by prior assumptions as to how to interpret these. They are comfortable reaching their own conclusions and creating their own syntheses, which may draw on the insights of teachers from multiple denominational camps (or none at all). All of the movements are, as I have noted, "broad tents." Many different religious and educational sensibilities are represented therein. But this very fact makes the connection between denomination and educational philosophy and practice more tangential. In an age in which access to multiple perspectives on virtually every issue, including religious ones, is routine, and in which individual choice among options—even the choice to give up one's right to choose— is taken for granted, it is hard for any ideological or programmatic movement to command broad or automatic deference.

A key question for many individuals involved in Jewish education is why denominational labels need to be attached to Jewish learning at all. In fact, Jewish education, despite operating so widely under denominational auspices, is in many ways already a bastion of nondenominationalism. Not only are significant segments of the educational domain avowedly communal, transdenominational, or pluralist, but even among educators who identify themselves denominationally, large numbers also view Jewish learning as a bridging force in Jewish life, almost a denomination-free zone. Staffs of community day schools, nondenominational youth movements (like BBYO and Young Judaea), and central agencies for Jewish education; attendees at educational conferences convened by transdenominational organizations like the Coalition for the Advancement for Jewish Education (CAJE), Partnership for Excellence in Jewish Education (PEJE), and Jewish Education Service of North America (JESNA); and faculty in Jewish education training programs typically come from and maintain affiliations with the full range of denominations. Yet, the vast majority have no difficulty in studying together, exchanging professional opinions, reading one another's writings, and viewing themselves as colleagues—even if they do have to mount multiple worship services when they gather. The same holds true for participants in the growing number of large-scale Jewish learning gatherings, like Limmud conferences, which some attend specifically because of the opportunity to encounter teachers and fellow students from multiple ideological streams. Gender roles in Jewish education too are more similar across denominations (except for some fringes) than in other areas of Jewish life. Women may not (yet) be Orthodox rabbis, but increasingly they are playing important roles as educators and even as religious guides in pararabbinic roles.

This sense that Jewish education by its very nature transcends denominationalism, that Jewish learning—Torah study—constitutes an arena where such distinctions both can and should be set aside, is a potent counterforce to the continuing prominent role of denominations organizationally. The emphasis on commonality, on finding what unifies Jews instead of divides them, gives this a moral, not merely a practical, dimension. From this standpoint, commonality is a positive value to eschew or at least to minimize denominational distinctions in our teaching. Part of Jewish education's mission becomes uncovering and highlighting precisely those elements that Jews have in common, which tends almost inevitably to raise questions about the real importance of those areas where they differ.[7] If the Jewish community shares the essentials, why place so much emphasis on the areas of disagreement? This is a position that holds great appeal to the many Jews, especially younger ones, who find denominational self-aggrandizement, divisions, and recriminations distasteful and are strongly tempted to adopt a "plague on all your houses" approach.

Pluralism and Denominational Education

The desire to approach Judaism without the "burden" of denominational labels and distinctions represents one challenge to the historical predominance of denominational Jewish education. Another challenge emanates from what is at first glance a very different position. This view holds that the objective in Jewish education should *not* be to disregard, diminish, or transcend denominational (or other) disagreements, but rather to teach respect for differing positions as legitimate expressions of Judaism. This pluralistic stance is embraced by a number of institutions and programs for both young people (for example, community day schools and Hillels) and adults (for example, many of the newer, academically grounded, intensive adult-learning programs). Some institutions also provide opportunities for diverse behavioral expressions of Jewish commitment (for example, multiple prayer services) as part of their commitment to pluralism. Others, though pluralistic in principle, operate on the basis of a consensus norm with regard to behavior (often a moderate traditionalism) in order to avoid excluding any part of the community from participating in the activities of the institution.

The empirical appeal of this position is evidenced by the rapid growth in recent decades of community day schools on both the elementary and secondary levels. (RAVSAK, the network of community day schools, is the fastest growing of all of the day school associations today, now numbering more than one-hundred-twenty members. Community high schools have been successfully launched in a number of major communities and have emerged as a dynamic force on the overall Jewish educational landscape.) The experience of these schools buttresses the claim that offering serious Jewish education outside of denominational frameworks is possible—though not without pedagogical and curricular challenges that many of these schools struggle with on a continuing basis. It should be noted that not all community day schools are *pluralistic*. As stated above, some are *communal* in their enrollment, including students from a range of affiliations (including secular—often Israelis who want the Hebrew language learning), but *traditional* in their ideology and practice. Also true is that some community day schools are more conscious and explicit than others in working out the implications of pluralism for their educational practice. Nonetheless, with community day schools a growing force, it seems likely that Jewish education under the banner of pluralism will become increasingly common.

This makes thoughtful consideration of what we really mean by *pluralism* important. In fact, there are several possible meanings. One version of pluralism is akin to relativism: all positions are considered equal because none has a greater truth claim than any other. In another version, pluralism is essentially equated with tolerance: individuals who take positions different from one's own (or the official position of the institution) are to be respected and permitted to do so, but the positions themselves may not be accorded the same respect. True pluralism is more complex than either of these. It walks a thin line, simultaneously encouraging individuals to take and defend particularistic stances (thereby rejecting relativism), while urging them to remain open to truth claims emanating from other such stances (thereby going beyond tolerance). This type of pluralism regards ultimate truth as approachable through multiple doorways, but recognizes that humans must choose and walk through one of these and cannot merely stand outside comparing and contemplating the value of each.[8]

In this approach to pluralism, there is clearly a place for denominationalism—or for any other well thought-through articulation of the meaning and implications of Jewishness. In fact, embracing a denominational stance may be strongly encouraged and the ideologies and programs associated with the denominations accorded great respect. Some denominational education, especially in the non-Orthodox sector of the community, itself adopts this type of pluralistic position, presenting its own denomination as the preferred, but not exclusive, doorway into Jewish life and tradition while acknowledging the strengths and contributions, as well as the limitations, of other pathways.

Pluralism has its critics who see it as incoherent and ultimately unsustainable, especially in its more relativistic versions, as a guiding philosophy for educating young people. Children, they argue, need to be given a consistent picture of what Judaism teaches, not a set of options from which they are unable to choose effectively. Inevitably, they contend, presenting Judaism as a set of alternative positions of equal validity undermines *all* of these positions. In addition, doing pluralistic education fairly and well is a major practical challenge, especially when at least one major segment of the religious community does not accept the premises of pluralism in the first place. To expose adults (or near adults) to diverse Jewish positions when they have already formulated a personal stance that can serve as a reference point for adopting and adapting new ideas may be salutary. But pluralism, these critics say, is neither a philosophically valid nor practicable basis for educating the next generation.

Despite this critique and despite the fact that pluralism need not negate the value and validity of denominational Judaism, the growth of pluralistic Jewish education seems inevitably to contribute to the overall weakening of the nexus between denominationalism and Jewish education. Forces both within and outside the Jewish domain—ranging from economic factors that apparently favor "community" institutions over more narrowly constituted ones,[9] to the dramatic increase in interfaith families (heightening awareness of multiple religious paths), to the influence of multiculturalism and postmodernity on attitudes toward truth—are driving this growth. The result is to add to the sense that Judaism is expansive and fluid, capable of being apprehended from many different perspectives, religious and nonreligious, and further, that appreciating and embracing this plural identity is a positive good. So even if one does choose to identify with a particular denomination (and this is, of course, not the only way of adopting a stance of one's own), one does so in the spirit of pluralism, with a recognition that this is a practical and provisional decision, not a declaration of fealty to an absolute truth. Educating Jews so that they can make this kind of thoughtful, respectful choice *may* indeed be done within a denominational context, but it need not be, and probably will be done so less often in the future. Thus, though pluralism and denominationalism are not enemies, they are uneasy friends at least as far as education is concerned.

Denominations and Twenty-First-Century Jewish Education

Another challenge to denominationalism's predominant role in Jewish education also comes not in the form of a frontal assault, but as a corollary effect of developments on the overall landscape of Jewish education and American Jewish life. The past quarter century has witnessed enormous geopolitical, social, cultural, scientific, and technological changes that have affected all Americans, including American Jews. New generations have grown up—Gen Xers, Millennials—who bring different sensibilities and experiences to everything they do, including how they approach religious and ethnic life and how they learn. Many of these changes have been widely noted: a growing personalism with respect to religion; the dominance of a consumer mentality in approaching nearly everything; a greater openness to and comfort with diversity; a preference for informality; a global consciousness; total ease operating in a digital world. For Jews, we can add to this list a disenchantment with large institutions, greater ambivalence about Israel and its role in Jewish life, a diminishing sense of boundaries separating Jews from others, and a refusal to be judgmental about the ways in which various Jews choose to express their Jewishness.

The impact of all of these changes has been clearly felt in Jewish education. The rise of digital technology and the business models associated with it has produced a new learning and teaching environment. Today, information is plentiful and easy to access, but not so easy to assess for its truth and value. Customers expect to be able to get what they want, when and where they want it, and to have a role in designing the final product. Learning is a multisensory experience. Connections can readily be formed across multiple boundaries, and virtual communities can complement and support "real" ones. These developments are changing the ground rules of education, and Jewish education will fail to adjust to them at its peril.

These changes themselves and the needed responses to them have little to do per se with denominations and their roles in Jewish education. They present both challenges and opportunities to *all* Jewish education, regardless of its ideological underpinnings or institutional sponsorship. And this is precisely the point. Denominational dominance in Jewish education grew out of a specific set of historical and social circumstances that made the linkage between the two, especially as mediated through the synagogue, a source of strength for both. Now, a different set of circumstances pertain, and the advantages of linking Jewish education to denominational ideologies, programs, and institutions must be demonstrated anew.

One should not assume that no such advantages exist or that education under denominational sponsorship cannot respond to today's challenges as or more effectively than any other educational effort. But, neither can one assume that it will. Elsewhere, I have proposed a number of design principles for twenty-first-century Jewish education. These grow out of three core concepts: making Jewish education more (1) learner focused, (2) relationship infused, and (3) life centered. Implementing these design principles will require that Jewish education change in a number of ways. It will need to be more experiential; more attuned to learners' real needs, concerns, and life circumstances; more conscious of the power of social groups and passionate teachers; available in many more forms and places; more open to allowing learners to help shape their own experiences; more adept at using technology; and more focused on issues that are consequential for both individuals and society.[10]

Nothing in this prescription excludes denominations, their educators, and their institutions from embracing these directions. However, a great deal of inertia must be overcome if they are to lead this transformational process. Most of the cutting-edge developments in Jewish education today, those that best embody these and other similar design principles, are not coming from the institutions affiliated with the major religious movements (there are some notable exceptions to this generalization).[11] Thus, like the ascendance of pluralism as a philosophical stance, the changing dynamics of Jewish education are weakening, de facto if not in principle, the nexus between education and denominationalism. As new educational arenas emerge and creative energies shift toward these, denominations become less consequential in defining and shaping the goals, the ideological underpinnings, the structural configurations, and the practical contours of Jewish education.

Conclusion: Denominations in the Educational Marketplace

Earlier I suggested that it would be premature to write an obituary for denominational Jewish education. I would reaffirm that contention, even after the analysis above. The continuing influence of denominations on Jewish education rests on several factors: First, the institutional infrastructures of the denominations remain formidable. Synagogues and denominationally affiliated schools, youth movements, and camps will continue to educate the largest proportion of American Jews. Alternative options may be nibbling away at this market share, but it will be a long time, if ever, before this situation changes substantially. The support structures of the denominations (training programs, education departments, professional organizations) also remain in place and are in some respects growing stronger. Those who staff and take most advantage of these frameworks tend to be enthusiastic partisans of their particular denomination. They promote its vision, its program, its materials, and ensure that these remain a vibrant presence in the educational marketplace. The debate over whether denominations are growing stronger or weakening may have a surprising answer: both, though for different groups of people. There is great vigor at the heart of each of the religious movements (even the recently much-maligned Conservative movement[12]), including educational energy and ideological ferment.

This is the second major factor that keeps denominations a significant force in Jewish educational life. They do embody visions of Jewish life that have the potential to catalyze serious educational activity. At the outset of this essay I noted that education is inherently ideological: it embodies a particular understanding of who we are and prescription for how life should be lived. For Jewish education this is all the more the case. In recent years, a good deal of attention has been drawn to the role of vision in guiding effective Jewish educational institutions and programs.[13] Although an institution's educational vision can and should emerge from a process involving its own leadership and constituents, a key source for that vision will most often be the classical texts, concepts, and values of the Jewish tradition itself as interpreted and applied by historical and contemporary thinkers. This is, at least in theory, the playing field on which the religious movements make their mark. Although one certainly can look elsewhere for a guiding vision for a school, a camp, or an adult learning program, many educators and laypeople will continue to look to the denominational movements and their ideologies for much of this guidance.

For these reasons, as well as others cited above, it is unlikely that the strong connection between denominations and Jewish education forged in the nineteenth century and cemented in the twentieth will be broken entirely in the twenty-first. However, for the many other reasons also laid out earlier in this essay, equally unlikely is that the denominations, their ideologies, and their institutions will enjoy the same degree of prominence over the next several decades as they did in the past.

The Jewish educational marketplace is a far more open one today and will only become more so. So too is the ideological marketplace. As Jews continue to adjust to a world in which choice is the dominant reality shaping all things Jewish, the denominations will ultimately thrive or wither based on how well they can compete, not just with one another, but also with the myriad of other options for being Jewish (and for not being Jewish) that are now available. The diversity of Jewish life is a fact (if you doubt it, check the number of categories needed to encompass the variety of ways in which respondents described themselves on the 2000–01 National Jewish Population Survey). Whether Jews identify with one of the major denominations or with some other movement or label or call themselves postdenominational or "just Jewish," their educational choices will continue to grow more numerous. One hopes that this competition will produce better and more differentiated products and services and not a rush to commoditization and lowest-price-wins.

What happens will depend in good measure on how educational producers for the American Jewish community respond, and no small part of this will be in the hands of the denominational movements. Though some in these movements may look back wistfully to the days when nearly every Jew was educated under their auspices, more, one may hope, will recognize the value of being challenged and use this as an opportunity to rethink and redesign. In the final analysis, the big questions for Jewish education are not about who is in charge or even where it takes place. The big question is how we in the Jewish community can ensure that the timeless teachings of our tradition continue to inspire and guide successive generations to live lives of dignity, purpose, and responsibility. This is a question to which the denominational and the postdenominational alike are challenged to provide compelling and effective answers. They will succeed if, in the end, they understand themselves to be not competitors, but allies in the sacred quest to help every Jew live *b'tzelem Elokim*, in God's image.

CHAPTER 11

Rabbinic Training and Transdenominationalism
Some Personal Perspectives

Arthur Green

You might say that from my earliest Jewish experiences, I was destined to be a transdenominational Jew. Raised in a Jewish atheist household, I was given the opportunity of a Jewish education as a concession to my rather traditional maternal grandparents, who expected that each male grandchild would celebrate a bar mitzvah (my sister, by contrast, was given not a day of Jewish education). Living in Newark, New Jersey, my parents chose the nearby "temple," which happened to be B'nai Abraham, under the leadership of Rabbi Joachim Prinz, whom they respected as a liberal communal leader. B'nai Abraham, a founding congregation of the Conservative United Synagogue of America, had left the movement soon after it hired Prinz, a Reform rabbi recently arrived from Berlin. To this day the congregation, now in suburban Livingston, remains proudly unaffiliated.

Much to my father's chagrin, I began to take Judaism rather seriously and found myself deeply drawn to the synagogue. Once I came to understand that the temple service was essentially a performance, conducted by the cantor and the (mostly non-Jewish) professional choir, I had little ability to pray there. I turned instead to my grandparents' synagogue in nearby Clifton, where prayer was infinitely more informal and participatory. This congregation was also undefined by denomination. It was an East European *shul*, the "regulars" still largely Yiddish speaking, but with mixed seating. The rabbi, a young immigrant yeshiva graduate, knew he could not pull it to Orthodoxy and made his peace with the situation, staying for many years in the unaffiliated pulpit.

161

My Jewish education came from those two institutions, the highly Zionist and Hebraist Hebrew School of B'nai Abraham and the "*davvnen*, schnapps, and herring" *minyan* at the Clifton Jewish Center. Neither one forced me to answer the question, "What kind of Jew are you?" I could probably have responded best in negative terms when I was a child. I knew I wasn't Reform, because our family had attended a cousin's bar mitzvah in a Reform temple and were duly scandalized by the lack of male headgear and all the rest. I wasn't Orthodox, because unlike the one Orthodox kid in my public school class, I still turned on lights and answered the phone on the Sabbath. You might think that would have defined me as Conservative, but it was not a label I would have chosen for myself. I was Jewish in the very natural way that urban Jewish kids, grandchildren of East European immigrants, were Jews in the 1940s and '50s. "What are you, kid?" was a question still asked by bullies on the Newark streets in those days, and "Jewish" was an answer that sometimes got you a bloody nose. The adjective "Conservative" would not have helped in that defining moment.

Although the temple was unaffiliated, we kids did get sent to Camp Ramah, which had a major influence on me. From there I joined the Leaders' Training Fellowship, supposedly the elite future leadership of the Conservative movement. But in my college years I swung wildly, first toward orthopraxy (under the influence of Rabbi Yitz Greenberg and then still-Lubavitcher Zalman Schachter) and afterwards away from observance altogether (influenced by Albert Camus, Friedrich Nietzsche, Franz Kafka, and a few others).

When I began to take Judaism seriously again as a young adult, the communities that served as models for me were the *Lehrhaus* of Franz Rosenzweig (thanks to Nahum Glatzer, my teacher at Brandeis), the circle of the Ba'al Shem Tov, and the hasidic communities of Bratslav and Kotzk. Again, none of these had denominational labels. Rosenzweig had openly eschewed any such categorization and I had learned to admire him for it. And would anyone dare call Rabbi Nahman or the Kotzker an "orthodox" thinker?

Being a rabbinical student at the Jewish Theological Seminary (JTS) in New York in those days gave me rather little exposure to the real Conservative movement, which hardly existed inside the walls of 3080 Broadway. Discussions among future rabbis, and they were often quite intense, were conducted on a rather rarified plane. Often they had to do with theology, including such tough issues as faith after the Holocaust, the morality of Jewish particularism, and especially the authority of *halakhah*, Jewish law. Already then I felt that a certain theological bankruptcy in the more conservative branches of faculty and fellow students (those who rejected both Mordecai Kaplan's theology and Abraham Joshua Heschel's politics) was leading them to replace theology with philosophy of law. "Just 'bracket' the questions of God and revelation," they would say, "and Judaism provides a wonderful, sensitive legal system and basis for behavior." Later I would discover thinkers from the liberal side of Orthodoxy, including David Hartman, saying much the same thing. I would have none of it. I would have had little attraction to Judaism if it were primarily a legal system. I was, and remain, a religious seeker. I crave passion, not conformity; intimacy with God, not normative behavior within the law. I was increasingly attracted to Jewish mysticism as my spiritual language, and that only added to my alienation from those who were setting the denominational tone. With regard to observance (*not* my most important religious question), I understood already in those years that I was a selective traditionalist on more-or-less spiritual and aesthetic terms, not a participant in a binding legal framework. My choice to resign from the Rabbinical Assembly, quite a few years later, just confirmed a reality many years in the making.

The later key stations of my religious life, including Havurat Shalom, Somerville, Massachusetts; Germantown's Minyan Masorti, Kehillat Yedidya in Jerusalem, the Newton Centre Minyan, and now our little local Minyan Olat Shabbat, are all similarly unaffiliated. Hillel Levine, activist and scholar of religion, noted many years ago that the *havurah* phenomenon grew mostly out of the soil of Conservative Judaism because that movement had a particularly huge gap between values preached and those practiced, setting the stage for a whiff of hypocrisy, rebellion, and the quest for a new alternative. There may be other reasons for this as well, including the fact that the movement was better at giving its future leaders access to the sources than it was at creating rationales for living within its own definition of the halakhic framework. Hence the defections to both right and left.

For my own religious life and struggles, the continuum of *maskil* to *hasid* was much more meaningful than that which ranged from Orthodox to Reform. I was never much interested in knowing how much a particular person observed, whether he would drive to Shabbat dinner or only to shul, whether she ate fish out or only salads. I *was* trying to figure out whether I was an insider or an outsider to the tradition. Was I a scholar, living with a historical awareness that no longer allowed me to have faith? That was the maskil within me, reinforced by the cynical joking that was common in my JTS and later AJS (Association for Jewish Studies) academic circles. Or was I a neohasidic devotee longing for God's presence and trying to make some form of *avodat ha-shem* (service of God) central to my life? I was reading hasidic sources intensively, and not just as an academic exercise. While disinclined for many reasons to join the contemporary hasidic community, at the edge of which I stood for some time, the religious seriousness and passion I found in those sources continued to attract me, despite everything the maskil in me knew. I have lived out something of that struggle every day for the past four decades, in periods of both greater and lesser religious observance.

By the 1970s I began to notice that I was not alone in my discomfort with the available denominational labels. My friends who were working as rabbi-directors in Hillel Foundations around the country were serving the most diverse and interesting Jewish communities anywhere, in those happy years before denominational groups began to appear on the college campus. Those communities emphasized study and personal seeking, and these could well be conducted across denominational lines. The same was true in the academic community of Judaic scholars formed around the Association for Jewish Studies. We AJS members might have worried about whether a particular author or scholar was apologetic rather than critical in presenting Jewish sources or a particular historical epoch, but we were hardly concerned with whether or not he (mostly, in those days) *davvened mincha* (prayed the afternoon service).

Emerging Signs

A decade or so later the transdenominational framework began to appear beyond the college campus.[1] I first noticed it in adult education settings when such more serious programs as Wexner Heritage, Melton, and later Hebrew College's own Me'ah all appeared on the scene without any denominational sponsorship. This was followed in the 1990s with the appearance of community day schools that sought to serve students whose family affiliations ranged from modern Orthodox to secularist-cultural. It began to feel that some of the best energies in the Jewish community were devoted to various sorts of educational efforts that cut across denominational lines.

Throughout this period, rabbinic education and placement remained almost exclusively in denominational hands. This was true despite the 1930s effort of Stephen Wise to create the Jewish Institute of Religion (JIR) in New York, intended to fill the wide space between the JTS definition of Conservative Judaism and the Cincinnati version of Reform. JIR existed without a label, as does its successor, the Academy for Jewish Religion. But the graduates had often struggled to find placement, and they had not significantly changed the face of the American rabbinate. Indeed, it seemed fitting to most observers that rabbinic training be denominational. Rabbis, after all, had to stand for something. Unlike academic scholars, commitment was essential to their self-definition and communal role. Wasn't the something that rabbis stood for best defined by the respective denominational platforms?

I recall a conversation I had with Rabbi Daniel Lehmann when he asked me to serve on an advisory board for the then-in-formation New Jewish High School in Boston (now Gann Academy). While agreeing to serve, I suggested to him that a transdenominational high school faced a grave problem. All the most compelling Jewish educational settings of the past had succeeded because of strong and clear vision. These included such diverse educational streams as Chabad, B'nai Akiva, HaShomer HaTza'ir, and Camp Ramah of the 1950s. What would the pluralism of the New Jewish High School imply? That there was no right way to be Jewish? My concern, as a committed pluralist, was that the ideology of pluralism might forcibly vacate all other ideologies. If that were the case, I feared the school might not have the clarity of vision that would allow for a convincing education. Jewish secondary education also has to stand for something, and that something has to be more than pluralism.

Little did I realize then that my questions to Lehmann were just a stage setting for the precise challenge I would be taking on five years later in defying the conventional wisdom and established traditions of contemporary Jewry by creating a new transdenominational program of rabbinic training at Hebrew College. Clear to us (President David Gordis, Provost Barry Mesch, and myself, in the initial conversations) was that at Hebrew College rabbinical students would be trained in critical study of the sources and would be exposed to a postcritical embrace of Jewish faith. We advocated a personal reengagement with the sources, despite all one might learn about the historical settings in which they were written. We knew that the rabbinate demanded some sort of faith commitment and we said that neither non-Jews nor avowedly secularist Jews could enroll in the rabbinical program. But the nature of that faith and the extent of commitment to religious observance would be each student's own responsibility, and we, the Rabbinical School faculty, would not dictate in areas of either theological or halakhic conscience. (With regard to ethical probity, and on the single issue of students' choice of Jewish marriage or life partners, we did set standards.) That left me asking the very same questions I had put to Lehmann: To what values, other than pluralism and diversity, is your school committed? Can a transdenominational program that educates rabbis stand for something? What kind of rabbis will these be, those who have studied together with colleagues who will find their place in other denominations or in none at all?

The initial four years of the educational experiment at Hebrew College (as of this writing we are eagerly anticipating the ordination of members of the first class of rabbinical students in June 2008), have taught those of us who shaped the initial program a great deal about this question. We are confident that the rabbis in this program will be *better* trained for having sat in classes alongside others who disagree with them on almost every issue imaginable. If one thing characterizes the Jewish community today, it is diversity. Two Jews not only have three opinions, as they say, but are likely these days to have different educations; childhood Jewish memories; views of law, religious beliefs, sexual orientations; and lots more. A rabbi has to minister to *all* of them. Where better to learn about how to respect and listen deeply to someone different than by sitting across the table from one another in the *beit midrash*? How better to sharpen your own understanding, to hone your own point of view, than by looking at the sources and discussing them openly, even arguing about them, in a mixed and diverse group of fellow students, where opinions and readings range across a wide spectrum?

The experiment has not always been an easy or comfortable one. Sometimes we faculty made assumptions about our students that missed the mark widely. As is true throughout American clergy education these days, classes at the Rabbinical School are peopled by individuals of a wide age range and very different in background, both professionally and in personal life experience. They do not always have an easy time listening to one another. But we have persisted in our belief that the forging of this diverse group into a community was vital to our enterprise, and the testimony of time has borne that out. By now I think it fair to say that students in our program have come to accept a certain set of values that characterize our community, even though each represents a particular blend and version of them, as we indeed hope they will. There is no single ideal type of Hebrew College rabbinical graduate, and all the values listed below are constantly up for appraisal and renewed conversation.

Common Values

The first value I would say the Rabbinical School of Hebrew College stands for is that of *klal yisrael*, the unity and wholeness of the Jewish people. We see ourselves as serving the entire Jewish community, including those who will not recognize the legitimacy of Hebrew College's rabbinic ordination. One of the great issues facing us as we look toward the Jewish future is the threat that our faculty and students will be divided in two because of differences in halakhic praxis, especially around issues of conversion, marriage, and personal status. While concerned about this growing wedge, we in the Rabbinical School are also unhappy about driving Jews away from Jewish life because we seem cool or ambivalent in the welcome we offer to them. Because Hebrew College is transdenominational, we do not have an institutional stance on specific issues (for example, may a rabbi officiate at mixed marriages? May a rabbi lead a marriage ceremony involving a divorcée who has not had a traditional *get*? Will a rabbi welcome a gay couple—in Massachusetts or elsewhere—to celebrate an *ufruf* in his or her synagogue before their marriage?). But we work to inform our graduates fully of the implications of these decisions both for the individuals involved and for Jewish unity. Our goal is to enable each graduate to make well-informed and thoughtful decisions about his or her own rabbinic practice. We welcome and encourage dialogue with all sectors of the rabbinic community and value keeping open lines of personal cooperation and work on shared concerns, even in areas of serious disagreement. Only by self-conscious and committed efforts can world Jewry be protected from the disaster of a full split along religious lines, and we hope that our graduates, with a commitment to true diversity within *klal yisrael*, will contribute to that effort.

A commitment to *klal yisrael* also requires faith in the unity of the Jewish people across geographical distances and political borders. It especially demands involvement with the challenges facing the state of Israel on every level: political, moral, cultural, and religious, to name but a few. We in the Rabbinical School believe that Israel and its tribulations will be a major item on the agenda of every rabbi over the coming decades, and we need to educate with this in mind. A rabbi must empathize with the Israeli dilemma as our own problem, not someone else's. Again, the school does not demand a particular point of view on any issue, and our students and faculty represent a wide range of opinions. But we do expect involvement and commitment to struggle with the questions, and that is why study in Israel and learning about issues of Jewish identity and Judaism as they develop in Israel are important to our program. Happily, our student body has been enriched from the beginning with members raised in countries other than the United

States, including Israel, and that has made an important contribution to the Jewish diversity we so cherish.

The Rabbinical School is firmly committed to other values as well, despite our refusal to adhere to a denominational self-definition. Let me describe these across the traditional rubrics of *Torah*, *avodah*, and *gemilut hasadim* (learning, worship, and acts of kindness), which the most classical of sources says are Judaism's three pillars.

Ahavat Torah, the love of traditional Jewish learning, is the hallmark of Hebrew College's program. It is the value most exemplified by our faculty, scholars, and teachers of text, and the love we most want to impart to our students and in turn have them share throughout the Jewish community. We find that text learning brings us together, even as we argue over the meaning of a passage. Talmudic sages used to speak about "doing battle" with one another over the meaning of Torah. But once the argument was over, the "warriors" again saw one another as friends and fellow seekers. Jewish life needs more of that spirit today. We at Hebrew College offer and model for our students a love of Jewish texts and their interpretation. This love embraces the widest variety of Jewish sources, from the Bible and Talmud through mystical, literary, and artistic teachings, down to Jewish thought as it is being re-created in our own day. It includes the pursuit of wisdom and truth, based on the sources, but also with an integrity that acknowledges our own personal experience and the era in which we live. We read the sources critically, understand their historical settings, but then seek to reembrace them as living Torah and to interpret or rephrase them so that they may speak to seeking Jews and others today.

Key to that appreciation of the sources is our *beit midrash*, which has become the living heart of our program. In addition to formal classes, each student spends ten to twelve hours per week in this supervised study hall, poring over texts and preparing for class with the help of a special *beit midrash* staff. While the staff's emphasis is always on building skills, helping students develop the ability to master and feel at home in the texts, it is here that some of the most important conversations among these future rabbis take place. There is something here of the Lehrhaus ideology, a sense that rabbinic education should be about access to the sources and a sharing of that access with the wider Jewish community. We are witness to a great hunger for serious Jewish learning among Jewish adults, almost all of whom are now graduates of fine university educations. The rabbi for the twenty-first century needs to have sufficient depth of text mastery (in the original Hebrew) so that she or he can select, translate, and present material on the high level that contemporary communities will demand.

Complementing a shared love of learning and the *beit midrash* is a deep commitment to the growth and development of the spiritual life as an important part of rabbinic training. Each rabbi needs to find his or her own way to an inner life of prayer, to thinking about God, to hewing out a deep inner well of empathy and caring on which he or she will draw daily throughout the rabbinic career. While these are deeply private matters, not discussed easily, rabbis know that having access to such a reservoir of faith is essential to finding and sharing the emotional strength required for the rabbinate. Rabbis who spend decades deeply involved with the lives of their congregants carry with them great burdens of personal pain. Techniques for developing the resources to deal with this aspect of the rabbinate, which are a growing focus in rabbinic education, should transcend all denominational lines. These include the Rabbinical School's prayer services, held each weekday in the *beit midrash* (attendance is required twice weekly), where a variety of approaches to prayer, ranging from the neohasidic to the very contemporary meditative, are offered. The emphasis in our worship is on *kavannah* and inwardness rather than on defending a particular prayer book or style of worship. Old techniques (hasidic *niggun* singing, and so forth) are welcome, as are new interpretations or readings, as long as they serve to open the heart and to make true prayer more accessible. Rabbinical School faculty include a number of exceptional *ba'alei tefillah* who personify and seek to teach the ability to make communal prayer an important and even transformative process.

Hebrew College also offers a voluntary program of spiritual direction to our students, one that offers them an opportunity for regular, confidential heart-to-heart conversations with a trained director, where they can share and articulate their own wrestling with the deepest and most personal spiritual questions. This program, in effect since the second year of the Rabbinical School, has won wide appreciation and praise from students.

The same is true in the realm of *gemilut hasadim*, expanded to include a commitment to social justice and activism in areas where one feels a moral call. Little denominational difference exists among Jews when it comes to what are called *mitzvot beyn adam le-havero*, the good deeds we do toward our fellow humans. We all believe in reaching out to the poor, the sick, and the needy. We care about the elderly and the disabled and want to help. Hebrew College's rabbinical students, including those who represent all points on the observance spectrum, are attracted to programs of social and economic betterment, both those focused within the Jewish community and some that reach beyond its borders. In an era when persecution of Jews is mostly a historic memory, and when large parts of the Jewish community live amid wealth and privilege unimagined by prior generations, rabbinic moral leadership will be key in redefining the nature of a Jew's obligations and role in society. Hebrew College's programs of social justice are meant to prepare rabbis to assert that leadership and vision. In this area we also have the special privilege of being close to our neighbors at Andover-Newton Theological School, and many of our programs in this area are shared with the students of that highly activist Protestant institution.

Learning, spirituality, and social justice: the intellectual, devotional, and ethical dimensions of what it means to be a rabbi. All of these, it turns out, are areas where Hebrew College's rabbinical students, for all their diverse viewpoints, can work together and build a single Jewish community. We feel that is a lot to share, giving us a sense of strong commitments and a clear vision of the rabbinate that we faculty and students are shaping together. Yes, there will be points of divergence. Some keep *kashrut* more strictly, others are more lenient. Some drive on Shabbat, others do not. Occasionally we will even choose to go into separate rooms to pray, although we try not to do that too often. But having worked hard to build a community around those three pillars we all share, the differences between us lose their sharp edge. Respect and affection for one another come to outweigh the differences between our chosen prayer books or specific practices. We work hard to be considerate of one another (food at communal gatherings is thus carefully labeled as to degree of kashrut, whether it was brought in on Shabbat or beforehand, for example) and try to include as wide an arc as possible within our embrace.

This emphasis on shared values across denominational lines does have its own bias. We in the Rabbinical School are indeed modeling that inwardness and sincerity in worship are more important than whether every word is said. Although kashrut is fully respected, we do model that sitting down at table with a wide variety of Jews is important. Shabbat is taught and modeled as a serious spiritual practice, which all students strive to observe in ever-growing ways, while remaining much challenged by the fact that as rabbis they indeed must look ahead to a career in which many will have to work at their jobs most fully on Shabbat. The concern is less with correct observance of each Sabbath law, which is left to the student's discretion, than with bringing the Shabbat spirit to the wide variety of communities students will lead. To do that, of course, the rabbi will need a rich well of Shabbat experience in his or her own life, and much of this has to be gained in rabbinical school. Periodic Shabbat retreats, shared meals as well as prayer services, singing and conversation long into the night are all vital parts of this rabbinic education.

We are neither so naïve nor so proud at Hebrew College to believe we have solved all the great challenges to contemporary rabbinic education. The gap between our educational ideal of mastering the rabbinic tradition and the rather different set of demands confronting rabbis in their actual careers is one we cannot resolve. The struggle with skill and language mastery and their place within the broader program plagues us as it does every program of rabbinic training. The constant competition for curricular hours (More intellectual history? More Bible? More management training? More personal growth-oriented courses?) confronts us as we shape each year's course of study. But we feel we have made some significant progress. A significant part of that lies in our seeing ourselves as an open, informal, diverse, and welcoming *beit midrash*. All the rest is commentary.

A Bigger Question

The perceptive reader will have noted a clear relationship between the two distinctive parts of this essay, the personal story and the institutional description. How could there not be? I was given the great privilege of creating a new institution for rabbinic training, defining its initial curriculum and priorities. As you would expect, these are significantly shaped by my own experiences and perceptions of Judaism and the contemporary rabbinate. As a scholar trained to study and explicate the Jewish past, I came to find greater challenge in thinking about the Jewish future and in trying to train a rabbinate appropriate to it, while still deeply rooted in the classical tradition. That rooting called for deep learning, upon which I have insisted. Openness to the diverse Jewish future has led to a nonrestrictive view with regard to personal observance and choices. I do want to show students that there are more important questions than "How much do you observe?" The maskil-hasid (outsider-insider) debate hopefully resounds louder within our walls than the Orthodox-Reform. Every rabbi today—indeed every seriously committed Jew—outside ultra-Orthodoxy has to ask the question, "How can I be honest with my own beliefs and still feel like an authentic insider to this ancient tradition?" I hope that our *beit midrash* will remain a good place to assk that question.

PART 4

Personal Reflections and Community Stories

CHAPTER 12

Reconciling Individualism and Community
A Common Challenge

Carl A. Sheingold

"Postdenominationalism" is a label with multiple meanings that cover a variety of trends and groups. If a common denominator underlies these, it would appear to be a disinclination to adopt a label associated with an existing denominational movement. This disinclination has been expressed in positive terms such as a desire for flexibility of thought and practice or in negative terms based on the presumption that affiliation with a movement restricts or even calcifies the freedom of belief or action of an individual or a group.

Beyond this common denominator is great variety. Some unaffiliated groups seek a higher level of intensity and quality in their Jewish life, particularly their prayer experiences, than they believe is possible in a mainstream synagogue. Others are seemingly motivated to maintain a more casual Jewish connection than they imagine an affiliated synagogue or movement might entail. Some seek flexibility to evolve. In other groups the disinclination to affiliate is connected more to the variety of members' past affiliations and the fear that affiliation with one movement would be too divisive—where the desire of individuals to hold on to old identities is the core reason the group refrains from collectively adopting a new one. Some are primarily committed to democratic process, often being resistant to rabbinic leadership or professional leadership of any kind. Others are built around charismatic "rebbe" leadership.

My view of this phenomenon is shaped in part by my role as executive vice-president of the Jewish Reconstructionist Federation, but also as a former and first executive director of the

National Havurah Committee in the early 1980s. I have followed the evolution of a prior incarnation of postdenominationalism and currently serve as a leader of a movement that for many years resisted seeing itself as a denomination and has always been highly decentralized. If some resist movement affiliation for fear of the depth of the impact of a label, I am aware, from inside a movement, how challenging it can be for movements to define what holds them together. It's not that I can't answer that question for the Reconstructionist movement. But there is an "eye of the beholder" aspect to this attribute of movements. And if my movement is the one in which the autonomy of individuals and groups is highly respected, I am sure my counterparts in other movements can identify with a sense of irony when confronted with images of uniformity and control as a price of movement affiliation.

Most important, as someone who exercises movement leadership at a time of postdenominationalism, I have to think about what a denominational movement really is and what its value is at its core. What is the core, *experiential* meaning of being a denominational movement, as compared to what may be attributed to the consequences of being part of one? The answer for me is precisely and specifically the fact that it is an organized network of groups that formally affiliate with it, where the groups in turn affiliate individual members. Movements have affiliates. To be sure, there are also commonalities of belief and, even more, of sensibility. There are boundaries. If the subject at hand were differences among the movements, these would be important. But the subject here is broader than that and, in my view, implicitly about the role of movements and the role of postdenominationalism, really postdenominational groups, in Jewish life today and in the future.

Seeking a Jewish Experience

In this context it is important to note that most Jews, and particularly uninvolved Jews, seek Jewish experience more than they seek opportunities to express belief. They are looking for meaning more than seeking to express a personal theology. They seek groups that are compatible in sensibility, more than they seek groups that espouse a particular ideology. In fact, a group's or movement's ideology may play a central role in creating the group culture or sensibility that appeals to someone. But that is not uppermost in the mind of the person deciding what group to join.

In my experience, the most profound and very real differences between the denominational movements are experienced when one walks in the door of a synagogue for services, more than when one reads the movement's platform. In fact, what one experiences when one walks in the door is typically not an accident and, indeed, is often profoundly connected to movement ideology. But those connections are not uppermost in the minds of most congregants or prospective congregants. That is not to minimize the differences among the movements, but rather to locate what the most important experiential differences are.

If the fact of affiliation is the defining characteristic of denominational movements (and their absence of postdenominational groups), what are the consequences? What primary, generic role do movements play? It is, I would suggest, that they provide pathways for groups and individuals to connect to other groups, to national and international expressions of Jewish community, to the evolution of Jewish history through the evolution of the movement (insofar as the movements have a deeper past than unaffiliated groups), among other things. In other words, a movement provides a pathway of connection to something larger than the group.

This has two major consequences. First, it provides the individual and the group with potential sources of meaning and expression and commitment beyond themselves. It also provides opportunities to experiment and learn from experimentation beyond one's own experience with the practical meaning of Jewish community. I will elaborate on this point for the remainder of this brief essay as I express my view of the actual relationship between denominationalism and postdenominationalism.

Finding Meaningful Community

For the sake of coherence, I will focus on a particular branch of postdenominationalism—the independent *minyanim* that have become an important part of Jewish culture in many urban centers. Given the depth of Jewish knowledge and commitment among many of their members, their role is of significant importance beyond themselves. They are, or are potentially, leadership groups. Also, they bear the most resemblance to the independent *havurot* that emerged in the last wave of postdenominationalism in the late 1960s and '70s, and thus would seem to have their roots in something deeper than a particular, contemporary cultural trend.

The central insight of Mordecai Kaplan, the founder of the Reconstructionist movement and a major source of influence beyond this movement, was that Judaism is an evolving religious civilization. In the spirit of Kaplan, we can think of all of modern Jewish life as experimental. It is not a new or historically unanchored or transitory experiment—at least for Kaplan and for Reconstructionists, on the contrary. But it is still as an attempt to define and find meaning in Judaism in historically new settings. Today the most important such settings are a democratic, pluralistic society in which Jews are more than welcome and, across the ocean, in a modern, sovereign Jewish state.

In this light, and as I look at the challenges involved, I am struck by the similarities between the independent minyanim and affiliated synagogues—not in their behavior or culture but in the challenges they confront. Getting only casually below the surface of the presence or absence of affiliation or movement labels, one quickly encounters generic challenges—tensions or polarities—that characterize all modern liberal religious communities. Within a pluralistic, inclusive context, are there boundaries? Within an inclusive context, what are the sources of quality control? Within a democratic context, what is the nature and source of leadership? Within a context with a relatively high focus on the present and direct experience, what is the future of the group and how will it be sustained? In the context of seeking not to be constrained, individually or collectively, by ideology or by labels, is there a source of coherence that can inform someone seeking to join the group or, indeed, shape the experience of its members? In an age when most Jews of most ideological stripes are more American than Jewish, what are the Jewish obligations of a group or individual beyond one's own experience? When does the American consumerist impulse promote quality (after all, much in the American competition for our time and energy is of high quality), and when does it lead to pallid, common denominator experiences and, indeed, moving from experience to experience without any real commitment? When is the search for quality elitist in a negative sense and when is it, rather, a search for new models and modes of experience that others can ultimately benefit from and, in that sense, a positive expression of leadership?

This list could go on. My point is that I do not know of any Reconstructionist synagogue, nor do I expect I could identify any independent minyan, that is not grappling with these issues. They may start from different places. Their different structures may have an impact on the way these tensions are experienced and confronted. But these generic issues are a result of living in the United States—seeking to reconcile individualism and community—rather than being part of a movement or not. Put differently, the central challenge is to find meaning and a meaningful and workable mode of Jewish community in a highly individualistic society.

I write this not to suggest that there is no difference between affiliated synagogues and independent minyanim or to imply that independent minyanim should give up their independence. I write it to suggest something positive. In an era of Jewish experimentation, we as a people need variety. The most important relationship we can have between movements and postdenominational individuals and groups is to learn from each other. Because movements involve affiliation and therefore relationships, they have a broader base of shared experience from which knowledge can be gained and vehicles to facilitate such sharing. Some independent groups have the potential to go deeper into discrete experiments, sometimes because of their smaller size or relative homogeneity; sometimes because of the positive implications of being more self-focused. I hope that independent groups can succeed and that we can learn from them. I hope that Reconstructionist communities can succeed and that others can learn from us.

Evolution will surely also operate in the formal and informal relationships between movements and the postdenominational phenomenon—collectively and individually. That will work itself out. In this context I am vividly aware of the historical evolution of the havurah movement of the late 1970s and '80s. Some of the havurot that were formed still exist; others don't. The National Havurah Committee still exists and other and newer institutions have their roots in this phenomenon. Some of the individuals involved are still involved in what might be thought of as countercultural Jewish life. Others have become leaders of what might be thought of as the mainstream. Indeed, some serve or served as leaders of denominational movements, which, in part because of their involvement, are no longer what they once were.

But in an important sense, I am suggesting that in some contexts these labels—denominational or postdenominational; mainstream or countercultural—are only partially useful. I will share an anecdote to illustrate my point. In the mid-1990s I was responsible for organizing what was then the Council of Jewish Federations' General Assembly. During those years Hillel organized participation by college students, some of whom were hoping that a protest could be mounted similar to the student rally at the 1969 General Assembly (GA)—a central event in the evolution of that era's Jewish counterculture. When I met with the students my major goal was to orient them to the GA and enable them to take advantage of it. I honestly didn't know whether I would welcome or not welcome a protest. I told the students that they would do what they would do. But I did want them to know that they and most of the other participants at the GA had something deeply in common: When they returned home from the GA, they would likely be and feel like a minority amongst Jews. A minority taking Jewish life seriously and seeking serious meaning from it. In that sense they were all fellow travelers in a common cause.

As a leader of the Reconstructionist movement, I regard the independent minyanim in exactly that way.

CHAPTER 13

A Personal Reflection on Contemporary Trends in American Judaism

Sanford (Sandy) Cardin

Few topics in contemporary American Jewish life are as polarizing as whether the four largest religious denominations—Orthodox, Conservative, Reform, and Reconstructionist—are a positive or a divisive force in the Jewish community. For "true believers," the denominations remain the primary prisms through which Jewish life should be refracted. For many detractors, the denominations have evolved into enterprises more interested in assuring their own survival and serving their own parochial interests than in helping forge a genuine sense of community in an increasingly diverse Jewish world.

As is the case in most debates of this sort, the truth lies somewhere in the middle. The denominations are not as influential as their leadership may wish us to believe, nor are they the bane of the American Jewish community. They are organizations that serve their constituents very well in some areas, even as they vastly overestimate their importance in others. And while recent studies suggest that the fastest growing segment of the American Jewish population is the one in which people would prefer to be known as "just Jewish" rather than as adherents of any denomination, evidence of the current strength of the movements is all around us.

Birthrates among the Orthodox are the highest in the Jewish community and strong communal norms—including the expectation that youth will attend day schools and subsequently a year in Israel upon graduation—have produced a Jewishly well-educated and highly Zionistic community. Even in an era of transition, the

183

Conservative movement has retained a strong core committed to intensive Jewish life and its well-developed camping system continues to produce highly Jewishly identified youth. Both rabbis and committed laypeople have engaged in serious discussions about creating practicing Conservative Jewish communities. With 896 affiliated congregations as members, the Union for Reform Judaism has never been larger. Its embrace of greater ritual practice, as well as its welcoming stance towards Jews in interfaith relationships, has enabled the Reform movement to attract an ever-growing number of adherents. The Reconstructionist movement, while still the smallest denomination, continues to mature. In recent years, it has established both a summer camp and a youth movement, and its innovative prayer book has been well received.

Congregational Affiliation Today

While all of this good news points to the strength of the movements among the constituencies they were created to serve, the picture is much different when viewed through the wider lens of the current state of affairs in American Jewish life. According to one study, less than half of American Jewry is affiliated with a congregation at any moment in time. That is not to say, however, that the majority of American Jews have never affiliated. It has been estimated that as many as 80 percent of American Jews join a congregation at some point in their lives, most likely around the time of a life-cycle event traditionally held in a synagogue (marriage, baby naming, b'nai mitzvah, and funeral), and then drop their membership shortly thereafter.

One interpretation of this phenomenon is that the majority of American Jews see congregational affiliation more along the lines of a fee-for-service arrangement than a meaningful connection to a particular denominational approach. What leads them to affiliate is their desire to fulfill a specific Jewish need, not a search for a specific ideology or theology to which they can relate (save and excepting, perhaps, for issues relating to patrilineal descent), and the fact that many depart so quickly suggests that little is taking place during their congregational encounters to engage them in deeper ways.

One reason denominational differences are no longer particularly relevant or meaningful to most American Jews, including a substantial percentage of liberal congregations' members, is the fact that most of the sociological, theological, and ideological reasons that led to the creation of non-Orthodox Jewry are either outdated or no longer pertinent because of shifts in the demography of American Jewry itself. The immigrant community in which the Jews of Eastern European descent affiliated with Orthodox and Conservative synagogues and the Jews of German and Central European descent are no longer identified as Reform; now that the community is composed predominantly of fourth and fifth generation Americans (recent Russian, Iranian, South African, and Israeli immigrants notwithstanding), many of whom are also intermarried, ethnic origin no longer plays a significant role in what kind of synagogue, if any, one decides to join.

It is therefore small wonder that recent trends in Conservative and Reform Judaism, for example, the Conservative embrace of egalitarianism and the intensified place of Jewish rituals among Reform congregations, reflect an ever more homogeneous set of American Jewish attitudes and practices that make denominational differences less and less significant or possible to discern. In fact, to the disinterested and casual observer of Jewish religious life—a category into which the majority of American Jewry can easily be placed—the practical differences between the liberal streams are very difficult to understand.

This is particularly true given that many Jews with congregational affiliations are neither aware of the theological and ideological roots that distinguish the denomination to which their congregation belongs nor do they often observe the ritual practices their movement legislates. Instead, they are much more familiar with discrete and limited ways in which the Judaism they know is practiced—the structure and melodies of their service, the number of days they observe (or not) the holidays, and perhaps the traditions of the youth group to which they belonged. The more American Jewish life begins to look the same, the less relevant denominationalism is to the majority of American Jewry.

The fact that the liberal movements arrived at what now appear to be very similar practices at various times and after following different ideological journeys may be an interesting historical phenomenon, but this is unimportant for most contemporary Jews. We are where we are, and continuing to dwell on theological and ideological differences is as relevant to many as trying to count the proverbial number of angels on a head of a pin.

It can also be destructive. The inter- and intradenominational struggles, tensions, and conflicts that dominate the headlines make it appear as though more divides than unifies the Jewish community. Disagreements surrounding the ability of rabbis to perform interfaith marriages, the status of converts to Judaism by rabbinical courts comprised of anyone other than Orthodox rabbis, and the opening of Jewish community centers on Shabbat are just three examples of the kinds of disputes the majority of American Jews consider petty and unimportant. This discord is what many unaffiliated Jews see and understandably decide to avoid.

Five Recommendations

The fundamental question, therefore, is how can the movements continue to provide their constituent congregations with the important programs and services they need while simultaneously promoting Jewish peoplehood across denominational lines? What follows are five modest recommendations, each of which depends on a commitment from the movements to give collaboration a much higher priority than it enjoys at present.

First, the leadership of the movements must learn to spend more time and attention celebrating what binds us as Jews rather than erecting ideological and theological fences. They need to figure out how to engage the "just Jewish" in ways that speak more to Jewish universalism, not with their own brand of particularism. Interestingly, this is a realm in which all of the denominations may want to take lessons from Chabad.

Second, the leadership of the movements must also find ways to work together more closely and more often. By identifying and working in the myriad of areas in which the movements are in total agreement, rather than by focusing on their differences, the movements are in a position to exemplify the kind of harmonious

Jewish world that is attractive to universalists without compromising their core principles.

Third, denominational leadership should be sure their seminaries produce broad-minded, inclusive rabbis, cantors, and educators committed first to the Jewish people and then to their denomination. Rabbis, no matter where they are trained, ultimately need to be able to serve all the Jews in their community as well as the greater Jewish community—*klal yisrael*—and need to understand the viewpoints of rabbis and fellow Jews of all stripes, who bring differing perspectives and ideological stances to the table.[1] Perhaps the denominationally based seminaries can learn from the experiences of the nondenominational seminaries. The students and faculty at the new seminary at Hebrew College in Boston and at the Academy of Jewish Religion (really two separate institutions in New York and Los Angeles) span the Jewish spectrum.

Fourth, especially since so many congregations are searching for new approaches to traditional membership paradigms, denominational leaders should clearly place the concept of Jewish peoplehood at the center of their ideology in an effort to attract the widest possible audience. They should view themselves more as Jewish leaders than as denominational spokespeople, all the while ensuring those congregations that choose to identify with their denomination will receive the help they need to serve their congregants and communities to the best of their abilities.

Finally, those movements with restrictive rabbinic placement, youth group, and camp enrollment policies should abandon those approaches in favor of a more open, inclusive approach. They should encourage their congregations to hire the best available rabbis and participate in the most effective youth programs regardless of denominational affiliation, and rabbis should be able to accept any pulpit without fear of retaliation or ostracism.

While some would argue that pursuing these ideas would undermine the influence of the denominations, it is more likely just the opposite would occur. By emphasizing Jewish peoplehood over denominational identity, the denominations would strengthen the very Jewish community they were created to serve and ultimately reap the benefits as more and larger congregations turned to them for guidance and assistance. People would begin to see them as part of the solution rather than part of the problem, and their influence would increase proportionately.

Among the basic tenets of the emerging field of leadership studies is that no one style of leadership is best for all kinds of situations. The Jewish world has changed dramatically in the past half century, and the demand for denominational allegiance that may have once made sense no longer resonates with the majority of American Jewry. Although the movements have made some important changes reactively, it is time for them to do much more than guard their turf. The American Jewish community needs them to place a higher priority on its universal challenges than on their particular concerns and to provide the leadership we need and deserve.

CHAPTER 14

Challenges to Jewish Community

Judy Beck

As director of a Synagogue Leadership Initiative at UJA Federation of Northern New Jersey in the suburbs of a large metropolitan Jewish community, I face the challenge of creating community in a service area where it often appears that the issues that divide American Jews denominationally seem to be greater than those that unite us. Two separate rabbinic boards are making the proverbial "Shabbat for themselves," and only a few very brave Orthodox rabbis seem to be able to bridge the denominational divide. They face being called inauthentic and marginalized by their more right-wing colleagues. I meet regularly with Conservative and Reform rabbis in the community and can see the pain on their faces when their Orthodox colleagues do not consider them authentically rabbinic, and yet they also cannot get beyond their own denominational differences. On behalf of female rabbis who serve in communal agencies, I have disseminated e-mails about social service programs, with the stipulation from these rabbis that their names be deleted from the announcement. They fear the Orthodox community might be offended by their rabbinic title and therefore might not patronize the social service agency they represent.

Obstacles to *Amcha*

Recently, I was asked to be a consultant for a congregation that was doing a strategic plan. One of the major issues that drove them was the perception that they might not be sufficiently Orthodox, which could have an impact upon their children whose prospects for marriage partners might therefore be limited in some elements of the Orthodox community.

From my vantage point, these symbolic but real issues have had deleterious effects on setting a Jewish communal agenda and enabling the broad community, including all of its sectors, to grow and flourish. Jewish education and outreach efforts are truncated because certain elements of the community feel "it is not our problem."

For years the galvanizing motto of the organized Jewish community was, We Are One. If the motto was ever true, for some segments of the community it is no longer so. We seem to be many different constituencies and communities. The issues that served to unite American Jews—anti-Semitism, the Shoah, the fate of Soviet Jews, the survival of Israel—are no longer viewed as central issues. The community has failed to find a new communal rallying point or to create an exciting vision to bring Jews together working for the common good. Therefore, we have reverted to our perceived winning strategies based upon self-interest and denominationalism that ultimately divide us.

As someone whose personal and professional life has been geared to collaboration and who grew up in a community where the Orthodox rabbi was out in the community recruiting unaffiliated Jewish public school students for Talmud Torah classes, where the Reform synagogue was the site for all Girl Scout activities, and where if you wanted to hear wonderful *chazzanut*, you could attend a Conservative or Orthodox synagogue in the neighborhood, this divisiveness causes me great angst. My perception is that the current state of denominationalism has more to do with the territoriality of the movements than the real needs of *amcha*, the broad collective of Jews.

Life-Cycle Needs

Several years ago, *The Jewish Journal* of Los Angeles reported the finding of a community demographic study done for the Jewish Federation of Los Angeles where mature individuals reported that in their Jewish journeys they had been members of several congregations. Conventional wisdom would suggest that these congregations would be of the same denominational stream. No. These individuals reported that they had been members of Orthodox, Conservative, Reform, and Reconstructionist congregations, although generally not at the same time. They joined congregations that most represented where they would fit ideologically at a particular moment in their lives. When they had moved on ideologically, they moved on to a new congregation.

Actually, that resonated with me. I remember the day in my childhood when my grandfather stated that he had decided to become Orthodox and change the pattern of his Jewish observance. The announcement was so momentous that I still remember it today. However, after my mother died he took my brother and me to the Conservative congregation so that I could say *kaddish*.

I decided to test my perception that denominationalism operates out of concern about turf more than concern for community by surveying a wide range of friends and acquaintances. The most unique response was the suggestion that there is no reason for denominations. The Jewish community should be restructured so that congregations are not denominationally connected but life cycle focused, meeting the needs of Jews at various stages in their lives. In this new framework, some congregations would be focused upon families with young children. When the children moved into the teen years the family would cycle into a congregation that had meaningful teen programming and would proceed to other congregations as life-cycle changes prompted them. While perhaps this is not a totally realistic proposal, it does reflect the reality that people at different stages of the life cycle have different needs, and that all institutions cannot be all things to all people.

After innumerable conversations, my unscientific focus group revealed that a congregation's denominational affiliation was not as important as other factors, as follows:

- The rabbi's vision is congruent with their view of the Jewish world and he or she has the ability to inspire them and reach out to them as individuals.
- The educational, social action, and social activities meet their needs and attract them.

- The Shabbat and holiday services are meaningful and spiritually fulfilling.
- The congregation is perceived as the place to be in the community.
- Their friends are going to a particular congregation, which has social ramifications as well as practical considerations such as car pooling.
- They sense that they are a part of a community that cares about them, and they care about the individuals in their community and love the social opportunities at the *Oneg Shabbat*, *kiddush*, or other activities.

It must be noted that the movement affiliation of a particular congregation does not necessarily define the attitudes and practices of its members. One cannot generalize and say "All Orthodox Jews do . . ." or "All Reform Jews do not . . ." In my discussion with a member of an Orthodox congregation, he indicated that he likes that service but then gets into his car after that Shabbat service is over and does whatever else is on his agenda. And then there is a Jew who had joined a Reform congregation because he thought it would require the least observance but is now kashering his kitchen. Then there is my Conservative friend who has children that span the spectrum from *ba'alei tshuvah* to unaffiliated and intermarried. These certainly are not atypical scenarios when one looks at Jewish communities across the country. Ultimately, even though many Jews tend to self-identify by the denominational affiliation of the institution they join or feel represents their attitudes, these people are much more than the dogma of that particular movement. They are individuals with desires, needs, and aspirations. As long as the congregation, of whatever stripe, reflects their worldview and meets their needs at that moment in time, these individuals will remain with that congregation without regard to its movement. The moment our needs—spiritual, educational, or social—are not being met or our worldview changes we move on.

An Evolving Whole

While the phenomenon of Chabad within the dynamics of the American Jewish community must be analyzed outside the framework of this essay, Chabad's proclaimed view of Jewish denominationalism as "A Jew is a Jew is a Jew" should be considered carefully. Peel away the outer layer of affiliation or lack of it and you find the *pintele yid*, the core elements of the Jewish soul, within so many who are unaffiliated or do not identify as Jews publicly. Each person represents one part of the Jewish whole, no matter where he or she is on the ladder of observance or nonobservance, religious belief or secular identity. All of us must be present at the Jewish table with all our variables.

Mordecai Kaplan, a Conservative rabbi whose first position was as rabbi of an Orthodox synagogue in New York, founder of the Young Israel movement in his early years, and then providing the philosophical cornerstone for Reconstructionism, was the one who posited that "Judaism is an evolving civilization." That concept would certainly recognize that movements in Jewish life have a legitimate place in expressing Jewish identity and varieties of Jewish expression at particular points in Jewish history. The question is how long do these labels remain relevant and how can individuals who choose to identify as "just Jewish" without labels be nurtured inclusively? The Jewish community must be unified by its commonalities and not separated by perceived differences. Only then will it grow and flourish.

CHAPTER 15

Does a Synagogue Need a Denomination?

Clifford Kulwin

I am a product of the Reform movement. I was born and grew up in a small midwestern city where the only synagogue was Reform. I was active in NFTY (North American Federation of Temple Youth), the Reform youth movement, kept up that affiliation while in college, and went to the Hebrew Union College, the Reform seminary. I served a Reform congregation in Brazil after ordination and became seduced by my fascination with the international Jewish community. For the next fifteen years, while devoting some time to a doctorate in Jewish history, I worked on behalf of the movement's international agency, for the last several years headings its efforts in countries outside of North America and Israel.

I dwell a bit upon my background because, on paper at least, I am not the one you would expect to be a spokesman for nondenominationalism. But that's precisely what I have become.

In the second half of 1998 an organizational restructuring took place, and it was time for me to seek a different professional direction. While several rabbinic positions available through the Reform Rabbinic Placement Commission looked interesting, all would have involved a significant relocation. Our family had lived in the same place for ten years, we had a large circle of friends, our children were comfortable, and quite simply, we did not want to move from the area.

Then, as if *bashert*, I received a phone call from a man whose name I did not know, calling on behalf of a synagogue I had never heard of—Temple B'nai Abraham in Livingston, New Jersey, close to my home. Their long-time rabbi was retiring, they were engaged in a search for a successor, and would I be interested in being considered for the position, he asked. I certainly was.

Temple B'nai Abraham, with nine-hundred member families, is, to the best of my knowledge, the largest, historically unaffiliated congregation in North America. The congregation was founded nearly 160 years ago in Newark, a split off from a Reform synagogue, which even today is just around the corner. Its founders wanted something slightly more traditional, and unsurprisingly, the congregation was an affiliate of the Conservative movement for much of its first century.

Change arrived in 1939 in the person of Joachim Prinz, a German rabbi who had taken his native country by storm, remaining there until well beyond the point he could count on his own personal safety. He was an intellectual and possessed eloquence and great charisma hardly matched among the rabbinate of his day. Although he was physically short, in an age in which congregational rabbis like Stephen Wise and Abba Hillel Silver led American Jewry, he towered above most of his peers.

If this description makes Prinz seem larger than life, he was and he had an ego to match. He did not like being part of someone else's framework. All this is important because one day, not long after he arrived in Newark, he said to his leadership regarding the Conservative movement, in essence if not verbatim, "What do you need them for? You have me!" The leadership, mesmerized by Prinz as it would be for some forty years, agreed, and about sixty years ago Temple B'nai Abraham disaffiliated from the Conservative movement, becoming the independent congregation it remains to this day.

Prinz remained rabbi of the synagogue until the mid-1970s. A long-time assistant rabbi, Barry Friedman, who, like me, was ordained at the Hebrew Union College, succeeded him. I succeeded Rabbi Friedman in 1999 and became the congregation's fourth rabbi in one hundred years.

I begin with this history for a reason. At Temple B'nai Abraham, its twentieth-century history begins with a history of its rabbinate. While, to put it mildly, the clergy is an important part of any congregation, it is especially so in the synagogue that does not have a label.

Being Independent and Unaffiliated

What does it mean to be an unaffiliated congregation? Let's first address what it means to be an affiliated congregation. Affiliation means that there is a label, which already tells one a good deal about the congregation before one walks in the door. It says something about the liturgy and the *minhag*; put another way, it says something about the nature of the congregation's services and even their possible length. Affiliation says something about when and how holidays will be observed, and the principles by which the congregation will conduct itself, and something about how the congregation sees itself politically in the Jewish and Zionist world. Obviously, many details can only be discovered through personal experience. But if all one knows about a given congregation is that one word that links it to a movement, then one already knows quite a bit.

But that's not the way it is with an independent congregation. Most of what we at Temple B'nai Abraham do is internally generated, sometimes to the point of exasperation. What *siddur* will we use? Should it include *musaf*? What will our food policy be? How do we approach issues of inclusiveness? Are we strict about synagogue weddings only after sundown at the end of Shabbat, even in summer? And what about weddings during *s'firat ha-omer*? Whom do we support in the World Zionist Organization elections? How do we determine who can be a member of the congregation?

The list goes on. Quite often, answering these questions can be laborious and frustrating. Happily, even more often, the process is both empowering and invigorating. Most of all, after hundreds of hours of board meetings and ritual committee meetings and officers' meetings, not once have I ever heard anyone lament the absence of a "higher" body to give us guidance. Everyone seems to agree we do just fine on our own.

These, of course, are some of the endless list of questions with which every synagogue grapples. But at Temple B'nai Abraham, we don't have a Rabbinical Assembly Committee on Jewish Law and Standards to guide us, we don't have a Union for Reform Judaism convention at which the president presents a policy agenda that we are expected to support, and we don't have a Jewish Reconstructionist Federation that promotes a certain sense of congregational feeling. We have our history, and we have ourselves. We are not a part of any external framework, something that many visitors have trouble comprehending. We are engaged in the ongoing act of self-definition in which every synagogue is engaged . . . just that for us, it is more so.

This lack of denomination puts special pressure upon the clergy. In a way that I think is unique, we are called upon to define the congregation and set its direction. Prinz brought independence to Temple B'nai Abraham, and he and his successors have engaged in a kind of clergy-lay partnership that I think does not exist in most other congregations simply because it does not need to. There a context exists, established by a synagogue's decision about where to affiliate. That doesn't answer all questions, of course, but it answers many.

To be sure, by not being affiliated, our congregation misses certain things. However, those things have to do with practical matters rather than issues of identity. We do not, for example, have a youth group associated with a national synagogue youth movement like North American Federation of Temple Youth or United Synagogue Youth. A few years ago we began hosting the local BBYO chapter and that has been a positive move, though its goals are not as in sync with ours as those of a synagogue youth movement would be. Nevertheless, it works just fine and seems to meet our needs for positive Jewish teen programming.

The key drawback, potentially quite serious, is that the denominations for the most part shut us out of their placement processes. We cannot advertise the professional openings the congregation has through any movement, which means that professionals— particularly rabbis, cantors, and educators—who are part of a movement are not only strongly discouraged from applying for professional positions with us but also may well face sanctions if they do so.

The movements take this seriously, and the reality is that the denominational professional associations of rabbis (and to a lesser extent cantors, educators, and synagogue administrators), who should be advancing the professional training of their members and promoting the philosophic approaches of their agendas, have taken on the characteristics of closed union shops that play hard-ball with anyone who deviates from their rules. If a professional seeks employment outside these frameworks, regaining the benefits of the system is very difficult if not impossible. One may well lose access to pension and insurance programs that are so significant in the contemporary professional world.

It is important to note that these two areas where not being af-filiated is a handicap have nothing to do with ideology or identity or belief or practice, but are organizational. To varying degrees, the movement institutions, whether one speaks of the seminaries, the professional associations, or the congregational organizations, have deliberately put up barriers. They have decided that a high wall of protection best serves their interests.

What Matters to People

Not having a youth group as part of a national synagogue youth organization is lamentable. Not being able to have official and often unofficial access to a pool of fine professionals is a serious handicap; and such things as advisory services or affinity group-ings of lay leaders would be useful. But we have managed to de-velop reasonable alternatives that work for us even if the process is not always completely smooth. However, while these issues and others enable us to be unaffiliated, the reason we are not missing out by being unaffiliated is somewhat different; to our members, and to those who would be our members, it just doesn't matter.

This took me a long time to learn. For forty years I thought of myself as a particular kind of Jew. Pretty much everyone around me thought of themselves as that same kind of Jew; but I never had reason to wonder if that was true of Jews as a whole.

Over the last several years I have had reason to wonder and I have come to a conclusion. For a large majority of non-Orthodox Jews, denominational labels, as an identity badge, are not impor-tant, and perhaps even irrelevant.

What do Jews want from a synagogue? They seek a Jewish place where they feel comfortable, where they feel safe, where they feel part of a community. They want to be with people they like, to be led by clergy they respect. By and large, they are not interested in labels.

This lesson was first taught me by the rabbi of the large Conservative synagogue in town, with whom I had lunch shortly after coming to Temple B'nai Abraham. In those days I still saw things through movement eyes and had not quite grasped what Temple B'nai Abraham was or could be. I said to him, "It must be nice to have a congregation of members who believe what you believe, who are part of a consistent ideological stream." He set me straight. "Don't be ridiculous," he said. "That may be true of 20 percent of the membership. But most of them came in through our nursery school and felt comfortable; they came in because friends were here and felt comfortable; they came in off the street and felt comfortable. For 80 percent of them, the fact that it was a Conservative temple in which they felt comfortable was happenstance."

I have come to believe he was correct. And if I sound guilty of the crime of "no saint like a reformed sinner," well, guilty as charged, and I am getting worse. Often, I have trouble reading movement magazines or other literature, because so much of it seems to be about the importance of getting people to live, for example, as "an authentic Reform Jew," as opposed to authentically as "a" Jew. This creates more walls rather than broader space of inclusion.

I know I am being simplistic. The movements' institutions and leaders are the source of much of the creativity and dynamism that animates Jewish life today. I also realize that because of what, for simplicity's sake, might be labeled "marketing reasons," they have to run a tight ship.

Nonetheless, I cannot help but think that if a mainstream congregation like Temple B'nai Abraham can, as it has for over half a century, flourish without a label, with healthy representation all along the age spectrum, with dynamism and verve, and, in a Jewish community of more than one hundred thousand, with more members in communal leadership roles than any other synagogue, then one has to wonder: Are denominations necessary? That is too big a question to take on here, but perhaps the question can be refocused for this discussion.

Is the denominational system as it exists today the best and most meaningful way to serve America's Jews? I simply say this: for at least one congregation and probably many others, the answer is probably no. Clearly, for reasons both ideological and practical, like-minded congregations need to work together for mutual support, learning, and creativity. But if my own belief is correct that denominational labels are not the main reason Jews join a particular synagogue, then Jewish community leaders should have the courage to imagine if there are ways of working together that might be done with greater effect on Jewish life. I believe that our community will not get there by continuing to rely on the institutional structures and frameworks that are, by now, many decades old. However, discussions like this are an excellent first step.

CHAPTER 16

Same Shul, New Shul
Affiliation and Focus

Cheri Scheff Levitan

The founders of Congregation B'nai Torah in suburban Atlanta were probably very similar to the founders of many other synagogues before them. They had a vision of building a spiritual and religious home where they and others could share Jewish philosophy, values, and practices. They settled in a geographic area with a growing Jewish population, raised the funds necessary to erect a building, and established the congregation's place in the community. Then the lay leadership sought rabbinic and other professional staff who would help them actualize their vision.

However, the initial impetus to establish a congregation or other voluntary institution is often far easier than managing its growth, maintaining its stability, and confronting its changing needs. After a decade-and-a-half of success, B'nai Torah found itself facing a series of challenges. An aging membership, financial instability, uncertain rabbinic leadership, and an identity crisis all promised to threaten the synagogue's future viability. These factors and others called for a dramatic strategic plan that would alter the downward-spiraling path upon which the congregation found itself. If the synagogue were to become a thriving, multigenerational congregation, it would have to reinvent itself and find new direction and identity.

Issues of Changing Demographics, Identity, and Leadership

Congregation B'nai Torah had been formed in 1981. The founding members, mostly raised with Orthodox backgrounds and traditions, established and maintained a synagogue committed to the ritual and worship practices of Traditional Judaism, with the exception of mixed seating. They had a strong desire to be independent and chose not to affiliate with any national organization. Through the course of twenty years, B'nai Torah's membership steadily rose to an all-time high of 540 member units.

In 1996, however, the Atlanta Jewish community started to change. The Jewish population began to grow steadily and spread out geographically. This growth translated into increased demand for new Jewish day schools, preschools, elder care services, community center programs, and synagogues. Over the next seven years, B'nai Torah struggled against the tide of change. Its membership dropped to 420; religious school enrollments plummeted; day school children, post B'nai Mitzvah teenagers, and their families slowly began to disengage from synagogue life; the rabbinic leadership floundered; and the lay leaders were at a loss.

I became president of B'nai Torah's board of trustees in June 2003 and began to analyze possible reasons for the synagogue's downward trends. Two main causes emerged. First and foremost, the congregation was suffering from an identity crisis. The public self-definition of "Traditional, with the exception of mixed seating" conflicted with the actual observance patterns of the majority of the members. For example, less than 25 percent of the congregation observed the laws of *kashrut* and less than 20 percent observed Shabbat or attended services regularly. The Jewish community saw the synagogue as positioned to the left of the Modern Orthodox world and to the right of the Conservative one, but the reality of its members was quite different. In addition, a steady growth of dissatisfaction among the membership and new levels of self-awareness gave rise to questions about the congregation's religious practices, philosophy, and future viability.

The second issue, exacerbating the first, involved the inability of the then rabbi to connect with or engage existing or prospective members. The growing lack of confidence in rabbinic leadership actually began in the last few years of the founding rabbi's eighteen-year tenure and continued through the third rabbi's term. The decision to discontinue a relationship with a rabbi is never easy, and the inevitability of launching a search for a new rabbi is never embraced with joy, but the board of trustees and I decided that engaging strong, focused leadership was the only way to begin turning things around.

A special meeting of the congregation was called to explain why the board of trustees voted to let the rabbi's three-year contract expire without renewal or extension; emotions ran high and many people expressed a range of strong feelings on the subject. While the rabbi at that time was a wonderful teacher and had a beautiful voice for leading services, he lacked the interpersonal and leadership skills necessary to engage the membership and help stimulate growth. By the end of the discussion, the main concern surrounded the anticipated difficulties and potential challenges of finding a rabbi who could really meet the needs of this very traditionally oriented congregation and move it forward.

The prospect of searching for a new rabbi and beginning to address the synagogue's concerns meant answering some important questions: Should we search for a rabbi with an Orthodox or a Conservative ordination? Would affiliating with a particular denominational movement help us define and embrace changes that we realized would be necessary to stimulate the renewal of the congregation? A committee was assembled to examine the pros and cons of affiliation. Focus groups and surveys of the members were conducted, and fact finding ensued. The national Orthodox, Traditional, and Conservative movements were all investigated. It became obvious to us that the answer for us was to join the Conservative movement.

Affiliation and Independence

The regional director of the United Synagogue of Conservative Judaism (USCJ) for the Southeast was invited to attend a meeting of the board and a subsequent town hall meeting with the congregation in August 2003. He made it clear that the Conservative movement could address that majority of the congregation's needs, including the following:

- Reconnecting young children and teenagers to synagogue life;
- More support systems and resources for lay leadership;

- Access to a pool of qualified rabbinic candidates;
- The desire for more creative programming and education;
- Ways to acquire professional development and administrative support; and
- Gaining access to regional or national organizations' programs and resources that would facilitate engaging various membership demographics.

The key discussion, however, involved B'nai Torah's ability to retain traditional ritual practices—full Torah readings, full repetitions of the *Amidah*, not counting women for a *minyan*, and so forth—while being a member of this movement. Although the movement promoted egalitarian practices, the director pointed out that other congregations like B'nai Torah existed, especially in Canada where such congregations were more the norm than the exception.

That November the congregation voted to affiliate with the United Synagogue of Conservative Judaism, with the understanding that no change would be made to the congregation's basic ritual practices and stated philosophy. The congregation did not bring the question of becoming egalitarian for any real discussion or vote. The overall hope, as a result of the vote on joining United Synagogue, was that this new association potentially could enrich and enhance the Jewish quality of our spiritual, social, educational, and family lives without sacrificing the values and patterns of observance that B'nai Torah had maintained with little change since its founding. Although this new direction appealed to many of the founders who considered themselves "traditionalist," some others did leave to join Orthodox congregations. B'nai Torah became Atlanta's newest Conservative synagogue with its unique traditional niche.

The search for a new rabbi began immediately with a trip to New York to meet with the director of the Joint Commission on Rabbinic Placement. The rabbi's advice and encouragement sent me back home full of optimism, armed with a how-to guide, and filled with clarity of purpose and process. I was confident that B'nai Torah was going to find the right rabbi! The search process went very smoothly and introduced us to some wonderfully qualified candidates. It enabled us to find a rabbi who would help our *shul* grow and flourish. On March 31, 2004, only three months after submitting our placement application to the Rabbinical Assembly, the congregation voted to engage its new rabbi, who accepted the position of spiritual leader and *mara d'atra* of B'nai Torah, effective July 1, 2004.

In addition to assistance with conducting a search, the staff and resources of USCJ helped us refocus our congregation's priorities and the way we function. We developed a new vision of our religious school and started a Kadima preteen youth group. A senior USCJ staff member was helpful in the areas of leadership development and congregational programming. Our executive director attended the convention of the North American Association of Synagogue Executives and returned with exciting new programs. Our Sisterhood joined the Women's League for Conservative Judaism and our Brotherhood joined the Federation of Jewish Men's Clubs. Their leadership groups returned from regional conferences both enthused and enriched with the ideas that were shared with them.

During that year Congregation B'nai Torah learned a great deal about our goals and ourselves. The needs of our community had shifted and a vision that once seemed so crystal clear had become blurred. We realized that we had been standing still, watching, as our young people moved toward other options that better satisfied their religious expectations and family needs, and we had been paralyzed. But our decision to join the Conservative movement, combined with our own experience and traditions that gave us roots, maturity, wisdom, and faith, enabled us to create a new legacy for the future. This transition gave us the insight and courage to implement fresh ideas and try new things. Utilizing a new support structure that we gained by joining the Conservative movement, we are better able to work together to recreate the energy and dreams that had been the foundation of our original spiritual home.

Three-and-a-half years later, in January 2008, after a process of study and serious discussion under the leadership of our rabbi, Congregation B'nai Torah voted to become more inclusive of women in ritual practices through a process that will evolve over time. Membership has grown to about 625 member units through the addition of numerous young families. The religious school is growing and the youth group programs are flourishing. The board is made up of many younger faces, and leadership development is at the top of its agenda. Finally, the strategic planning committee has determined that a modernization and expansion of the facility and the addition of a second clergy person are necessary to support the growth and changing needs of the congregation. B'nai Torah and its rabbi have become a dynamic central presence in the Atlanta Jewish community.

CHAPTER 17

The TBZ Story

Moshe Waldoks

The rejuvenation of Temple Beth Zion (TBZ), a moribund Conservative synagogue in Brookline, Massachusetts, into a vibrant independent congregation offers a model in achieving success beyond denominational labels and parameters.

Denominationalism may have served its purpose in the early and middle years of the twentieth century, but these models, which for the most part emerged out of the German Jewish experience, did a disservice to the vast majority of Eastern Europeans Jews who came to the United States between 1880 and 1924. The tripartite division of Jewish life in nineteenth-century Eastern Europe was less Orthodox, Conservative, and Reform than traditional, maskilic, and revolutionary. Within each of these divisions, it was possible to maintain still other distinctions: traditional—hasidic or mitnagdic; maskilic—observant or nonobservant Hebraist or Yiddishist; revolutionary—socialist or communist, Bundist or Zionist. While strands of all of these aspects of Eastern European Jewish life were maintained in the United States in various ways, the pressure of denominational affiliation ultimately defined and possibly narrowed the big tent of Jewish life that postdenominational or nondenominational Jewish life can offer.

Integral Judaism

Independent Jewish congregations continue to appear throughout the Jewish world. They are the models in the necessary transformation of the synagogue into its newest and most important role, as *centers for integral Judaism*, a Judaism not divorced from our core identities. These centers will be inviting to Jews who are looking for a community without labels, who are seeking a home where they may bring all of themselves and find an environment where they can integrate all of their disparate parts. In the Jewish community, few addresses other than the transformed synagogue offer this opportunity. For most Jews, the questions they have are answered by local Jewish institutions, not specific denominational forms of Judaism.

The power of synagogues lies in their ability to provide the platform and vantage point to decipher the complicated nature of the world and its vagaries. The removal of "turf" is a prerequisite for the synagogue to continue to be the direct delivery system of access to Jewish traditions, their beauty, and their complexity.

A New Kind of Synagogue

There are no easy answers to the opportunities and dilemmas that freedom provides us in the United States and in the State of Israel. One positive response can be the collapsing of the denominations into a newly reconstituted Jewish people and redefined independent synagogue.

TBZ is a model of trying to create a community that is not defined by any adjective other than Jewish. The place of the charismatic rabbi is often central, but not always necessary, to the establishment of an independent congregation. In the case of TBZ, my role consisted of facilitator and motivator of intensive Jewish experiences through study and prayer. My ordination emphasized the "rebbe" aspect rather than the "*rav*" aspect of my leadership.[1] I often quipped that if you were looking for a rabbi to tell you if a chicken was kosher or not, I could refer you to a rabbi who does that, but if you are having a relationship with a chicken, come and talk to me. Along with the rabbi, TBZ brought together a wide array of individuals from different backgrounds eager to establish a community that went beyond the usual labels and expectations. The style of this lay group could be characterized as "chaordic," that is, over a rumble of chaos order was maintained. The bubbling up of ideas from the bottom to the top, the creation of a consensus model of governance whenever possible, and the commitment of lay leadership to experimentation served the vibrancy of the TBZ transformation well. The lack of synagogue experience in most of these lay leaders was an important asset. This ability to see new things without preconceived notions added to the vitality of the TBZ transformation. We have capitalized on the nature and quality of the people we attracted.

The congregation began to grow quickly once we made it clear that we would not be affiliated with any of the existing Jewish movements. The Brookline community already had a fair representation of all of the denominational synagogues: two Reform, two Orthodox (hasidic and modern), and one Conservative. Surrounding areas provided both Reconstructionist and Renewal alternatives as well. Certainly, there was room for another congregation that would appeal to those who did not find full satisfaction in any of these choices.

When I began my part-time employment in January of 1998, the congregation had approximately 50 elderly members, with 12 or so of them actively involved in maintaining the congregation. By 2007 the congregation had grown to more than 600 individual members and approximately 140 children, including approximately 175 single units and 200 family units. Family units run the gamut of definitions and parameters: single parents, gay couples, elderly couples, families with children, and couples without children.

The older leadership of Temple Beth Zion, predominantly one or two members who were children of the original founders, had mixed feelings about giving up on revitalizing the synagogue as a traditional, preegalitarian Conservative *shul*. This led to a period of eighteen months or so when I officiated once a month at a "straight" *davvenning* and once a month at what was then called a Nishmat Hayyim service. The other two weeks were lay led.

Soon it became clear that the Nishmat Hayyim services were growing while the traditional services remained stagnant. Seeing that change was on the way, a number of the older members began to feel threatened and voiced their dissatisfaction, particularly at the laxity in the dress code on the Nishmat Hayyim Shabbats. The regulars attended services every week. They were also showing concern about the introduction of women into key roles in the services. A few of these members departed, others adjusted, and still others became strong supporters of our revitalization project. We are still blessed today by regular attendees in their eighties and nineties.

From Spectators to Participants

If any thread continues throughout the decade of TBZ transformation, it is the enhancement of the *tefillah* experience from a spectator model into a participatory and accessible model. This was helped greatly by reorganizing the physical structure of the sanctuary. The process was a difficult one, pitting old timers against newer members. For a period of time the sanctuary was only halfway "de-pewed." By the end of 2003 the entire sanctuary reflected the new TBZ attitude: accessibility. Partitions between the *bimah* and the congregation were removed, the reading table went down onto the sanctuary floor. The rabbi and officers sat among the congregation rather that over and above them.

Physical accessibility was an important aspect of the congregation's transformation and growth. A handicap accessible entrance and elevator were constructed that obviated the need to climb a steep staircase at the front of the building. Another important improvement was installing air conditioning in the sanctuary. As of the fall of 2007, we have raised more than a million dollars in the three renovation campaigns we have run.

Another example of accessibility was the decision to keep dues low and to provide abatements when necessary. The motivation for this was to maintain and encourage diversity in the congregation. The annual *Kol Nidrei* appeal looks to those with greater means to make up for those with lesser means. So far this deficit-defeating measure has been successful. In the fall of 2007 we were able to hire an assistant rabbi to help develop our family education programming.

Accessibility also meant choosing the right *siddur*, *humash*, and *mahzor*. For Friday night and the high holidays we created our own prayer books. For Shabbat and festival mornings we decided on *Siddur Hadash* (A New Prayer Book, published by Prayerbook Press), mainly because of its gender-neutral translation and many transliterations. We did not assume our congregants were all fluent in Hebrew. We also introduced as much communal singing as possible so that within a short time the basic service would become familiar to regular attendees.

Transforming Worship

But the most important part of the transformation was to be found in the services themselves. The rabbi starts the service with a meditation, sitting on a stool in front of the reading table facing the congregation. This introduction of meditative practice was invaluable in giving the *mitpallelim* the notion that *l'hitpallel* was indeed a reflective act, and that it was necessary to balance the transcendent nature of the *tefillot* with the immanence of listening to the small, still voice within. With the concentration on *neshima*, one could be in touch with the *neshama*.

Meditation leads to chanting, first in English, "Holy One of Blessing—Your Presence fills creation," then either to candle lighting all together on Friday night or other appropriate parts of the liturgy.

Our Friday night siddur incorporates meditations on the text written by Rabbis Rami Shapiro, David Wolfe Blank *z"l*, and Zalman Schachter-Shalomi. Many of these meditations amplify the nature of the Ineffable and the limitations of language to encapsulate the experience of the Divine. Every service offers *kavannot*. On Friday nights, the service includes an opportunity to do a *heshbon hashavuah*—a way of retrieving the positive from each day of the previous week and jettisoning the negative—to bring into Shabbat the gift of our best selves to *Shabbat Hamalka*, the consort of the Jewish people. We frame the hymn "*Lecha Dodi*" as a wedding celebration and an opportunity for enthusiastic singing and dancing.

Encouraging participants to leave their seats on a number of occasions during the service is vital and enhances the psalmist's notion that all of our limbs be actively involved in prayer and praise. We have also instituted a movement to fill the inner parts of the sanctuary during the silent meditation by offering congregants the opportunity to position themselves in front of either one of two magnificent quilts representing the kabbalistic notions of *hesed* and *gevurah*. Services are often capped by introductions of visitors and the practice of congregants blessing each other with the *birkat kohanim*.

Shabbat Torah services are marked by group *aliyot* based on content of the Torah readings that morning. This is another opportunity for getting congregants to be more active and less passive.

A Nexus of Tradition and Creativity

By being an independent congregation, we have leeway to be as creative or as traditional as we want to be. While this may be true of denominational congregations, we at TBZ have found it to be one of its motivating principles. TBZ has made its mark in this nexus of tradition and creativity. We are, in a sense, a feminist-hasidic shul, a *shteibel*, if you will. For some, this is a contradiction in terms. We also see ourselves as an unorthodox shul where attendees are open to surprises.

Could all of this have been done within a conventional denominational structure? Perhaps, but I doubt it for a number of reasons. The first is the most obvious—not being attached to any specific denomination immediately removed many preconceived notions of the way things should be. Second, it removed, for many, the discomfort they had experienced in the denominations they had grown up in and no longer felt attached to. This removal of a turf definition was vital in getting many of our congregants through the door. Many had not been affiliated at all since leaving their home of origin; others were seekers searching for more intensity than they found in conventional settings. Third, the absence of denominational affiliation allowed many congregants to feel more confident in articulating their Jewish worldviews, especially when they veered away from the denominational doctrines of their upbringing. A significant number of congregants had sought spiritual sustenance in other traditions (for example, Buddhism) before "returning" home. My acceptance of all those who had sought their connections elsewhere and a lack of judgment about their journeys added to the comfort felt by those seeking a spiritual home within Judaism.

For many of my congregants, the question that TBZ's independence answers is, Why be Jewish? When I was growing up in the 1950s and '60s, the question was how to be Jewish. This search for meaning overrides any specific practices they will or will not take on. For most of my congregants, their belonging to an independent shul is a boost to their own sense of Jewish choice—the capacity to make intelligent choices in an ever-widening marketplace of ideas.

Another hallmark of TBZ has been its emphasis on Jewish learning with a wide and open lens. We study the entire gamut of Jewish expression. We are aware of the theological and practical nuances of the movements, but urge our congregants to reach their own opinions. As in many liberal congregations, we avoid doctrinarism. This is reflected in our weekly Shabbat Torah study where we offer a multifaceted awareness of Torah and its multidimensionality. While choosing the Conservative movement's *Etz Hayyim* (Tree of Life, published by the Jewish Publication Society) as our humash, we bring in commentaries from a variety of sources and leave our sessions often with more questions than when we began. This vital, unending questioning is the hallmark of our interpretative tradition.

As we approach the end of the first decade of a century inaugurated by the attacks of September 11, 2001, the congregation is grappling with redefining our community parameters. Recent studies have pointed to the generation of Jews in their twenties eager for Jewish expression, primarily through Jewish versions of American popular culture, in venues other than the synagogue or the Jewish community center. The phenomenon of "nightclub" Jewish gatherings raises still new challenges to the synagogue as both *beit tefillah* and *beit midrash*. While the synagogue cannot be all things to all people, it is possible to reintegrate the roles it plays in community building for twenty-somethings as they marry (later and later) and look for a rootedness not possible through one-time, feel-good entertainment events. Within the postdenominational synagogue, future generations of Jews will find their opportunity to continue shaping and reshaping our tradition. In the spirit of *netzach yisrael lo-yishaker*, the eternity of Israel is no falsehood; the Jewish people will continue to transform itself.

PART 5

Independents and the Transitional Generation

CHAPTER 18

A New Generation of Seekers

Zachary I. Heller

In the late 1960s and through the 1970s, American Jewry witnessed the founding of the *havurah* movement. Independent groups, mostly of young people, sought greater freedom of expression in prayer, expanded settings for the study and exploration of texts, and heightened opportunities for spiritual exploration and devotion in a more intimate and informal communal setting than what was to be found in the synagogues of the existing movements or denominations.[1] While the National Havurah Committee continues to coordinate the activities of groups whose roots, if not actual history, can be traced back to those founded in and by an earlier generation, history often has a way of repeating itself in a cyclical manner.[2] A generation later, in the first decade of the twenty-first century, a similar attempt has arisen. Independent groups are creating more intimate settings that give expression to the religious needs of a new generation of seekers. In some ways this development is a throwback to the prayer rooms known as *shteiblach*. These prayer rooms were often the locus for worship for an early Jewish immigrant generation or for Hassidic groups that needed a local place of daily worship, other than the center of their Hassidic dynasty's rabbinic court where they gathered only on special occasions.

These independent *minyanim*, often known also as emergent spiritual or sacred communities, have begun to flourish in this decade.[3] The authors of the Synagogue 3000 (S3K) study of the phenomenon correctly note in their introduction that "these terms do not always capture the important variations within the broader category. Whatever these communities are called and whatever they call themselves, on one point of terminology they all seem to agree: they tend to avoid the term 'synagogue' and 'congregation,' thereby signaling their interest in differentiating themselves from previous generations' regnant form of local Jewish community building." By S3K's count, more than eighty communities founded since 1997, which may meet these basic criteria, are functioning with some regularity in the United States and Canada, with others identified in Israel and other countries.[4]

Characteristics of Emerging Spiritual Communities

These communities reflect several different approaches and conditions. One "set" of these emerging independent communities can be described as groups of young people, generally in their twenties and thirties, and generally the products of the day schools, youth groups, and summer camps of the Conservative and Reform movements. They seek to replicate the sense of intensity, knowledge, community, and fealty to tradition they experienced in their movements' educational institutions and programs. They claim that they do not find these ideal, or as others may say, "idealized," qualities in the synagogues in which they grew up or those in the urban settings in which they now live.

They are self-starters who look for a fully Hebraic service that follows the full rubric of the traditional service and generally is egalitarian in terms of gender. These groups sometimes attract participants from Orthodox families and educational training who opt for this type of service and worship community. With some exceptions, the groups are lay led. As they grow, they find rabbis and teachers of their own generation who become their teachers and educational resources, but generally these teachers do not assume a formal rabbinical position.

Some products of the Reform movement join these traditionally oriented groups. Others have started their own groups that mirror aspects of their experience in Reform camps and programs, or they have joined those seeking their own path in creating more experimental settings.

A second set of these emerging independent communities are those groups whose members are predominantly from Orthodox backgrounds and education. These groups are attempting to push the boundaries of Orthodox practice regarding gender while maintaining their adherence to what they view as accepted Modern Orthodox approaches to traditional practice. They are often modeled after a prayer group in Jerusalem founded by Tova Hartman, known as Shirah Hadasha.[5]

This phenomenon maintains the separation of the sexes during prayer with only a low divider, but places the reading table in the middle at the front of the setting so that both sides have equal access. Women are permitted and encouraged to lead some parts of the service, have *aliyot*, and read from the Torah scroll, as well as perform other functions previously reserved only for men in traditional settings.

This type of group has become enough of a phenomenon that two young Israeli scholars, Michal and Elitzur Bar-Asher, currently studying and teaching in the United States, were approached to do a serious study of classic and recent literature and prepare a resource. They wrote *Guide for the "Halachic Minyan"* for such groups, delineating the parameters and practical guidelines for such services, and it has been circulated to many of these groups.[6]

While the first two typologies indicate a specific orientation that brought many of these groups together, a third type of emerging Jewish community includes those that started with little definition but a generally traditional orientation. These groups wanted to bring young Jews together in rather uncharted territory and develop a prayer group that would find its own direction based upon common agreement. One such minyan in San Francisco (Mission Minyan) has not two but three seating sections with separations—one for women only, one for men only, and one for mixed seating—somewhat reminiscent of many early twentieth-century Conservative synagogues that tried to please multiple constituencies by providing different options for them.

Several other emerging spiritual communities have organized around the charismatic personality of a potential rabbinic leader. Often these are Jews in the community who have been distanced from Jewish observance and synagogue participation. In their view, a denominational identity would be the kiss of death for a nascent congregation. They are attracted by warm and inviting worship combined with study and an active social action program. What distinguishes these communities from a regular denominationally affiliated congregation? Here too we find the informal organizing structure, the opportunity for charting their own course, selecting their own emphasis, but with the guidance of a rabbi.[7]

Variations on these themes exist; for example, communities whose programs generally do not have a primary focus on worship but seek to bring together groups of young people for Jewish experiences. Some of them have the support of existing religious institutions and communal agencies and their professional staffs.[8]

A final type to consider, Kehillat Hadar, is one of the original groups often viewed as an archetype of the emergent Jewish communities. An egalitarian worship and study group that meets biweekly on the Upper West Side of Manhattan, Kehillat Hadar has expanded its horizons in several directions. Mechon Hadar (the Hadar Institute) is devoted to "revitaliz[ing] communal life—animated by prayer, study, and social action—among young Jews in America. Mechon Hadar offers Jews the opportunity to deepen their learning, broaden their skills, and intensify their experiences on the road to enhancing their Jewish lives and building stronger Jewish communities." Mechon Hadar has launched two major initiatives: The Minyan Project that "provides education, consulting and networking for independent prayer communities" and Yeshivat Hadar, "a full-time community open to men and women looking to engage in intensive Torah study, prayer and social action." The latter is geared to intensive adult study for personal enrichment rather than professional career preparation. Mechon Hadar anticipates that Yeshivat Hadar will be expanded from a current eight-week summer study program to a year-round opportunity as of September 2009.[9]

Professor Jonathan Sarna, eminent scholar of American Jewish History at Brandeis University, succinctly summarizes this phenomenon when he suggests that Hadar and similar emergent Jewish communities are the products of several factors in American Judaism: (a) the development of a highly educated laity in the Orthodox world; (b) the intensive study of texts in the growing day school movement of the Modern Orthodox, Conservative, and even Reform movements; (c) the egalitarianism that had its origins in the non-Orthodox world but has had a ripple effect in Modern Orthodoxy as well; and (d) the effects of intensive summer camp and youth group experiences and experiences of study in Israel. It must be noted that these emergent communities and groups, unlike their antecedents, purposely steer clear of any denominational identification and affiliation.[10]

At the annual meeting of the Association for Jewish Studies, held in San Diego in December 2006, Professor Riv-Ellen Prell of the University of Minnesota opened her remarks at a roundtable discussion of this subject with the following anecdote:

> A fall 2006 issue of the *Jewish Daily Forward* featured a personals advertisement which caught my eye because the word *havurah* appeared in it. Rather than simply presenting himself as a SJM (single Jewish male) or DJM (divorced Jewish male), this hopeful candidate described himself in terms of his desire to find a woman who shared his interest in havurah-style worship, and commitment to community outside the boundaries of traditional denominations or congregational life. I begin with this example in order to affirm that the issue that scholars variously describe as post-denominationalism or trans-denominationalism has powerful resonance. The advertisement makes clear that Jews and Christians not only create new forms of community and join different configurations of religious associations; they also identify with them, define themselves in terms of them, and in a deeply personal way seek out love in relationship to them.[11]

Personal Commitment—A Critical Factor

Among the important implications of these groups are that young people, who generally do not take synagogue membership seriously until later in life, have now begun seeking a venue for Jewish religious expression for which they take personal responsibility. In most cases, they share in sustaining it financially through dues that are substantially less than those of the synagogues of their youth, which were paid by their parents, or those of local formal congregations that maintain a building and a professional staff. Second, as this generation of seekers moves out of its current neighborhoods, where they live amidst a generational culture, they will carry what they develop with them. In their new suburban neighborhoods or other locations, where they will find room to raise families or will be closer to employment, they may seek to transfer the ethos and newly minted traditions of these emerging independent minyanim to the synagogues and schools available to them. If those institutions are not hospitable to them and willing to accept their openness, their values and norms of behavior, then, this observer is willing to predict, they will seek to replicate what they have been party to. They will find new outlets for the values and norms that they and others have found so compelling. That scenario will challenge the established synagogues of all movements, not by virtue of the numbers these young people represent, but by virtue of the quality of their Jewish expression and their leadership potential.[12]

CHAPTER 19

On Independent Jewish Communities and the Movements

Gordon Tucker

Long ago, the Talmud (in Yevamot 14a) tried to deal with the reality of diverse Jewish communities that adhered to different practices. Having accepted as fact that the schools of Shammai and Hillel acted on their incompatible interpretations of Jewish law, the Talmud asked this question: does this not violate the accepted understanding of Deuteronomy 14:1, according to which there is not to be sectarianism within the Jewish people? The answer the Talmudic sages gave, given their reality, could hardly have been yes. And in truth, the Talmud there exonerates communities that choose their own religious authorities and practices from the charge of destructive sectarianism, provided that each locus of authority is itself coherent and not riven by irresoluble dissent. That discussion raised the curtain on a tension that has probably never been absent from Jewish life ever since: the need for homogeneity that leads to communal coherence, on the one hand, and the natural tendency toward differentiation (and thus heterogeneity), on the other. How much of each should be balanced against the other? Back then, it seems, there was already a sense that too much of one would suppress creativity and evolutionary adaptation, and too much of the other would hopelessly splinter a nation that had lost its center-creating homeland.

Diversity and Cohesion: A Hoary Tension

I don't know that it is entirely correct to say, as we in the Jewish religious community are accustomed to do, that "movements" in Jewish life are a creation of the nineteenth century. For example, speaking of various philosophical and pietistic schools throughout the centuries as movements would seem to make sense. The same would be true for the "sects" of two millennia ago. (I use quotation marks because of the well-known phenomenon that no one identifies as a member of a sect. Just as a "clique" is a club that you *don't* belong to, so is a "sect" a *movement* that you don't belong to.) But let us in any event confine our attention for present purposes to the movements that did arise beginning in the nineteenth century, because they are the ones still with us. How shall we evaluate their contributions and their value today?

The conditions of modernity added their own twist to the age-old tension between diversity and cohesion. The rapid passing of premodernity's politically integral Jewish communities set into motion centrifugal forces strong enough to create two related needs: (1) the need for combined and concerted efforts, going beyond local communities, to counteract the potential alienation from Judaism that greater individual autonomy brought with it, and (2) the need for greater ideological definition, so as to make plausible the Jewish limits on autonomy that were being urged on these now modern Jews. And this is what the modern movements contributed to the Jewish landscape: local communities struggling with similar cultural and sociological trends felt a kinship with one another in their effort to sustain and stabilize a substantive Jewish life; and they had available a theological and philosophical footing on which to base the practices by which they were, in part, defined. To put it another way: the modern movements provided a way of accommodating, but also domesticating, the pull to diverse, autonomous religious expression as well as the pull to homogenization. They did this by creating broad coalitions, by providing some quasi-centralized thinking about shared goals and ideals, and by generating ideological discussions that, when done well, helped rationalize the concrete commitments urged upon coalition members. This was, and is, unquestionably a good thing, albeit not entirely unprecedented.

I must emphasize that this by no means solved all the problems traceable to the hoary tension between the desires for both diversity and cohesion. *Nothing will ever fully resolve that tension,* which constitutes religious societies, because that tension constitutes human societies generally. And thus, it is no surprise at all that the "conventional" movements of Jewish life today sometimes seem to be affording their member communities and individuals too much autonomy at the expense of better definition. It is no also surprise that they sometimes are thought to be attempting too much imposition of uniformity (for example, in liturgical publications). And finally, it is no surprise that they, often enough, are thought to be committing both errors simultaneously. Can you serve a core constituency and build up its commitment while at the same time successfully broadening the overall membership?

One example from my own recent experience will illustrate the incorrigibility of this age-old tension as it plays out within a single congregation. My (relatively large) Conservative synagogue participated a few years ago in the Synagogue 2000 program, a project intended to help congregations meet the special challenges of the twenty-first-century populations for which they would need to create spiritual homes. The program stressed two central goals: (1) making the synagogue a more spiritually fulfilling and uplifting place, and (2) making the synagogue a welcoming, user-friendly place, which would draw people in. It is not a stretch to say that most congregations found that the two desiderata were locked in tension with one another. To be spiritually fulfilling generally involves doing and promoting such things as singing the kinds of soulful melodies that are rarely the common heritage of the minimally initiated (that is, they are not the ones taught in religious school), allowing worshipers the time and space to intensify their involvement in prayer, and having a bare minimum of interruptions in the service's flow. All of these features are sought after and appreciated by a fairly homogeneous community that can assume a relatively common level of experience, competence, and commitment across individuals. On the other hand, being welcoming and user-friendly means always putting yourself into the minds of those who are not yet there, in terms of shared interests and skills. But being encouraging to heterogeneity in this way cannot fail to be a serious impediment to an atmosphere of spiritual depth. In my congregation, dealing with the tension was a continual challenge, though we did learn things from the experience.

Demographic Cohesion and Well-Defined Core Practices

Into this virtually inescapable landscape the "Indies"—the catchall term I will use from this point on for the independent *minyanim* and Jewish spiritual communities—have made their entrance. They have been enormously successful in building quickly a large constituency of young Jews, in augmenting both the skills and commitment of their members in impressive ways, and in attracting a good deal of attention within the Jewish world's leadership and funding cadres. Anyone who has experienced *davvenning* with these minyanim—or their study retreats and other educational, spiritual, and communal events—will testify to the vibrancy and energy that the Indies have generated for themselves. The envy that they have given rise to among the leaders of the more conventional institutions because of these achievements is, no doubt, a good thing. For envy among seekers of knowledge, we are told, increases wisdom; and the Indies have obviously discovered and exploited what have generally been elusive keys to the enthusiasm and engagement of significant numbers of young Jews with multiple talents and potentials.

One aspect of this particular success, however, seems to conform well to the dynamic that, I have argued, has been with the Jewish community for millennia. The Indies have, apparently, opted for the benefits that accrue from greater homogeneity, and have, in a way, bracketed the realities of multiplicity and diversity to be dealt with later. Recall that greater uniformity in a community generally gives an enormous boost to the possibilities of intensity and spirituality. And greater homogeneity is certainly enjoyed by most, if not all, of the emerging independent young communities. Note well: I do not at all suggest that individual members of the Indies are content to suppress their individualities in favor of some cookie-cutter image of an ideal Jew. On the contrary, the young people in question are among some of the best educated, most motivated, and most self-assured Jews we have ever created as a people. But I do want to note two important things: (1) some objective facts about the demographics in question and (2) the ways in which the Indies define *openness*.

On the first matter of demographics: In general, these emerging independent communities primarily consist of twenty-somethings (for this purpose, I also include people in their early thirties) who are either single or married, or otherwise partnered, with fewer than two children. These are the conditions under which maintaining a household in a Jewishly populated, energetic, and exciting urban area today is still widely possible (albeit with some financial stretching). Thus a much higher than usual degree of similarity in life experiences exists among members of the Indies, and that similarity tends to augment— even if subtly—some of the dynamics of peer influence. The result in each case is a community with an elevated level of cohesiveness; with respect to what adherents are seeking and what they bring to the quest (in both background and aspiration), that they are on the same page is far more the norm than the exception.

On the second matter of openness: The autonomy bestowed on all of us by modernity, and which is legitimately cherished especially by the demographic group described above, is surely a given. The way in which Indies have chosen to address that autonomy is as an opportunity to invite individuals to choose voluntarily to embrace the community's specific set of core practices. For example, if one such minyan were committed to egalitarian *davvenning*, it would advertise and project its openness to including anyone who also wishes to make that commitment. It would not, however, be anxious to have among its members a minority that has chosen them as their best fit, but that would actually prefer nonegalitarian *davvenning*. Such a minority would never, of course, be excluded. But they would quickly get the message that they would be happier at a minyan with core practices matching their own preferences. And this, note well, is a perfectly benign message in a milieu (remember, the Indie landscape is generally urban) in which other independent minyanim with competing practices not only can start up nearby, but the complementarity and competition that such a proliferation entails are also celebrated rather than resented.

What I have described in the previous paragraph is not a vulgar "our way or the highway" attitude. Far from it. Nor is it a hypocritical lip service to openness that is belied by practice. Not at all. This type of openness is a strategic decision to exploit all of the sociological factors before us today in order to maximize the real benefits that come from a greater homogeneity (as laid out earlier in this essay), and to encourage adherents to explore and deepen their commitments—and to express themselves—within the parameters of a well-defined set of core practices. And it can be done. Those to whom those core practices do not speak can find (or have found) communities of worship and study with core practices that they can comfortably call their own. This is because those same sociological factors (demographics, geography, educational realities, and so forth) provide ample opportunities to do so. The impressive—though as yet short-term—results of this strategic decision speak for themselves.

The Inevitable Forces of Heterogeneity

But now the following question arises: Are the Indies really so different *in kind* from the more conventional religious communities from which they distinguish themselves? As a thought experiment, consider a hypothetical description of a movement-affiliated synagogue, which I will call B'nai Israel. It is, perhaps, somewhat unusual, but hardly impossible to imagine. B'nai Israel is situated in an urban, or very close-in suburban, area with a sizable Jewish population and comprises several hundred families who have, in one way or another, come to believe in the approach to Jewish living and culture taught in the institutions of the Conservative movement. The adults in most of these families are in their early to midthirties with very young children and have histories at Conservative religious schools, Solomon Schechter Day Schools, United Synagogue Youth, Camp Ramah, the movement's Israel programs (including the Conservative Yeshiva in Jerusalem), and so on. Other families in the community have taken on this way of living without the early benefit of those institutions, because of their exposure to it through friends and their having found deep meaning in the beliefs and practices they now embrace. B'nai Israel has a high awareness of the life-enriching possibilities in observing *halakhah*, and thus nearly all the community's homes observe *kashrut* and Shabbat. Skills in worship abound, and services (which follow the Hebrew text of the Conservative *siddurim* and are egalitarian) are thus spirited, competently led not only by clergy but also by a broad cross section of the membership, and marked by uplifting music and meaningful teaching of Torah. Many regular educational opportunities are not only provided by professionals and lay members of the community, but also are well attended. And social action projects—inside the Jewish community and beyond—are also de rigueur.

A seemingly justifiable assumption would be that the segment of the twenty-something population that is today attracted to the Indies with similar core practices would be just as happy to be part of B'nai Israel. In other words, nothing in the movement affiliation of B'nai Israel would tend to negate its attractiveness to the population under consideration. B'nai Israel is a synagogue that, like most real synagogues, formed itself with a particular core community and some core practices in mind (the latter of which are often spelled out or referenced in bylaws), and grew over the years.

What makes B'nai Israel unusual (though not *impossible* to imagine) is not that it has a movement affiliation, not that it numbers hundreds of households, not that it has many people committed to living out the synagogue's core values and practices, but rather that it has much more homogeneity than is common in movement-affiliated synagogues. Its age range is relatively narrow, the backgrounds of the members cluster around a particular band within the "Jewish life-experience spectrum," and thus a great deal of agreement exists within the community on goals and aspirations. No doubt, many affiliated synagogues started in a way somewhat similar to B'nai Israel. What makes B'nai Israel unusual is that it *stayed that way.*

In the usual course of events, people age, their children grow up and have diverse needs and interests, their own attitudes and beliefs are affected by their life experiences, their careers make different demands on them, their spouses have their own life experiences and career demands, and in addition to all of this, people from outside the community decide, for a variety of reasons, that they find enough about the community congenial that they decide to join. These are the forces of heterogeneity.

The classic conundrum that social and economic libertarians are wont to toss out at their egalitarian counterparts is: "OK, you've achieved your social structure in which everyone is equal. Now, how are you going to keep it that way, given that people—when they are free—make all sorts of decisions and enter into all sorts of transactions that upset equality?" This is a very hard challenge to answer in political philosophy, and the analogous challenge is hard to answer here. The very autonomy the Indies recognize as a part of contemporary culture, and that they celebrate and seek to build upon, eventually must upset the homogeneity that provides much of the energy surge that is their hallmark and their great contribution to Jewish life today. This thought experiment would seem to suggest that the best course may be not to make an aspirational virtue out of nonaffiliation and independence, but rather to use the intensity the Indies have successfully harnessed as a way of energizing the more heterogeneous communities in which the Jewish people are destined to live, absent coercion or very artificial restrictions on community membership.

Balance Without or Within

I believe the independent community phenomenon is best looked upon not as something completely new in Jewish life, but rather as a particular way of approaching the unavoidable and venerable balancing act between uniformity and diversity in community structure, an approach that contemporary conditions in the large Jewish population centers in North American cities, and in Israel, make possible. In a sense, Jewish life from Sinai on has always been about people becoming "freely bound" (to use American political philosopher Michael Walzer's felicitous phrase) to the Jewish commitments they take on. And the fact that the Indies both celebrate autonomy and empowerment and yet often enough feature authority figures (young ones, to be sure) to whom adherents look for guidance and direction, underscores this continuity with the Jewish community's history of institutional structure. The greater energy and intensity that come from organizing around core defining norms have, for the time being, trumped the potential benefits of coalition building. But the large movements—and the synagogues they comprise—have *their* core defining norms as well (for example, "If you're not comfortable with mandated kashrut in the synagogue, you might find that you will be happier in a Reform community"). The difference seems to be that the rewards of greater internal sameness play much less a preemptive role in movement institutions, as a matter of strategic choice, given the realities of life. The balancing effort is ubiquitous; the ways of executing that effort vary. And the independent minyan movement (if we can use that word) has opted, for now, to have diversity expressed more across community lines rather than within them.

What about the future? Several questions, at least, beg to be posed. First, to what structures will the Indie constituents turn when they have their second children and find that economic necessity pulls them out of the urban centers to places where—for reasons that need little elaboration—"letting one hundred flowers bloom" is much less practical? And if they create their own independent communities, what effect will that have on efforts to reach and include those Jews who are not ready to commit to the tighter internal uniformity that is currently the signature of such communities?

Second, if it is true that broad ideological self-definition (such as the one again being looked for in the Conservative movement) plays a critical role in creating rationales for constraints on autonomy, then another question is this: Will an imagined large collection of Indies have to face the choice between failing to provide such structures, on the one hand, and giving up their independence in furtherance of greater ideological unity, on the other?

Third, what is given up when the energetic blessings of homogeneity come at the expense of diversity within a community? Might not the close proximity of members with significantly different and competing orientations toward such things as worship, observance, study, and Zionism (to mention just a few focal points of Jewish living) contribute to the life of a community a leavening arising from dueling perspectives? I have certainly found such contributions to be very real and very constructive in my own synagogue community. Can multiplicity of perspectives *across* community lines further some of those goals as effectively when the habits of *internal* debate are much less necessary?

Being neither a prophet nor the son of a prophet, I shall refrain from making a prediction about whether the particular organizing strategy of the Indies will have long-term staying power and perhaps even eclipse the approximately 150-year run the modern movements have had. One thing is clear: both the traditional and newer institutions will have much to learn from one another—and from experience—in the years and decades ahead. And in that process, recognizing the great deal that they have in common with one another, and with Jewish institutional history, can only help.

CHAPTER 20

The Riverway Project
One Model for Reaching a New Generation of Young Adults

Jeremy S. Morrison

Named after the location of Temple Israel of Boston, the Riverway Project (RWP)—at this writing, in its eighth year—is an outreach and engagement initiative for unaffiliated Jews. The RWP seeks to connect greater numbers of adults in their twenties and thirties to Judaism and to the synagogue through a variety of entry points.

Methods

The content of RWP initiatives is derived from the stated needs and desires of the participants. Temple Israel began the program in late spring 2001 with house meetings conducted with unaffiliated Jews living in the neighborhoods in which we have now established circles, small-group meetings in homes. At these meetings we asked participants about their connections to Judaism, their reluctance to become affiliated with a synagogue, what of Judaism they would like to try, where they would like to try it, what we could do to help, and similar questions. Participants responded that they were seeking Shabbat meals and services in an intimate setting, serious learning about Judaism, and social action projects. They wanted to start with activities in their own neighborhoods, and they sought a mix of ages and types (for example, married and single, older and younger; interfaith couples) to join together. Additionally, participants wanted any social connections to flow from these activities, rather than focusing on the social or dating aspect. Many found it awkward to go to events with the goal of meeting partners and many found it off-putting to go "cold" into a large synagogue.

A serious and critical approach to text study is one of RWP's main methods for connecting adults in their twenties and thirties to each other, to Judaism, and to Temple Israel. Over time, we have developed stratified learning opportunities.[1] We began with Torah and Tonics on Tuesday (which continues today): a bimonthly opportunity to study the Torah portion of the week. No Hebrew or prior knowledge is required for this drop-in learning experience. Building on our participants' increased comfort with and interest in study, we created a neighborhood-based educational experience called Mining for Meaning. "Mining" is a four-session course designed to deepen RWP participants' understanding of Jewish rituals, how they may function in one's life, and how they came to be. Each session includes in-depth text study utilized to elucidate the historical roots of particular rituals as well as a how-to workshop (discussions, demonstrations regarding particular rituals and how they may be adapted to one's life). Most recently, in partnership with two other Boston-area organizations, Combined Jewish Philanthropies and Hebrew College, we offered a new model of Me'ah, designed for this age group and taught by instructors in their thirties.

Engendering Ownership

Since the RWP's inception, we have sought to create leadership opportunities consistent with the quest for Jewish meaning that motivates most of the RWP participants. Rather than replicating the leadership models of many synagogues with fixed committees that oversee various types of programs (such as the ritual committee or the education committee) we have, instead, fostered a relational model of partnership between professionals and participants—and among the participants themselves—engaging all who are interested in the process of creating authentic Jewish experiences.

For example, one of the goals of the Mining experience is to create ongoing, self-sustaining learning circles (what we are now calling Still

Mining for Meaning) with participants becoming confident teachers of text for one another. In different neighborhoods, participants have continued studying together theology, liturgy, and *parashat hashavuah*. Typically, each monthly session is taught by a member of the circle who, beforehand, meets with me or with a colleague to prepare a lesson plan. Furthermore, these gatherings are organized around the ritual of *Havdalah*, which also is led by participants.

Two years ago we created an ever-changing leadership group of twenty to twenty-five core participants that meets quarterly to evaluate, brainstorm, and plan. This group does not function as an advisory committee or focus group. Rather, to be part of this leadership team means to be an owner of RWP experiences. By initiating new activities and improving current ones, this group of leaders is deeply involved in strengthening the RWP community. They are visionaries as well as implementers who serve as the hosts, greeters, teachers, and musicians at RWP gatherings.

The coordinator of the RWP and I serve as organizers who facilitate connections between participants based on common interests. As the founder of the RWP, I developed a model and infrastructure for building Jewish community within this cohort. However, determining the content of RWP gatherings is a joint effort. What I teach as a rabbi in the community, when I teach, and how Judaism is taught emerges through dialogue with participants.

The People

The population of RWP participants is heterogeneous. The majority is over age twenty-five. The range of professional pursuits is vast, including artists, graduate students, entrepreneurs, architects, teachers, doctors, and lawyers. Approximately 50 percent of participants are married or in ongoing relationships; about 25 percent of participants are in interfaith relationships. A growing percentage of participants have infants or toddlers. For many, the RWP is either their first encounter with organized Jewish activity or marks a return to Jewish communal life after a hiatus that began when the participant left home for college. If a participant's family was affiliated with a synagogue during his or her childhood, it was most likely Reform. Roughly 15 percent of participants describe their Jewish background as Conservative, Reconstructionist, Humanistic, or secular, and an estimated 2 percent of RWP participants report that they are from Orthodox homes. What unifies most RWP participants is a low level of Jewish knowledge and a beginner's experience of Jewish ritual, which distinguishes this population from many participants in independent *minyanim*. Few have studied Jewish texts before engaging with the RWP; most have only a rudimentary or no understanding of Hebrew.[2]

The RWP has connected with a sizeable, diverse, and dynamic group of adults in their twenties and thirties. Approximately 1,500 people have, to varying degrees, affiliated with RWP programming. Several hundred individuals have become members of Temple Israel. However, as would be expected among any large cachement of adults in this age group, the RWP's population is always in transition. After three to five years, many of our core participants either move to new cities or become further engaged with the synagogue in new ways as they grow older, have children, and assume roles as participants or leaders in the larger Temple Israel community. Consequently, the RWP is constantly in the process of renewing its base by building relationships with new participants and developing new leaders. Ideally, the RWP—and the synagogue as a whole—are continually in a process of transformation: we seek to adapt our methods, structures, and programs to ensure that they are consistent with both Jewish tradition and the ever-changing ideas, and lives, of the members of our community.

Meaningful Judaism

The RWP consists of worship, study, and social justice activities conducted both within the Temple Israel's building and in various locations throughout the Boston metropolitan area. In an attempt to engage unaffiliated Jews in the creation of Jewish community in both informal and institutional settings, RWP provides a panoply of connecting points, including casual Shabbat experiences in participants' homes, low-cost opportunities to formally join this urban congregation, and regular opportunities for Torah study.[3] On average, four to six RWP gatherings are held each month.

A hallmark of the RWP is a network of neighborhood circles situated in four urban areas in and around Boston. The circles meet in homes for Shabbat meals or services, study sessions, or Havdalah. Although the circles are designed to be a tool for creating communities of Jews living in a particular neighborhood, the activities of each circle are open to all Jews in their twenties and thirties living in Boston. Consequently, each event draws participants from different parts of the city, and the circles serve to form a wide network of qualitative relationships among our target population. Each circle has twelve to eighteen core members. A rabbi leads the *Kabbalat Shabbat* services within the circles, while the participants organize, with the aid of a coordinator, and lead their own Shabbat dinners and other study and ritual gatherings.

In conjunction with RWP programming occurring around the city, the RWP also holds programs at Temple Israel, designed to introduce participants to synagogue life and to integrate them into the larger Temple Israel community. These activities include holiday celebrations; study sessions; social action initiatives; Riverway Tots, a biweekly, pre-Shabbat experience for parents with children ages infant to three; and Soul Food Fridays, a monthly Friday night service at Temple Israel solely for those in their twenties and thirties.

Synagogue Transformation

The presence of a sizeable and growing population of adults in their twenties and thirties has brought new energy and enthusiasm into the synagogue, and the RWP is serving as a model within the larger Temple Israel community for adding depth and quality to the Jewish life of its members.[4] Our interfaith, new member, and adult education activities are now developed through the methods that we utilize in the RWP. And slowly Temple Israel is becoming a synagogue community comprised of qualitative relationships among its participants.

By developing meaningful pathways to connection with Judaism, the RWP has engaged several hundred adults in their twenties and thirties in this dynamic and creative process. The Riverway Project has transformed their conceptions of the synagogue experience and, I hope, has ensured that they will seek out Jewish community throughout the course of their lives.

Notes

Introduction

1. Samuel C. Heilman, *Sliding to the Right: The Contest for the Future of American Jewish Orthodoxy* (Berkeley, CA: University of California Press, 2006).

Chapter 1

1. Haym Soloveitchik, "Rupture and Reconstruction: The Transformation of Contemporary Orthodoxy," *Tradition* 28, no. 4 (Summer 1994).

2. Jon Butler, "Three Minds, Three Books, Three Years: Reinhold Niebuhr, Perry Miller, and Mordecai Kaplan on Religion," *Jewish Social Studies* 12, no. 2 (Winter 2006): 17–29. The halfway covenant defined salvation as extending not just to those predestined individuals but to their children as well. See Edmund S. Morgan, *Visible Saints: The History of a Puritan Idea* (Ithaca, NY: Cornell University Press, 1965).

3. Moshe Halbertal, *People of the Book: Canon, Meaning, and Authority* (Cambridge, MA: Harvard University Press, 1997), 168.

4. Jonathan D. Sarna, *American Judaism: A History* (New Haven, CT: Yale University Press, 2003).

5. Stephen J. Whitfield, *The Culture of the Cold War* (Baltimore: JHU Press, 1996), 88.

6. See recent works on lived religion such as David D. Hall, *Worlds of Wonder, Days of Judgment: Popular Religious Belief*

in Early New England (New York: Knopf, 1989); Robert A. Orsi, *The Madonna of 115th Street: Faith and Community in Italian Harlem, 1880–1950* (New Haven, CT: Yale University Press, 1985), and Orsi, *Thank You, St. Jude: Women's Devotion to the Patron Saint of Hopeless Causes* (New Haven, CT: Yale University Press, 1996).

Chapter 3

1. James G. Heller, *Isaac M. Wise: His Life, Work and Thought* (New York: Union of American Hebrew Congregations, 1965), 395.

2. Jakob J. Petuchowski, "Liberal Halakhah and Liturgy," in *Liberal Judaism and Halakhah*, ed. Walter Jacob (Pittsburgh: Rodef Shalom Press, 1988), 20. Petuchowski observes that although Wise was well aware that few members of the laity would understand the Hebrew, the purpose of the preface was to disarm potential Orthodox opposition to those departures from the traditional siddur in *Minhag America*.

3. W. Gunther Plaut, *The Growth of Reform Judaism* (New York: World Union for Progressive Judaism, 1963), 87.

4. Steven M. Cohen, "Non-denominational and Post-denominational: Two Tendencies in American Jewry," *Contact: The Journal of Jewish Life Network/Steinhardt Foundation* 7, no. 4 (Summer 2005): 7–8.

5. Tobin Belzer and Donald E. Miller, "Synagogues That Get It: How Jewish Congregations are Engaging Young Adults," *S3K Report*, S3K Synagogue Studies Institute, Spring 2007, 7.

6. Ibid.

7. Calvin Goldscheider, *The American Jewish Community: Social Science Research and Policy Implications* (Atlanta: Scholars Press, 1986), x.

8. Ibid., 86–87.

9. Ibid., 106.

10. Steven M. Cohen and Arnold M. Eisen, *The Jew Within: Self, Community and Commitment Among the Variety of Moderately Affiliated* (Boston: The Wilstein Institute of Jewish Policy Studies, 1998).

11. Ibid., 76.

12. Arnold M. Eisen, "Constructing the Usable Past: The Idea of 'Tradition' in Twentieth-Century Judaism," in *The Uses of Tradition: Jewish Continuity in the Modern Era*, ed. Jack Wertheimer (Cambridge: Harvard University Press, 1998), 460–61.

13. Michael A. Meyer, "Tradition and Modernity Reconsidered," in *Uses of Tradition*, 468–69.

14. Cohen, "Non-denominational and Post-denominational," 8.

15. Reconstructionist Placement Guidelines, Reconstructionist Rabbinical Association, November 2002, 1.

Chapter 4

1. See *U.S. Religious Landscape Survey 2008* (Washington, DC: Pew Forum on Religion and Public Life, 2008), 13; http://religions.pewforum.org/pdf/report-religious-landscape-study-full.pdf (accessed February 26, 2008).

2. Boston Faith and Justice Network, http://www.bostonfaithjustice.org (accessed December 2008).

3. Ibid.

4. Wade Clark Roof as cited in Stewart M. Hoover, "The Cross at Willow Creek: Seeker Religion and the Contemporary Marketplace," in *Religion and Popular Culture in America*, eds. Bruce David Forbes and Jeffrey H. Mahan (Berkeley: University of California Press, 2005), 145.

5. Quoted from Dave Schmelzer's website, http://www.spoke.com/info/p8IuQ8X/DaveSchmelzer.

6. Alpha is a Bible study series developed by Nicky Gumbel, assistant curate at Holy Trinity Brompton, London.

7. Ralph D. Winter, "The Two Structures of God's Redemptive Mission," in *Perspectives on the World Christian Movement: A Reader*, eds. Ralph D. Winter and Steven C. Hawthorne (Pasadena, CA: William Carey Library, 1981), 178–90.

8. Petros Vassiliadis, "Ecumenical Theological Education and Orthodox Issues for the 3rd Millennium," *Ministerial Formation*, no. 90 (July 2000): 15–21.

9. Quoted from the Lindisfarne Community's website, http://www.icmi.org.

10. Charles Trueheart, "Welcome to the Next Church," *The Atlantic Monthly* 78, no. 2 (August 1996): 37–58.

11. Todd Johnson, "The Changing Face of Global Christianity," in Daniel Jeyaraj, Robert Pazmiño, and Rodney Petersen, *The Antioch Agenda: Essays on the Restorative Church in Honor of Orlando E. Costas* (New Delhi: Indian Society for the Promotion of Christian Knowledge, 2007), 26.

12. Jonathan D. Sarna, *American Judaism: A History* (New Haven, CT: Yale University Press, 2004), xix–xx, 41.

13. Paul M. Barrett, *American Islam: The Struggle for the Soul of a Religion* (New York: Picador, 2007); Hassan Qazwini, *American Crescent: A Muslim Cleric on the Power of His Faith, the Struggle against Prejudice, and the Future of Islam in America* (New York: Random House, 2007).

14. William H. Swatos Jr., *Into Denominationalism: The Anglican Metamorphosis* (Storrs, CT: Society for the Scientific Study of Religion, 1979).

15. Hannah Adams, *A Dictionary of All Religions and Religious Denominations, Jewish, Heathen, Mahometan, Christian, Ancient and Modern*, 4th ed. (1817; repr., Atlanta: American Academy of Religion, 2000). The standard survey of denominations in the United States includes Jewish as well as Christian groups. See Frank S. Mead as revised by Samuel S. Hill, *Handbook of Denominations in the United States*, 10th ed. (Nashville: Abingdon, 1985).

16. Milton J. Coalter, John M. Mulder, and Louis B. Weeks, eds., *The Organizational Revolution: Presbyterians and American Denominationalism* (Louisville, KY: Westminster John Knox, 1992); cf. Philip Schaff, *The Principle of Protestantism* (1845; repr., Eugene, OR: Wipf & Stock Publishers, 2004); see, for example, Donald G. Mathews, "The Second Great Awakening as an Organizing Process, 1780–1830: An Hypothesis," in *American Quarterly* 21, no. 1 (Spring 1969): 23–43.

17. Richard F. Lovelace, *Dynamics of Spiritual Life: An Evangelical Theology of Renewal* (Downers Grove, IL: IVP Academic, 1979).

18. N. J. Demerath, ed., and others, *Sacred Companies: Organizational Aspects of Religion and Religious Aspects of Organizations* (New York: Oxford University Press, 1998).

19. Jim Wallis, *The Great Awakening: Reviving Faith and Politics in a Post-Religious Right America* (New York: HarperOne, 2008).

20. The movement extended from the late nineteenth century into the early years of the twentieth century, arguing that the ends of the church are not only the proclamation of the gospel but also the promotion of social righteousness. See Francis Greenwood Peabody, *Jesus Christ and the Social Question: An Examination of the Teaching of Jesus in Its Relation to Some of the Problems of Modern Social Life* (1900).

21. H. Richard Niebuhr, *The Social Sources of Denomination-alism* (1929; repr., Gloucester, MA: Peter Smith Publisher, 1984).

22. The history of the ecumenical movement is documented in the following three volumes: Ruth Rouse and Stephen Charles Neill, eds., *A History of the Ecumenical Movement, 1517–1948* vol. 1 (Philadelphia: Westminster, 1967); Harold E. Fey, ed., *A History of the Ecumenical Movement, 1948–1968* vol. 2 (Philadelphia: Westminster, 1970); and John Briggs, ed., and others, *A History of the Ecumenical Movement, 1968–2000* vol. 3 (Geneva, Switzerland: WCC Publications, 2004).

23. Schaff was one who developed the influential "branch theory" of church history, which looked to a common source and final reconciliation of church differences; see George H. Shriver, *Philip Schaff: Christian Scholar and Ecumenical Prophet* (Macon, GA: Mercer University Press, 1987).

24. Garth M. Rosell, *The Surprising Work of God: Harold John Ockenga, Billy Graham, and the Rebirth of Evangelicalism* (Grand Rapids: Baker Academic, 2008); cf. David Wells and John Woodbridge, eds., *The Evangelicals* (Nashville: Abingdon, 1975).

25. Martin Marty, *Righteous Empire: The Protestant Experience in America* (New York: Dial Press, 1970).

26. Robert Wuthnow, *The Restructuring of American Religion* (Princeton, NJ: Princeton University Press, 1987).

27. See C. Peter Wagner, *Your Church Can Grow* (Glendale, CA: Regal, 1976), ch. 1.

28. See George Barna's *The Frog in the Kettle: What Christians Need to Know about Life in the Year 2000* (Ventura, CA: Regal Books, 1990); *Marketing the Church: What They Never Taught You about Church Growth* (Colorado Springs, CO: Nav-

Press 1988); and *User-Friendly Churches: What Christians Need to Know About the Churches People Love To Go To* (Ventura, CA: Regal Books, 1991).

29. Scot McKnight, "Five Streams of the Emerging Church," *Christianity Today*, February 2007; also see Brian D. McLaren, *The Story We Find Ourselves In* (Hoboken, NJ: John Wiley, 2003), and McLaren, *Everything Must Change: Jesus, Global Crises, and a Revolution of Hope* (Nashville: Thomas Nelson, 2007).

Chapter 5

1. To be sure, Baeck was ultimately ordained at the Hochschule in Berlin. However, his motive for transferring from Breslau to Berlin after three years of study at his father Samuel Baeck's Breslau alma mater was not theological. Instead, he moved because he desired to work with historians at the University of Berlin in completing his doctorate, and he therefore finished his rabbinical studies at the Hochschule.

2. Cohen and Eisen, *The Jew Within*, 13ff.

Chapter 8

1. This is Project STAR's definition of who they are from their website: "When your 'business' is transmitting tradition with integrity, how do you manage needed change? That is the question that STAR works with synagogues to answer. Judaism has long been a balancing act of preserving core practices and values and absorbing contemporary influences. It is the contemporary influences of a very changing Jewish population and society that synagogues must address in order to thrive in the 21st century"; see "About STAR" at http://www.starsynagogue.org/.

2. Various factions in Israel, in partnership with the Jewish Agency for Israel and the United Jewish Communities, have tried to impose the term *stream*, an English translation of the Hebrew word *zerem*, rather than *movement* or *denomination*. While zerem fits fairly well in Hebrew, it does not translate well. Its use was an attempt to deal with the implied pluralism and equality of the term *movements* to which the Orthodox, particularly in Israel, objected.

3. This conceptualization would be analogous to John Dewey's, Horace Kallen's, and Jane Addams's early twentieth-century theory of cultural pluralism in opposition to that of the melting pot.

4. Rebellious Jewish students marched on the General Assembly of the then Council of Jewish Federations in Boston in 1969; the all-feminist issue of *Response* magazine was published in the summer of 1973; in 1968 Havurat Shalom was organized in Somerville, Massachusetts, and by 1973 Rabbi Harold Schulweis had organized thirty *havurot* at Valley Beth Shalom, a Conservative synagogue in Encino, California; the Jewish Theological Seminary made the decision to ordain women in 1983. In that same year the Reform movement adopted its resolution on acceptance of patrilineal descent for Jewish identity.

5. See Slingshot's website, http://www.slingshotfund.org/.

6. Cohen is referring to the ten years between the 1991 and 2001 National Jewish Population Surveys. The quote is from the *Contact* article "Non-denominational and Post-denominational," 7.

7. At one time or another we in the Jewish community have probably all heard someone say with a laugh, "I'm Reconformadox" or "Orthoderv." This transdenominational language is still couched in the terminology of the major movements.

8. Cohen, "Non-denominational and Post-denominational," 8.

9. I am indebted to the late Professor Vivian Klaff who spent a whole day with me in Delaware developing the tables on which this analysis is based.

10. The same can't be said for many other countries. In much of South America, Jewish sports centers and clubs are central to Jewish communal life. In Israel, schools and youth movements are more powerful than synagogues in the maintenance of Jewish identity.

11. The most complete explication of charismatic authority appears in Max Weber, *The Theory of Social and Economic Organization*, trans. A. M. Henderson and Talcott Parsons (New York: The Free Press, 1947), 358–92. As Weber writes, charismatic authority "cannot remain stable, but becomes either traditionalized or rationalized, or a combination of both" (ibid., 364).

Chapter 9

1. Mordecai M. Kaplan, *Judaism as a Civilization: Toward a Reconstruction of American-Jewish Life* (1934; repr., New York: The Jewish Publication Society of America Reconstructionist Press, 1981).

2. Sarna, *American Judaism*, cf. 206.

3. Alan Deutschman, "Building a Better Movie Business," *Fast Company*, December 2005; Chris Anderson, *The Long Tail: Why the Future of Business Is Selling Less of More* (New York: Hyperion, 2006).

4. David Kaufman, "The Synagogue as a Mediating Institution," in *Re-Envisioning the Synagogue*, ed. Zachary I. Heller (Boston: Hollis Publishing, 2005), 3–37.

5. For example, see the *National Jewish Population Survey 2000–01: Strength, Challenge and Diversity in the American Jewish Population* (New York: United Jewish Communities, 2003), which documents high levels of secular education, suggesting that American Jews are likely to live their personal and professional lives at the vanguard of this new world.

6. To cite several illustrations of philosophers and theologians who are in the tradition of uncovering Jewish values in Jewish legal texts, see the works of Philo of Alexandria, Saadiah Gaon, Moses Maimonides, and Rabbi Samson Raphael Hirsch. Also see the writings of Bachya Ibn Pekuda and the teachings of Rabbi Israel Salanter for illustrations of teachers concerned with the improvement of personal character and values.

7. See, for example, Elliot N. Dorff and Louis E. Newman, eds., *Contemporary Jewish Ethics and Morality: A Reader* (London: Oxford University Press, 1995); Joseph Telushkin, *A Code of Jewish Ethics: You Shall Be Holy, Vol. 1* (New York: Bell Tower, 2006); Louis Jacobs, *The Book of Jewish Values* (1960; repr., Chappaqua, NY: Rossel Books, 1983).

8. Byron L. Sherwin and Seymour J. Cohen, *How to Be a Jew: Ethical Teachings of Judaism* (Northvale, NJ: Jason Aronson, 1992), xi.

9. See Egon Mayer, Barry Kosmin, and Ariela Keysar, *American Jewish Identity Survey 2001* (New York: The Graduate Center of the City of New York, 2001), 39–45.

10. Thanks to Rabbi Yitz Greenberg, a major thought leader on contemporary Jewish life, for his insights about essential Jewish values and their application to modernity and to Dr. David A. Teutsch, whose book *A Guide to Jewish Practice* (Wyncote, PA: Reconstructionist Rabbinical College Press, 2000) served as a foundation for my attempt to present classical Jewish values in contemporary terms.

11. See Talmud Bavli Berakhot 31b and Tamid 29a.

12. David A. Teutsch, "Reinvigorating the Practice of Contemporary Jewish Ethics: A Justification for Values-Based Decision Making," *The Reconstructionist* (Spring 2005): 4–15.

13. This observation is based on my unscientific review of approximately thirty denominational and nondenominational synagogue websites during the writing of this paper.

14. I would like to thank Betsy Platkin Teutsch, a friend and colleague, for bringing this concept to my attention.

15. Project for Public Spaces; http://www.pps.org/info/placemakingtools/placemakers/roldenburg.

16. Scott Bedbury, *A New Brand World: Eight Principles for Achieving Brand Leadership in the Twenty-First Century* (New York: Penguin Group, 2002), 49–50, 124–25.

17. Or literally, wisdom on a cup—note how Starbucks coffee cups are now imprinted with pithy maxims about life wisdom. Starbucks also sells relaxing music CDs and books.

18. Observations made at a presentation by former Starbucks chief marketing officer, Scott Bedbury, Nov. 14, 2006, in Chicago, sponsored by BMO Capital Markets.

19. Coffeehouses may provide other insights that can help synagogues. Aharon Appelfeld, *Od Hayom Gadol* (Jerusalem: Keter, 2001), writes, "Sometimes, I feel as if the coffee house is a port in which all of the gates of the imagination are open. You sail to distant lands, connect with people whom you love and you begin anew. Sometimes, toward evening, the coffee house is like a secular house of prayer in which people are sunk in meditation."

20. See, for example, Jeffrey A. Spitzer, "The Synagogue and the Study House," MyJewishLearning.com; http://www.myjewishlearning.com/history/Ancient_and_Medieval_His-

tory/539_BCE-632_CE/Palestine_in_the_Hellenistic_Age/Syna-
gogue_and_Study_House.shtml.

21. Avi Weiss, "The Synagogue as a Home and the Role of
the Rabbi," *Re-Envisioning the Synagogue*, ed. Zachary I. Heller
(Boston: Hollis Publishing, 2005), 162–68. While Weiss's description of the synagogue as a *bayit* is helpful, his suggestion about the
role of rabbi as *abba* or *ema* is problematic because of the potential for reinforcing the tendencies of some rabbis to infantilize their
congregants instead of fostering their unique individual growth.

22. On the local congregational level, there is much creativity and vibrancy. The question is whether the denominations can
better catalyze this energy into something greater and lead their
member congregations with greater vision.

23. For example, in the Conservative movement, Emet v'Emunah,
the statement of basic Jewish belief developed in 1988; in the Reform movement, "A Statement of Principles for Reform Judaism" in
1999; and ongoing publication of the Reconstructionist movement's
series of guides to Reconstructionist Jewish practice.

24. This observation does not contradict the most current research on denominations and their distinct differences, conducted
by Steven M. Cohen, "Members and Motives: Who Joins American Jewish Congregations and Why," *S3K Report*, Fall 2006. Cohen has captured a snapshot of the differences in behavior, feelings,
and attitudes of denominationally affiliated Jews. My claim is not
that denominations do not make a difference, but that leaders of
the Conservative and Reform movements are actually driving the
trend toward convergence. It is too soon to know whether the current denominational differences in outcomes of Jewish behaviors
and attitudes will persist, given a closing of the gaps in key areas
of ideology and practice.

25. *Highlights of the CFJ 1990 National Jewish Population
Survey* (New York: Council of Jewish Federations, 1991); *The
National Jewish Population Survey 2000–01: Strength, Challenge
and Diversity in the American Jewish Population*; Ira M. Sheskin,
How Jewish Communities Differ (Storrs, CT: Mandell L. Berman
Institute–North American Jewish Data Bank, 2001).

26. The Reform movement may prove the exception to this
rule and has committed to expanding its services both in the Unit-

ed States and throughout the Jewish world. However, an expansion of service is not identical to creating an overarching vision of contemporary Jewish life. Other changes in self-perception, organization, and vision are required if the Reform movement wants to play the role that the Chabad-Lubavitch movement does for the liberal Jewish world or lead the other movements in this effort.

27. For example, see the following online articles: Sue Fishkoff, "New Congregations Getting 'Net Results,'" February 15, 2007, JTA at http://www.jta.org/cgi-bin/iowa/news/article/20070215cong regationsInternet.html; Uri Cohen, The Aperture, http://uricohen. wordpress.com/; and jspot.org, a project of Jewish Funds for Justice, http://www.jspot.org/. Also see Shifra Bronznick, "DIY Judaism: A Roundtable on Independent Minyan Phenomenon," *Zeek: A Jewish Journal of Thought and Culture*, Spring/Summer 2007.

28. Some notable examples include the American Jewish World Service (AJWS), Taglit-Birthright Israel, the Coalition on the Environment and Jewish Life (COEJL), Rosh Hodesh: It's a Girl Thing (sponsored by Moving Traditions), Hazon, Jewish Milestones, and JDub Records.

29. Unfortunately, the number of federations that have turned the rhetoric of Jewish renaissance into innovative funded realities is miniscule.

30. While the Reform movement is experiencing growth, there appears to be a correlation between its growth and the numerical decline of the Conservative movement. Additionally, in his study on denominationalism, Steven M. Cohen, *A Tale of Two Jewries: The "Inconvenient Truth" for American Jews* (Jewish Life Network/Steinhardt Foundation, 2006) has shown that membership affiliation in Reform congregations follows life-cycle patterns, with people joining and then dropping membership as life-cycle milestones are crossed. Finally, 26 percent of Reform congregations are comprised of interfaith marriages, leaving the sustainability of membership open to question. Of course, communal attitudes toward outreach could positively influence sustained involvement of interfaith families, making the children of interfaith marriages more likely to remain involved in Reform synagogues.

31. Mayer, *American Jewish Identity Survey 2001*, 35.

32. Leonard Saxe, "How Many Jews? Synthesizing Data to Understand American Jewry," *Contact*, Summer 2006, 5–6; Nathan-

iel Popper, "New Studies Put U.S. Jewry Over 6 Million Mark," *The Jewish Daily Forward*, Dec. 22, 2006.

33. Jewschool, www.jewschool.com; Jewlicious, www. jewlicious.com; jspot, a project of Jewish Funds for Justice, www. jspot.org; and Jewcy, www.jewcy.com.

34. Jay Michaelson, "Old Labels Feel Stiff for 'Flexidox.'" *The Jewish Daily Forward*, Oct. 13, 2006.

35. Bronznick, "DIY Judaism," 24.

36. While all different, IKAR (Los Angeles), Kehillat Hadar (Manhattan), East End Temple (Manhattan), Congregation B'nai Torah (Atlanta), and the Washington, D.C., Minyan all represent centers of creativity and use volunteer talent.

37. For an example of this, see Temple Emanuel, Newton Centre, Massachusetts, www.templeemanuel.com.

38. The author thanks the many colleagues who reviewed this chapter.

Chapter 10

1. Numbers 16.

2. Steven M. Cohen, "Non-denominational & Post-denominational," 7. Between the 1990 and 2000–01 Nation Jewish Population Surveys (NJPS), the number of adult Jews who did not identify with any major denomination rose from 20 to 27 percent. This movement away from denominational identification was noted already in analyses of the 1990 National Jewish Population Study: "Among the 18–24 group, 10 percent identified themselves as 'just Jewish'/secular. This percentage is the highest of any age group, possibly pointing to an underlying movement away from denominational identification." See Sidney Goldstein, "Profile of American Jewry: Insights from the 1990 National Jewish Population Survey," *American Jewish Year Book* (New York: American Jewish Committee, 1992), 130. Also see Jonathan Ament, "American Jewish Religious Denominations," Report 10, United Jewish Communities Report Series on the National Jewish Population Survey 2000–01 (New York: United Jewish Communities, 2005). The 2000–01 NJPS found that while only 20 percent of adults said they were raised as "just Jewish," 26 percent claimed to be

"just Jewish" at the time of the survey. Many self-described non-denominational Jews have generally low levels of Jewish identity by conventional measures. Among this group are some who have relatively strong Jewish identities but consider themselves postde-nominational. The two categories are quite different, but share a lack of interest in being associated with a specific denomination.

3. See, for example, the discussion of "The Rise of the Syna-gogue School" in *A History of Jewish Education in the United States*, ed. Judah Pilch (New York: American Association of Jew-ish Education, 1969), 124–27; and the section on "The Shift to Synagogue Schools" in Gil Graff's *"And You Shall Teach Them Diligently": A Concise History of Jewish Education in the United States, 1776–2000* (New York: JTS Press, 2008), 67–69.

4. In discussing diminishing denominationalism, a distinc-tion needs to be made between "elites" and "folk." Each religious movement has a strong core of activist members who take their denominational identities seriously and care about the well-being and vitality of the movement with which they are affiliated. These activists tend to be especially intense in their identification at times of conflict and when they believe their movement is being dispar-aged by others (for example, during the "Who is a Jew?" con-troversy). At such times, even the rank-and-file members of the movements are likely to be more conscious of their affiliation and their differences from other Jews. But many Jews remain largely untouched by these differences, identify only tepidly with one side or the other, or adopt a "plague on all your houses" attitude. Thus, there is no real contradiction between the phenomenon of declin-ing denominational identification among the Jewish populace as a whole and the interdenominational tensions cited by authors like Jack Wertheimer in *A People Divided: Judaism in Contem-porary America* (Waltham, MA: Brandeis University Press, 1997) and Samuel Freedman in *Jew vs. Jew: The Struggle for the Soul of American Jewry* (New York: Simon & Schuster, 2000).

5. On these differences, see the analysis of factors influencing children's Jewish schooling based on data from the 2000–01 NJPS. Laurence Kotler-Berkowitz, "The Jewish Education of Jewish Chil-dren: Formal Schooling, Early Childhood Programs and Informal Experiences," Report 11, Report 10, United Jewish Communities

Report Series on the National Jewish Population Survey 2000–01 (New York: United Jewish Communities, 2005), 14–16.

6. Jack Wertheimer, ed., *Family Matters: Jewish Education in an Age of Choice* (Waltham, MA: Brandeis University Press, 2007). On the larger personalization of American Jewish religious life, see Cohen and Eisen, *The Jew Within*.

7. In the last few years a renewed effort has been made to articulate the tenets of what some are calling a "common Judaism" (a reference to John Dewey's classic work, *A Common Faith*). The philanthropist Michael Steinhardt and the scholar-teacher Rabbi Yitz Greenberg have been the most noted proponents of this effort. See Michael H. Steinhardt, "My Challenge: Towards a Post-Denominational Common Judaism," *Contact* 7, no. 4 (Summer 2005): 14–15. See also the interview with Michael Steinhardt and Yitz Greenberg, "Jewish Movement, Jewish Renaissance: A Forum," in *Contact* 6, no. 1 (Autumn 2003): 3–8, and the article by Rabbi David Gedzelman, "What Does the Hour Demand? Creating a New Movement in American Jewish Life," in the same issue, pages 9–11.

8. Important work on the understanding of pluralism and its relation to particularism has been done in the Jewish-Catholic context by the team of Sara S. Lee and Mary C. Boys. They have convened several groups of Jewish and Catholic educators to work on this issue and coauthored a book on this process, *Christians and Jews in Dialogue: Learning in the Presence of the Other* (Woodstock, VT: Skylight Paths, 2006). Many conceptual issues that apply to interreligious pluralism also apply within specific faith traditions such as Judaism, where ideological divisions among the denominations are pointed and not readily harmonized.

9. A modest but interesting debate is developing in the Jewish community on the relative merits of consolidated institutions like community day schools that have the potential to appeal to broad audiences (and achieve some economies of scale) versus a number of "boutique" programs that are more finely tailored to specific diverse audiences. For those interested in maximizing overall participation, the latter may have some actual advantages (by appealing to a larger number of niche markets), but also incurs potential costs related to the capacity to deliver qualitative edu-

cational excellence due to the diffusion of resources among many small programs, each of which has fixed infrastructure costs. In the day school world, at least, the tendency seems to be to push for widening the (potential) appeal of individual institutions by making them transdenominational. However, this has raised concomitant interest in finding ways to accommodate ideological diversity within umbrella institutions.

10. For an elaboration of these concepts, see the working paper of JESNA's Lippman Kanfer Institute, *Redesigning Jewish Education for the 21st Century* (New York: JESNA, 2007).

11. See the initial list of noteworthy innovative programs in *Redesigning Jewish Education for the 21st Century*, appendix 2.

12. An example is the network of Conservative Jewish activists, lay and professional, that calls itself Shefa and whose statement of self-identification is "the Conservative Movement dreaming from within" (www.shefanetwork.org).

13. See, notably, the work on vision in Jewish education emanating from the Mandel Foundation and its associated institutions, especially Seymour Fox, Israel Scheffler, and Daniel Marom, eds., *Visions of Jewish Education* (Cambridge, UK: Cambridge University Press, 2003); and Daniel Pekarsky, *Vision at Work: The Theory and Practice of Beit Rabban* (New York: Jewish Theological Seminary of America, 2006).

Chapter 11

1. I do not include here reference to such communitywide functions as Jewish Federation agencies, fundraising structures, and Jewish community centers, which obviously existed long earlier, but usually under secular auspices.

Chapter 13

1. It was with this specific value in mind that the Charles and Lynn Schusterman Family Foundation recently decided to develop—in partnership with the Hebrew Union College (HUC)–Jewish Institute of Religion, Jewish Theological Seminary (JTS), Synagogues: Transformation and Renewal (STAR), and the Center

for Leadership Initiatives (CLI)—an unprecedented interdenominational rabbinic fellowship program. Slated to start with a pilot phase in the fall of 2008, the project will enable eight outstanding students (four from HUC and four from JTS) to experience a collaborative rabbinical education that is expanded in scope and deeper in areas of critical need to the American Jewish community. All alumni of the program will also be encouraged to join the STAR network of rabbis and invited to participate in all appropriate continuing education programs for rabbis offered by STAR.

Chapter 17

1. Moshe Waldoks, or Reb Moshe as he has been known since receiving *semikha*, was given *semikha* by three well-known and well-respected rabbis: Rabbi Zalman Schachter-Shalomi, of Hasidic lineage, and Rabbi Arthur Green and Rabbi Everett Gendler, both ordained by the Conservative movement's Jewish Theological Seminary of America. Rabbi Green and Rabbi Gendler each went on to explore different paths of Jewish expression in their personal and professional careers.

Chapter 18

1. Riv-Ellen Prell, *Prayer and Community: The Havurah in American Judaism* (Detroit: Wayne State University Press, 1989).

2. This is not to suggest that while the rooted *havurot* are now most often composed of families and may be multigenerational, they do not have some younger members who could well be participants or members of the new independent *minyanim* described here.

3. See Rodney L. Petersen's chapter, "American Dissonance: Christian Communities in the United States and Their Cultural Context," in this volume.

4. Steven M. Cohen and others, *Emergent Jewish Communities and Their Participants: Preliminary Findings from the 2007 National Spiritual Communities Study* (S3K [Synagogue 3000] and Mechon Hadar, 2007), 1. Available online at http://www.jewishemergent.org/survey/.

5. Tova Hartman, *Feminism Encounters Traditional Judaism: Resistance and Accommodation* (Waltham, MA: Brandeis University Press, 2007).

6. Kobi Nahshoni, "New Guide for the Halachic and Egalitarian Minyan," YnetNews.com, February 10, 2008; http://www.ynet.co.il/english/articles/0,7340,L-3505012,00.html.

7. Conversation with Rabbi Sharon Brous of IKAR in Los Angeles.

8. See chapter 20, "The Riverway Project" by Rabbi Jeremy Morrison, which describes this phenomenon.

9. See the Mechon Hadar website: www.mechonhadar.org.

10. Conversation with Jonathan D. Sarna, summer 2008.

11. From Professor Prell's written text that she graciously shared with the author.

12. For a broad discussion of this subject, see *Zeek: A Journal of Jewish Thought and Culture*, Spring 2007, available online.

Chapter 20

1. For a further discussion of Torah and Tonics on Tuesday and the RWP's approach to study, see Beth Cousens, Jeremy S. Morrison, and Susan P. Fendrick, "Using the Contextual Orientation to Facilitate the Study of Bible with Generation X," *Journal of Jewish Education* 74, no. 1 (January 2008): 6–28.

2. Ibid., 8.

3. All of the RWP programs are either free or cost the participant seven to twenty-five dollars. One does not need to be a member of Temple Israel to participate in RWP programming. However, demonstrating its commitment to adults in their twenties and thirties, Temple Israel has established an introductory, one-year membership of thirty-six dollars, or seventy-two dollars per couple, for those age thirty-five and under.

4. The inception of the RWP coincided with the commencement of our social justice initiative known as *Ohel Tzedek* (Tent of Justice). Both of these endeavors are premised on relational-based models of organizing, and together the RWP and Ohel Tzedek have profoundly altered how Temple Israel transforms itself.

Glossary

Unless otherwise stated, all non-English words are in Hebrew. Pronunciation: kh, ch, and ḥ are a guttural sound.

aggadic: Relating to the aggadah, the interpretive tradition of Jewish lore

aliyot, pl. of *aliyah:* Honor at the Torah

amcha, amkha (alt.): Populist term for collective of the Jewish people

Amidah: Core prayer of Jewish worship services

Ashkenaz (sing.), Ashkenazim (pl.), Ashkenazi (adj.): Jews from Central and Eastern Europe

avodah: Jewish worship

ba'alei tefillah: Worship leaders

ba'alei tshuvah: Those who have returned to religious observance

bashert: Destiny or destined mates

beit kenesset: Place of communal gathering

beit midrash: House of study

beit tefillah: House of prayer

bimah: Lectern or reader's desk used in a synagogue

birkat kohanim: Tripartite priestly blessing (Num. 6:22–26)

chazzanut: The cantorial arts

davven, davvenen (alt.), davvenning: Praying (Yiddish)

davvened mincha: Recited the afternoon prayer

get: The document of divorce

gevurah: Strength

halakhah, halacha (alt.): The way to go (lit.); the primal path and structure of Jewish law

halakhic: Pertaining to Jewish law

Ḥanukkah: Dedication (lit.); the Jewish festival commemorating the Jews' victory over the Hellenists in 163 BCE and the rededication of the Temple in Jerusalem

ḥaredim: Right-wing, ultra-Orthodox Jews

HaShomer HaTza'ir: Young guard (lit.); a socialist and early Zionist youth movement founded in Eastern Europe on the eve of World War I

ḥasid (sing.), ḥasidim (pl.): Pious (lit.); adherent to Ḥasidism

ḥasidic: Referring to Ḥasidism

Ḥasidism: A Jewish mystical movement, founded in the eighteenth century in Eastern Europe by the Baal Shem Tov, that reacted against Talmudic learning and maintained that God's presence was in all of one's surroundings and that one should serve God in one's every deed and word

Havdalah: Distinction or separation (lit.); the ceremony that concludes the Sabbath and festivals

ḥavurah (sing.), ḥavurot (pl.): Fellowship(s) (lit.); name for groups who together share prayer, study, and the celebration of holidays and life-cycle events

hazzan: Cantor; a prayer leader with deep knowledge of the liturgy and trained in the vocal arts who leads the congregation and enhances the service musically

hesed, chesed (alt.): Acts of lovingkindness

ḥevruta: Partnership (lit.); two study partners, generally referring to the traditional method of studying a section of the Talmud or other classic texts

ḥumash: Five books of Moses; the Bible

kabbalah: That which is received (lit.); used as the name for the Jewish mystical tradition and its classic texts

Kabbalat Shabbat: Welcoming the Sabbath (lit.); the opening elements of the Sabbath evening service

kaddish: Part of the liturgy that emphasizes faith and is either a demarking element in the liturgy or is recited by mourners

kashrut: Fit (lit.); the system of Jewish dietary laws and practices

kavannah: Focus upon prayer or some other religious action (lit.)

kavannot, pl. of kavannah: Intentions; also, literary texts, often out of the mystical tradition, written to help the worshiper focus

kehillah, kehilla (alt.): Community

kiddush: Sanctification (lit.); prayer said over wine on Shabbat and festivals

kippah: Skull cap

klal yisrael: Broad community of Jews

Kol Nidrei: All vows (lit.); first element of the Yom Kippur evening service (Aramaic)

l'hitpallel: To pray

mahzor: Cycle of prayers (lit.); prayer book for festivals and high holy days

mara d'atra: Master of the place (lit.); a designation for the official rabbi of a community (Aramaic)

maskil, maskilic: One who identifies with the eighteenth-and nineteenth-century Enlightenment

masorti: Traditional (lit.); term used in Israel and elsewhere for the analog of the North American Conservative movement

mechitzah: A divider (lit.); separates the sexes in synagogue worship according to Orthodox practice

midrash, midrashic: Process of interpretation

Mikra'ot Gedolot: A compendium of classic commentaries on the biblical text

minhag: Custom

minyan (sing.), minyanim (pl.): Quorum of ten individuals needed for public worship; in the Orthodox tradition a minyan is restricted to males and in the liberal movements is not gender defined

mitnagdic: Pertaining to mitnagdim

mitnagdim: Opposed (lit.); the countermovement to Hasidism

mitzvah (sing.), mitzvot (pl.): Religious commandment or obligation

musaf: Additional element of Sabbath and festival liturgy

neshama: Soul

neshima: Breath

niggun: A tune (lit.); melody without words in the hasidic tradition

Oneg Shabbat: Delight of the Sabbath (lit.); communal gathering to celebrate the Sabbath

parashat hashavuah: The Torah reading for the week in an annual cycle of readings

rav: rabbi

semikha: Rabbinic ordination

Sephard (sing.), Sephardim (pl.), Sephardic: Pertaining to Jews of Sepharad, the Iberian Peninsula and Mediterranean basin

s'firat ha-omer: Counting the forty-nine-day period beginning the second night of Passover

Shabbat: Sabbath

Shabbat Hamalka: Sabbath Queen

Shammai and Hillel: Two leading figures of early rabbinic Judaism

shivah: The seven days of mourning

shteibel (sing.), shteiblach (pl.): Small houses of worship (Yiddish)

shul: Synagogue (Yiddish)

siddur (sing.), siddurim (pl.): Prayer book

tallit: Prayer shawl

tefillah (sing.), tefillot (pl.): Prayer(s)

tzedakah: Charity

ufruf: Calling up (lit.); in Orthodox Judaism, calling the groom up to the Torah on the Shabbat before his wedding; in the other movements, both the bride and groom are frequently called up together (Yiddish)

yeshivah (sing.), yeshivot (pl.): A place where one sits (lit.); place of study

Yevamot: A tractate of the Talmud

z"l: May his (or her) memory be for a blessing

Contributors

Judy Beck is director of the Synagogue Leadership Initiative at the Jewish Federation of Northern New Jersey. She is the major programmatic liaison with the synagogues and their leadership in this prime suburban area of New York.

Sanford Cardin, long a significant Jewish community activist and keen observer of Jewish life, serves as president of the Charles and Lynn Schusterman Family Foundation.

Arnold M. Eisen has served as Chancellor of the Jewish Theological Seminary of America in New York, the academic center of Conservative Judaism in America, since 2007. Previously a professor of Jewish thought and noted scholar at Stanford University, he has written extensively on contemporary Jewry and Jewish thought.

David Ellenson, a Reform rabbi, holds a Ph.D. in Jewish history and is a noted scholar of German Jewry and the issues surrounding the rise of denominational divisions. He is president of the Hebrew Union College–Jewish Institute of Religion, the multicampus seminary and academic center of Reform Judaism.

Rela Mintz Geffen, immediate past-president and professor emerita of sociology at Baltimore Hebrew University, has written and lectured extensively on the sociology of the American Jewish community.

David M. Gordis is president emeritus of Hebrew College in Newton Centre, Massachusetts, which he led from 1993 to 2008. The college includes transdenominational rabbinical, cantorial, and educator training programs as well as other academic and certificate programs. He is the founder and director of the National Center for Jewish Policy Studies and a noted scholar of ancient rabbinics as well as analyst of contemporary Jewry.

Arthur Green, noted Judaic scholar, especially in the fields of theology and mysticism, served as president of the Reconstructionsit Rabbinical College, professor at Brandeis University, and currently is rector of the Rabbinical School at Hebrew College, where he was the founding dean. He is also professor of philosophy at the college.

Lawrence Grossman is editor of *The American Jewish Yearbook* and associate director of research for the American Jewish Committee. He has written extensively on contemporary Judaism.

Zachary I. Heller, the editor of this volume, was a congregational rabbi in New Jersey for more than thirty years before becoming the associate director of the National Center for Jewish Policy Studies. He also served in many national and international leadership roles including as president of the World Council of Synagogues from 1989 to 1993.

Hayim Herring, rabbi and Ph.D. in the field of management, is Director of STAR (Synagogues: Transition and Renewal). He is considered one of the major experts in the study of the contemporary synagogue and has developed a wide-ranging network of programs to reimagine and reinvigorate the contemporary synagogue and provide extensive in-service training for rabbis.

Clifford Kulwin is rabbi of Temple B'nai Abraham, a major non-denominational congregation in Livingston, New Jersey. He previously served for many years as a senior staff member of the World Union for Progressive Judaism.

Cheri Scheff Levitan, director of Jewish Life and Learning at the Marcus Jewish Community Center, Atlanta, Georgia, served as president of Congregation B'nai Torah in Atlanta (Sandy Springs) from 2003 to 2005 and spearheaded its transition from an independent congregation to one affiliated with a denomination.

Jeremy S. Morrison is a rabbi of Temple Israel in Boston, a leading Reform congregation. Through the Riverway Project, which he directs, hundreds of previously unaffiliated Jews in their twenties and thirties have deepened their connections to Judaism. He is also a doctoral student in Bible and the Ancient Near East at Brandeis University.

Rodney L. Petersen, an ordained minister, is executive director of the Boston Theological Institute, a consortium of the graduate departments of religion and theology as well as theological schools in the greater Boston area, including much of New England. He holds a Ph.D. from Princeton Theological Seminary and specializes in history, ethics, and conflict resolution.

Sanford Seltzer, a rabbi, was part of the central administration of the Reform movement in Judaism for many years. He has been associated with Hebrew College as Director of the Interreligious Center on Public Life and for several years also served as Associate Dean of the Rabbinical School. He initiated the conference that stimulated the development of this volume.

Carl A. Sheingold is executive vice president of the Jewish Reconstructionist Federation. He previously spent thirteen years as a senior staff member of United Jewish Communities and its predecessors. He also was a professor of management in the Hornstein Jewish Professional Leadership Program at Brandeis University.

David B. Starr holds both rabbinic ordination and a Ph.D. in Jewish history and is an assistant professor of Jewish history at Hebrew College, Newton Centre, Massachusetts. He also serves as Vice President for Community Education and Dean of Me'ah, a national, intensive program of Jewish adult learning designed and sponsored by the college.

Gordon Tucker serves as senior rabbi at Temple Israel Center, White Plains, New York. He has previously served as dean of the Rabbinical School at the Jewish Theological Seminary of America (Conservative), where he currently serves as adjunct assistant professor of philosophy. He holds a Ph.D. in philosophy from Princeton University and has garnered great scholarly acclaim by virtue of his translation and annotation of Abraham Joshua Heschel's magnum opus, *Heavenly Torah*.

Moshe Waldoks, rabbi of Temple Beth Zion (TBZ) in Brookline, Massachusetts, is a leader in the Jewish Renewal movement. He earned his Ph.D. in Jewish intellectual history at Brandeis University and is also well known as coeditor of the *Big Book of Jewish Humor*.

Jonathan Woocher, after serving for many years as chief executive of JESNA (Jewish Education Services of North America), retired from its administrative duties and now is its chief ideas officer and heads its Lippman Kanfer Institute.